Contending Approaches to the American Presidency

Contending Approaches to the American Presidency

Editor

Michael A. Genovese

Loyola Chair of Leadership
Loyola Marymount University

Los Angeles | London | New Delhi
Singapore | Washington DC

CQ Press
2300 N Street, NW, Suite 800
Washington, DC 20037

Phone: 202-729-1900; toll-free, 1-866-4CQ-PRESS (1-866-427-7737)

Web: www.cqpress.com

Cover design: Auburn Associates, Inc.
Composition: C&M Digitals (P) Ltd.

♾ The paper used in this publication exceeds the requirements of the American National Standard for Information Sciences—Permanence of Paper for Printed Library Materials, ANSI Z39.48-1992.

Printed and bound in the United States of America

15 14 13 12 11   1 2 3 4 5

Library of Congress Cataloging-in-Publication Data

Contending approaches to the American presidency / Michael A. Genovese, editor.
     p. cm.
     ISBN 978-1-60871-706-4 (pbk. : alk. paper) 1. Presidents—United States. 2. United States—Politics and government. I. Genovese, Michael A.
     JK516.C59 2011
     352.230973—dc23

                                                                        2011022394

To Gabriela

How did I get so lucky?

Contents

About the Contributors

David Gray Adler is the James A. McClure Professor and Director of the James A. and Louise McClure Center for Public Policy Research at the University of Idaho, where he holds a joint appointment in the College of Law and the Department of Political Science. He teaches Constitutional Law in the College of Law. A recipient of teaching, civic, and writing awards, Adler has published in the leading journals of his field, and he has lectured nationally and internationally on the Constitution and presidential power. The author of more than 100 scholarly articles, essays, and book chapters, Adler's books include the following: the two-volume work *American Constitutional Law*; *The Constitution and the Conduct of American Foreign Policy*; *The Presidency and the Law: The Clinton Legacy*; and *The Constitution and the Termination of Treaties*. His forthcoming books include these: *The Steel Seizure Case, Presidential Power and Foreign Affairs: The Legacy of Curtiss-Wright,* and *The Constitution and Presidential Power*. His scholarly writings have been widely cited by political scientists, historians, and law professors, and they have been invoked by both Republicans and Democrats serving in all three branches of government. He has consulted with members of Congress from both parties on a variety of constitutional issues, including impeachment. Adler's lectures have aired on C-SPAN, and he has done scores of interviews with, among others, reporters from *The New York Times, The Washington Times, The Washington Post, The Wall Street Journal, Los Angeles Times, Newsweek, National Review,* National Public Radio, and the BBC. He earned a BA from Michigan State University and a PhD from the University of Utah.

Ryan J. Barilleaux received his PhD from the University of Texas at Austin in 1983. His professional interests lie in the study of the American presidency. As a member of Miami University's faculty since 1987, Barilleaux served as chair of the Department of Political Science from 2001 to 2009. Barilleaux commits his research to presidential and executive politics, American politics, and religion and politics. He has written such books as *Power and Prudence: The Presidency of George H. W. Bush* (2004) with M. Rozell, *The President as World Leader* (1991) with B. Kellerman, *The Post-Modern Presidency* (1988), and *The President and Foreign Affairs* (1985). He has also edited *The Unitary Executive and the Modern Presidency* with C. S. Kelley (2010) and *Presidential Frontiers: Underexplored Issues in White House Politics* (1998).

Thomas E. Cronin is the McHugh Professor of American Institutions and Leadership at Colorado College. He was president of Whitman College from 1993 to 2005 and was acting president of Colorado College (1991). He earned a PhD in political science from Stanford University and is author, coauthor, or editor of over a dozen books on politics and government, including *The Paradoxes of the American Presidency* (3rd ed., 2010), *On the Presidency* (2009), *Inventing the American Presidency* (1989), *Direct Democracy* (1989), and *The State of the Presidency* (1980). He has been a moderator, since 1973, of more than a dozen Aspen Institute executive seminars.

Michael A. Genovese received a PhD from the University of Southern California in 1979. He currently holds the Loyola Chair of Leadership Studies, is a professor of political science, and is director of the Institute for Leadership Studies at Loyola Marymount University. Professor Genovese has written 27 books, including *The Paradoxes of the American Presidency*, coauthored by Thomas E. Cronin (3rd ed., 2009); *The Presidential Dilemma* (2nd ed., 2003); *The Encyclopedia of the American Presidency*, winner of the New York Public Library "Best of Reference" work of 2004 (2004); and *Memo to a New President: The Art and Science of Presidential Leadership* (2007). He has won over a dozen university and national teaching awards, including the Fritz B. Burns Distinguished Teaching Award (1995). Professor Genovese frequently appears as a commentator on local and national television. He is also associate editor of the journal *White House Studies,* is on the editorial board of the journals *Rhetoric & Public Affairs* and the *International Leadership Journal,* has lectured for the United States Embassy abroad, and is editor of Palgrave Macmillan Publishing's "The Evolving American Presidency" book series. Professor Genovese has been The Washington Center's "scholar-in-residence" at three national political conventions and the 2008 presidential inauguration. In 2004–2005, Professor Genovese served as president of the Presidency Research Group of the American Political Science Association.

Gene Healy is a vice president at the Cato Institute. His research interests include executive power and the role of the presidency. He is the author of 2008's *The Cult of the Presidency: America's Dangerous Devotion to Executive Power* and the editor of the 2004 collection *Go Directly to Jail: The Criminalization of Almost Everything.* Healy has appeared on PBS's *NewsHour with Jim Lehrer* and National Public Radio's *Talk of the Nation,* and his writing has been published in the *Los Angeles*

Times, The New York Times, the *Chicago Tribune,* the *Legal Times,* and elsewhere. He is also a weekly columnist for the *Washington Examiner.* Healy holds a BA from Georgetown University and a JD from the University of Chicago Law School.

Melanie M. Marlowe received her MA in Political Science from Claremont Graduate University in 2002. She is currently a visiting assistant professor at Miami University in Oxford, Ohio, where she teaches the following classes: Constitutional Law, the American Presidency, and American Founding Political Thought. While earning her doctorate, she researches a variety of topics related to the presidency and Congress: concurrent powers, federalism, piracy, presidential war powers, and judicial deference to the executive and legislative branches. Marlowe contributed a chapter titled "The Unitary Executive and Review of Agency Rulemaking" in *The Unitary Executive and the Modern Presidency* (2010), and she edited a volume with Carol McNamara on the Obama presidency titled *The Obama Presidency in the Constitutional Order* (2011).

Robert J. Spitzer received his PhD from Cornell University in 1980 and is Distinguished Service Professor of Political Science and Department Chair at the State University of New York at Cortland. He is the author of 13 books and hundreds of articles, essays, and papers on many topics related to the American government, and he edits the book series on American Constitutionalism for SUNY Press. His areas of specialty include the American presidency and gun control. His recent books include *Saving the Constitution from Lawyers: How Legal Education and Law Reviews Distort Constitutional Meaning* (2008), *The Politics of Gun Control* (5th ed., forthcoming), *The Presidency and the Constitution* (2005), *President and Congress* (1993), and *The Presidential Veto* (1988). He is also a regular contributor to The Huffington Post.

Preface

"Today I authorized the armed forces of the United States to begin a limited military action in Libya."

President Barack Obama, March 19, 2011

"I decided." Does the president have the authority to, on his own, order American forces into combat? Does not the Congress possess the sole constitutional authority to declare war?

The president called the bombing raid on Libya a "humanitarian" mission, but a war by any other name. . . . The president acted, and acted boldly, against Libya. Yet, boldness is one thing; constitutionality another. Did President Obama have the right, absent congressional authorization, to send American forces into harm's way?

Most presidents argue "yes." Many member of Congress say "no." The Court has often sided with the Congress. Confused? How could one not be?

Welcome to a book designed to help the reader better understand the American presidency, an office complex, paradoxical, and confusing.

We usually bring two sorts of biases to our decisions regarding the legitimacy of presidential actions. The first is a partisan bias. We tend to support a president of our own party while we criticize a president of the opposing party even if their behaviors are virtually identical. These partisan blinders are very forgiving to our party comrades, yet quite harsh when examining the other party.

The second bias we often employ is ideological or positional. A liberal might generally favor the bold exercise of presidential power, while a libertarian might rankle at the sight of a president exercising broad independent powers. An advocate of the unitary executive might defend presidential unilateralism, while a constitutionalist may argue that to be legitimate, Congress must give its approval.

Is there a way out of this confused and confusing dilemma? Perhaps by more openly airing our biases, exposing them to the light of day and open intellectual investigation, we might better understand both where *we* are coming from and on what basis the president makes claims of power.

This book makes more explicit many of the implicit intellectual and ideological assumptions we tend to make about the American presidency. It does so in an effort to allow the reader to see more clearly, judge more accurately, and discriminate more appropriately. It gives you, the reader, a clearer roadmap to understanding the various contending approaches to the American presidency.

Acknowledgments

There are many people I wish to thank for their assistance in completing this project. Charisse Kiino, my editor at CQ Press, was an absolute joy to work with. She was professional, kind, and encouraging. Also, the contributors to this volume performed extraordinarily, and if this book "works," it is largely due to their efforts. My administrative assistant at the Loyola Marymount University Institute for Leadership Studies, Brian Whitaker, and researchers Kelsey Flott, Matt Candau, and Rebecca Hartley, worked tirelessly for their mean boss. Deepest thanks to you all.

Toward Understanding the American Presidency

Michael A. Genovese

LIBERALS VERSUS CONSERVATIVES, Constitutionalists versus Unitary Executive Presidentialists, Moderates versus Libertarians, these diverse viewpoints make up the blood sport that has become our politics in an age of Fox News, cable television, and slash and burn talk radio. These cleavages are also evident—albeit in a somewhat more temperate form—in the study of the American presidency.

Today, students of the presidency can be forgiven if they find the institution both confused and confusing. In fact, while looking at the presidency, those who aren't a bit schizophrenic just aren't thinking clearly. It *is* a paradoxical institution, full of contradictions and clashing expectations.[1] And given that few authors openly reveal their ideological or partisan preferences, readers often have a difficult time understanding what values, goals, and political orientations animate writings about the presidency. As scholars, we try to be neutral, fair-minded social scientists, yet we are also human. Clearly we are not trying to manipulate our audience, yet in not making more explicit the values and assumptions that may occasionally creep into our work, we may end up confusing our readers as well as illuminating them.

Because of this, citizens sometimes end up applying the wrong or even contradictory evaluative standards to the office. They want strong leadership to combat terrorism, yet they insist on a presidency bound by democratic and constitutional controls. They demand that the president be our national problem solver, yet they bristle when the government intrudes too much into our lives. They want more services yet lower taxes. And the list goes on and on.

In an effort to remedy such confusion, this book makes more explicit the assumptions—often hidden—behind various approaches to understanding the American presidency. This is not a book devoted to partisan intellectual combat. It is about laying bare the ideological and constitutional assumptions about the presidency. We will familiarize readers with a number of different approaches to understanding politics and the presidency and apply these approaches to questions of presidential power and reform of the presidency. These chapters cover six approaches: *Liberal, Conservative, Moderate, Constitutionalist, Libertarian, and Presidentialist (Unitary Executive)*. These different approaches define the conflict or clashing perspectives that animate the current political debate concerning the presidency.

In doing this, we hope the reader will better understand the contrasting values behind the different approaches to presidential power, more clearly sort out and choose from among these varied conceptions of the presidency, and develop more consistent measures for evaluating the office. A more accurate, nuanced, and realistic understanding of the scope and limits, as well as the ideological underpinnings of the presidency, can serve to both constrain and empower the office along more explicit and rational lines.

This book helps the reader see how different people, coming from different starting points, view the presidency. The future of the American presidency is contested territory. It remains to be shaped, constrained, or empowered. It is not a static office set in stone but a dynamic, elastic office that is repeatedly reborn and reformed.

By examining the presidency from varied and distinct vantage points, the discerning reader will be better able to compare and contrast, exercise critical thinking skills, and pose thoughtful questions concerning presidential power and leadership. Would a Libertarian presidency fit the needs of a global superpower? Does a constitutional presidency restrict presidential power in a way that might interfere with our ability to fight a war against terrorism? Is a Unitary Executive compatible with the view of the framers? How does a Liberal or Conservative presidency serve the needs of the nation? And is a Moderate presidency capable of solving the massive problems confronting the United States?

There is an ongoing debate over where the presidency fits in the constitutional order of the United States. Did the framers invent a big, powerful, and independent executive, a kind of "magnificent lion who can roam widely and do great deeds so long as he does not try to break loose from his broad reservation"?[2] Or did the framers make the president errand boy to the Congress, able *only* to execute the laws of the legislature? Or is the truth buried somewhere in between? This book shines a light on that debate, asking you to draw your own conclusions. As this book makes clear, Gene Healy, a Libertarian, sees expansive presidential power as poison. So too, but for different reasons, does David Gray Adler, the Constitutionalist. Melanie Marlowe, embracing a Unitary Executive view, sees power as necessary and proper. Our other contributors fall somewhere in between.

The only constant in the American presidency is change, and as the old Yiddish saying goes, "Only a wet baby welcomes change." It is up to us to decide how the presidency of tomorrow will look. The office will reinvent itself in the coming years—it always does. We can be passive observers (and perhaps victims) of that change, or we can demand that the office conform to our design and thus we can become the masters of our future as well as of the presidency. And if *we* are going to reinvent the presidency, it is incumbent upon us to make a thoughtful, rational, and positive contribution to this ongoing debate.

The discerning reader may well ask, why choose these perspectives and approaches to understanding the presidency? And is there a bit of a "conservative bias" in this selection of approaches? Where, for example, is a chapter on how a Socialist might look at the presidency? These are fair questions, all.

These perspectives were chosen because they represent the most common and most important ideological, constitutional, and/or intellectual approaches to understanding the American presidency. If there seems a conservative bias, it is because largely the United States is a moderate to conservative nation. There is no significant socialist "left" in America. If this were a book about a European prime minister, there would surely be a chapter from a Socialist perspective.

These clashing perspectives on the presidency do not always unfold neatly along an ideological spectrum. It is better to view these approaches along two contrasting dimensions: Big Government versus Small Government and Monarchical versus Rule of Law tendencies. We can then (see Figure 1–1) better conceptualize the dimensions along which these perspectives can be compared and understood.

FIGURE 1–1 Comparative Perspectives on Monarchical/Size of Government Dimensions

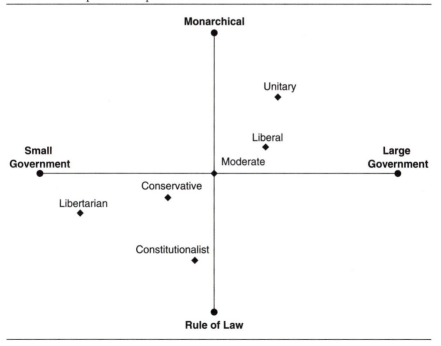

Before we can sort out the contemporary debate, we need to put the presidency into context and perspective. That is the goal of this introductory chapter. We briefly examine the origins and invention of the presidency, the president's constitutional power and how the framers understood that power, the historical development of the office, and the controversies pertaining to presidential power in an age of terrorism. This background will allow the reader to place the contemporary debate within a historical and developmental context.

The Revolt Against Executive Power

The American Revolution took place in the middle of the transformation from the divine right of the king to government by the people. As liberal and constitutional democracy emerged, the ruler (king) was seen as the problem to be solved, not as the solution to the people's problems.

To the colonists, the king became the focal point of virtually all complaints and criticisms. At the time of the colonists' break from Great Britain, antimonarchical sentiment was strong. Thomas Paine's pamphlet, "Common Sense," was a broadside against the arbitrary power of the monarch stigmatizing England's George III as "the Royal Brute of Britain." Thomas Jefferson's Declaration of Independence was, in addition to being an eloquent expression of democratic and revolutionary faith, an exhaustive laundry list of charges leveled against the tyrannical king.

Antiexecutive feelings were so powerful that when the post-Revolutionary War leadership formed a new government, the Articles of Confederation and Perpetual Union contained no *executive!* Yet, so weak and ineffective were the Articles that Noah Webster said they were "but a name, and our confederation a cobweb."[3] Over time, the absence of an executive proved unworkable, and slowly the inevitability of an executive with some authority became more commonly accepted.

At the Constitutional Convention, James Wilson was the first to raise the possibility of an executive officer for the new government, and his suggestion was met, according to James Madison's notes, with "an embarrassed pause"—so antiexecutive were most of the delegates that even the thought of a new kingly officer led to harsh looks and stunned silence. Edmund Randolph of Virginia broke the silence, reminding the delegates that there would be "no semblance of a monarch" here.

Alexander Hamilton addressed the convention of June 18, 1787, and delivered a lengthy speech praising the British system as "the best in the world." "The British monarchy is," he said, "the only good model of executive power available." But the framers knew that to create an American monarchy invited yet another bloody revolution, and Hamilton's hopes were quickly dashed. The new government would have no strong, independent executive. The new nation was reluctant, yet willing, to accept the necessity of an executive, yet the fear of tyranny contin-ued to lead them in the direction of a limited and constrained constitutional executive office.

The ideas from which the framers drew in inventing the presidency are diverse and complex. They took a negative example away from their experiences with the king of England. This fear of the executive imbedded in the framers a determina-tion not to let the new American executive squint toward monarchy. Several Euro-pean political theorists opened the framers' imagination to new possibilities for governing. John Locke's *Second Treatise on Government* (1690) and Montesquieu's *The Spirit of the Laws* (1748) were especially influential.

From their understanding of history, the framers drew several lessons. In studying the collapse of Greek (Athenian) democracy, the framers deepened their already strong suspicion of direct democracy. Thus, they were determined to pre-vent what some framers referred to as "mobocracy." A tyranny of the masses was just as frightening as a tyranny of the monarch, as the French Revolution was soon to confirm. From their examination of the Roman Republic and its collapse from the weight of the empire, the framers understood how delicate the balance was between the Senate and the will of an emperor. An emperor armed as tribune of the people, bent of imperial pursuits, commanding a large army, led to tyranny just as surely as monarchy and mobocracy.

The framers also drew from the Native Americans. While the framers looked across the Atlantic and saw nothing but hereditary monarchies, they looked to upstate New York and could see a sophisticated, democratic, egalitarian govern-ment in action: the Iroquois Confederation. This union of six tribes/nations, organized along lines similar to a separation-of-powers system, was the model for Ben Franklin's 1754 Albany Plan of Union, and it was much studied by several key framers.

The experience with colonial and postcolonial governors further added to the framers' repertoire of knowledge. Those states with weak executives, states domi-nated by the legislature with a defanged governor, seemed less well run than states like New York, with a fairly strong, somewhat independent governor. Such exam-ples softened the fears of executive tyranny and opened their eyes to the possibility of a controlled but effective executive office. Thus, over time, the antiexecutive sentiments began to wane, and there developed a growing recognition that while executive tyranny was still to be feared, an enfeebled executive was also a danger to good government.

Under the Articles, the national government was weak and ineffective. Soon, in each state, revolts of debtors threatened property and order. The most famous of these was led by Daniel Shays and know as Shays' Rebellion (1787). These mini-revolutions instilled fear into the propertied classes. Some longed for the imposed order of a monarchy. "Shall we have a king?" John Jay asked George Washington during Shays' Rebellion. This was not the first time Washington had been approached with such a suggestion. Several years earlier, in 1782, army units stationed in Newburgh, New York, openly spoke of making Washington monarch. But Washington unearthed the conspiracy and quickly put an end to it.

As the framers met in Philadelphia, most of those present recognized (many quite reluctantly) the need for an independent executive with *some* power. But what? No useful model existed anywhere in the known world. They would have to invent one.

Inventing the Presidency

The Revolution against Great Britain was largely a revolt against executive authority. Historian Bernard Bailyn said the rebellion made resistance to authority a divine doctrine.[4] The colonists were for the most part independent, egalitarian, and individualistic. Their symbols and rallying cries were antiauthority in nature and when it became necessary to establish a new national government, it was difficult to reestablish the respect for authority so necessary to support an effective government. Putting Humpty Dumpty back together proved a Herculean task.

Reconstructing executive authority out of the ashes of a revolution against the tyrannical king was a slow, contentious process. By 1787, when the framers met in Philadelphia to revise the Articles of Confederation, there was general agreement that a limited executive was necessary, but what kind of executive? Should it be one person or several? How should he be selected and for how long a term? And most importantly, what powers and limitations would he have?[5]

No decision at the convention was more difficult to reach than the scope and nature of executive power. The framers went through proposals, counterproposals, decisions, reconsiderations, postponements, and reversals, until finally a presidency was invented.[6] The confusion reflected what political scientist Harvey C. Mansfield Jr. referred to as the framers' "ambivalence of executive power."[7] Initially, most of the delegates were considered "congressionalist," hoping to create a government with a strong congress and a plural executive with limited power. Delegate George Mason proposed a three-person executive, as "no more than an institution for carrying the will of the legislature into effect."[8] But there were also advocates such as Alexander Hamilton, who supported a strong, independent, unitary executive. However, there was little support for this view, and Hamilton was forced to retreat. In this book, Melanie Marlowe argues otherwise. She sees the framers as creating a unitary executive with considerable independent power.[9]

James Madison, referred to as the father of the U.S. Constitution, had surprisingly little impact on the invention of the presidency, going so far as to write in a letter, dated April 16, 1787, to George Washington shortly before the convention, "I have scarcely ventured as yet to form my own opinion either of the manner in which [the executive] ought to be constituted or of the authorities with which it ought to be clothed."[10] Probably the most influential framer on the invention of the presidency was James Wilson of Pennsylvania. At first, Wilson sought the direct popular election of the president, yet he eventually lost that battle and instead helped develop what became the Electoral College. He also greatly influenced the choice of a single over a plural executive.

In the end, the framers wanted to strike a balance in executive power. They feared that making the presidency too strong would jeopardize liberty; making the office too weak would jeopardize good government. Yet how to achieve this balance remained a thorny issue. Unlike the Congress and judiciary, for which the framers found ample precedent, the presidency was truly new, invented in Philadelphia, different from any executive office that preceded it. The president would not be a king or a sovereign. He would swear to protect and defend a higher authority: a constitution.

The framers faced several difficult questions in inventing this office. First, how many executives? Should it be a single (unitary) or plural executive? Initial sympathy for a plural executive gave way to a single executive, primarily because it was deemed the best way to assign responsibility (and blame) for the execution of policy. The second question was how to choose the executive. Some proposed popular election, which was rejected because the framers feared the president might become tribune of the people or be able to inflame the passions of the masses. Others promoted selection by Congress. This was rejected on grounds that it might make the president the servant of Congress and would undermine the separation of powers. Finally, the framers invented an Electoral College as the best of several unappealing alternatives.

Next, for how long a term should the executive serve? Should the president serve for life, a set term, two years, four years, six years? If for a fixed term, should he be eligible for reelection? After much debate, the framers decided on a four-year term with reeligibility as an option. The president could be removed—impeached—for certain, not very clearly delineated offenses.

The trickiest question related to how much power this new president should be given. The president would not be a king, and the debates at the convention are peppered with antimonarchical sentiments. Charles Pickney of South Carolina was opposed to giving the president authority over war and peace because it "would render the Executive a Monarchy, of the worst kind, to wit an elective one." James Wilson of Pennsylvania concurred, arguing that "the prerogatives of the British Monarchy," are not "a proper guide in defining the executive powers. Some of the prerogatives were of a legislative nature. Among others that of war and peace." James Madison, speaking after Wilson agreed, said, ""Executive powers . . . do not include the rights of war and peace . . . but should be confined and defined—if large we should have the evils of elected Monarchies."[11]

The framers knew what they didn't want—an office resembling the monarchy they had just overthrown. They were less clear precisely on what they did want. Taming, not liberating, the prince, was their goal. The new president would be guided by the rule of law under a constitution—a constitution he would be required to take an oath to uphold.

The framers repudiated the English Monarchy and with it monarchial prerogative.[12] The new president was authorized to act only on the basis of law and never against it. The revolutionary rhetoric that animated the break with England is replete with condemnations of arbitrary power. Thomas Jefferson's Declaration of Independence, Thomas Paine's "Common Sense," and Samuel Adams's "The Rights of the Colonists" bristle at the arbitrary powers exercised by the King of England. As Paine reminded the colonists in "Common Sense," "in America the law is king. For as in absolute governments the King is law, so in free countries the law ought to be King; and there ought to be no other."

The framers could not reach a consensus on the president's power. They thus decided to create a bare skeleton of authority, and they left many areas vague and ambiguous, with gaping silences throughout Article II. These gaps would later allow advocates of a strong presidency—Presidentialists—to fill in the missing pieces with a view of presidential power that embraced expansive power.

Inventing a presidency was one thing; operationalizing it was quite another. Any examination of the invention of the American presidency that did not stress the importance of George Washington would be remiss. Every day, as the debates took place, the men at the Convention looked at the man presiding, secure in the knowledge that whatever else became of the presidency, George Washington would be the first officeholder. So confident were they of Washington's skills, integrity, and republican sentiments, that they felt comfortable leaving the presidency unfinished and incomplete. They would leave it to Washington to fill in the gaps and set the proper precedents.

The problem, of course, was that Washington would not always be president. Thus, while the framers trusted Washington, could they trust all of his successors? Leaving the presidency unfinished opened the door for future problems in the executive that Presidentialists exploited. Ben Franklin pointed to this when he noted, at the convention on June 4, 1787, "The first man, put at the helm, will be a good one. Nobody knows what sort may come afterwards."[13]

Washington is thus the chief reason why the office of the presidency was left somewhat elastic by the framers. The office was half finished with the expectation that Washington would fill in the blanks. And in some ways he did. But this also left openings that future presidents would exploit on the road to expanding executive power.

Maddeningly, the presidency that emerged from the Philadelphia Convention was an office with "very little plainly given, very little clearly withheld . . . the

Convention . . . did not define: it deferred."[14] This meant that the presidency would be shaped, defined, and created by those who occupied the office and by the demands of different eras. The framers invented a very "personal presidency," and much of the history of presidential power stems from the way individual presidents have understood and attempted to use the office to attain their goals. As Alan Wolfe has written, "The American presidency has been a product of practice, not theory. Concrete struggles between economic and political forces have been responsible for shaping it, not maxims from Montesquieu."[15] The unsettled nature of the presidency was a marked characteristic of this office and, to some, it was the true genius of the framers. The Constitution was less an act of clear design and intent and more a "mosaic of everyone's second choices."[16] The presidency, left unfinished and only partially formed at the Convention, had yet to be truly invented.[17]

While most scholars argue that the framers created an office limited by both laws (the Constitution) and structure (the separation and sharing of powers), some argue otherwise. The Unitary Executive view of the presidency—when taken to the extreme—sees the president possessing a vast reservoir of independent, unilateral, and constitutional authority—especially in war. This view (see Chapter 6 in this book) gained some visibility during the presidency of George W. Bush, when lawyers from the Justice Department's Office of Legal Counsel posited an expansive interpretation of presidential power, used to justify many of the more controversial actions of the administration. While still a minority view within the academic community, this ""Presidentialist" view continues to carry some weight among policy-making circles. Thus, the scope and limitations of presidential power remain contested territory.

The Presidency as a Constitutional Office

The framers invented a presidency of some strength but little independent power. They put the president in a position to lead (influence, persuade) but rarely command (order). The chief mechanisms established to control as well as to empower the executive are as follows: (1) *Limited Government,* a reaction against the arbitrary, expansive powers of the king, and a protection of personal liberty; (2) *Rule of Law,* so that only on the basis of legal or constitutional grounds could the government legitimately act; (3) *Separation of Powers,* so that each of the three branches of the government would have a defined sphere of power; and (4) *Checks and Balances,* so that each branch could, where necessary, limit or control the powers of the other branches of government.

As a bulwark against tyranny, the separation of powers is no panacea, but it is an important structural impediment to the establishment of one-man-rule. The framers did not invent an especially efficient system, yet efficiency was not the primary goal of the framers. As Justice Louis Brandeis reminds us in *Myers v.*

United States, this system was "adopted by the Convention of 1787, not to promote efficiency but to preclude the exercise of arbitrary power."[18]

Of course, there is no such thing as a pure or perfect separation, and as Madison noted in the *Federalist Papers,* some blending (or sharing) of power must occur if one branch is to truly check and balance another. Too rigid a separation "would be subversive of the efficiency of the government, and result in the destruction of the public liberties."[19] Thus powers are both separated and shared, blended and distinct. This partial separation allows each branch to exercise some powers concurrently. The goal of separation was not to incapacitate the government— they did, after all, want a government that could operate effectively—the goal was to better safeguard the exercise of power. As Justice Robert Jackson describes it, "While the Constitution diffuses power the better to secure liberty, it also contemplates that practice will integrate the dispersed powers into a workable government. It enjoins upon its branches separateness but interdependence, autonomy but reciprocity."[20]

Ironically, separation of power is never literally mentioned in the Constitution, not in the sense that we use the term in a checks and balances system. It is largely implied from the structure of power established in Articles I (Congress), II (Executive), and III (Judiciary) of the Constitution. These articles establish three separate branches, yet they require syncopation or collaboration of the branches if the government is to legitimately act. Shared and overlapping powers demand that the branches find ways to join what the framers have separated.

Article I of the Constitution is devoted to the Congress, the first and constitutionally the most powerful branch. Article II, the executive article, deals with the presidency. The president's power cupboard is—compared to the Congress— a bit threadbare. Section 1 gives the "executive power" to the presidency but does not reveal whether this is a grant of tangible power or merely a title issued to a single executive. As you will see later in this book, Davie Gray Adler has a different interpretation of the "executive power" than is presented here. Adler does not see very much independent power conferred or vested in the presidency as a result of Article II, Section 1. Section 2 makes the president Commander-in-Chief of the armed forces yet reserves the power to *declare* war for the Congress. Section 2 also gives the president power to grant reprieves and pardons, power to make treaties (with the advice and consent of the Senate), and the power to nominate ambassadors, judges, and other public ministers (again, with the advice and consent of the Senate). Section 3 calls for the president to inform Congress on the state of the Union and to recommend measures to Congress, grants the power to receive ambassadors, and imposes upon the president the duty to see that the laws are faithfully executed. These powers, while significant in and of themselves, do not suggest a strong independent institution and certainly not a powerful national leadership position.

Presidential Power in the Constitution

Presidential power, viewed solely from a constitutional perspective, is paradoxically both specific and obscure: specific in that some elements of presidential power are clearly spelled out (e.g., the veto power, a pardon power), obscure in that the limits and boundaries of presidential power are sometimes ill-defined or open to differences in interpretation (e.g., the president's power in foreign matters). In an effort to understand presidential power, the Constitution must be our starting point, yet it provides but a few definitive answers.

As historical circumstances changed, so too did our understanding of the Constitution. The scope and meaning of the executive clause (Article II, Section 1) has changed to meet the perceived needs of the times and the actions (demands) of strong presidents. The skeleton-like provisions of Article II left the words open to definition and redefinition by courts and presidents. The wording gives room for an aggressive chief executive, a sometimes compliant Congress, and an often willing Supreme Court to shape the shifting parameters of such powers. To a large degree, history has rewritten the Constitution. For two centuries, we have been debating just what the words of the Constitution mean, and this debate still rages on. The words are "flexible" enough to mean different things at different times, in different situations, yet not so flexible as to prove meaningless. Thus one can see the elasticity of the office. Over time, a more "expansive" view of the presidential power has taken precedence over a more "restrictive" view. The Presidentialists have largely won the argument. The history of the meaning of presidential power through the Constitution has been one of the expansion of power and the enlargement of the meaning of the words of the Constitution.[21]

The Constitution gives us a vague outline of the powers of the president, not a full picture. For, the presidency is more than the Constitution leads us to believe. As Haight and Johnston write, "The Presidency is above all an integrated institution, all of whose parts interlock with one another. Any description that discusses these parts individually cannot help being partially misleading."[22]

Presidential power exists in two forms: formal and informal. To fully understand presidential power, one must know how the formal and informal powers work and interact and how the combination of the two can lead to dominance by a president who, given the proper conditions and abilities, can exploit his power sources to full advantage.

The formal powers of the president revolve primarily around the constitutional powers to "command" and areas where the president may take direct action.[23] Perhaps the best example of the formal power of the president is the pardoning power. The Constitution grants the president sole power over pardons, and as controversial as many pardons have been (e.g., President Ford's pardon of former President Nixon, President George H. W. Bush's pardon of former Secretary of

Defense Casper Weinberger in the midst of his Iran-Contra trial, and Bill Clinton's pardon of Marc Rich), the president has been able to maintain nearly absolute control over pardons. Additionally, presidents claim to have the following:

- *Enumerated powers* (those expressly granted in the Constitution)
- *Implied powers* (those that may be inferred from power expressly granted)
- *Resulting powers* (those that result when several enumerated powers are added together)
- *Inherent powers* (those powers, especially in a field of external affairs that the Supreme Court has declared, do not depend upon constitutional grants but grow out of existence of the national government)

The informal powers of the president find their source primarily in the "political" and "personal" as opposed to the "constitutional." They are the powers acquired through politics and those resulting from individual skill, judgment, vision, and political circumstance. Richard Neustadt, in *Presidential Power*, discussed the informal power of the president to "persuade." Neustadt feels that the power to persuade is the most important of all the presidential powers, but the informal powers require skill at persuasion, political manipulation, coalition building, self-dramatization, and political mobilization.[24]

The president's formal powers are limited and (almost always) shared. The president's informal powers are a function of individual skill, situation, and political circumstance. While the formal powers of the president remain fairly constant over time, the president's informal powers are variable and dependent on the skill of each president.

What the Framers Gave Us

The framers of the U.S. Constitution created—by design—what has been called an "antileadership" system of government. This may sound grating to the modern ear, but upon reflection, it is clear that their primary goal—rather than to provide for an efficient system—was to create a government that would provide security and not jeopardize individual liberty. Freedom and security were their goals and governmental power often their nemesis. The framers created an executive institution, a presidency, that had limited powers.

For James Madison, chief architect of the Constitution, a powerful government might well become a dangerous government. Seeing himself as a student of history, Madison believed that human nature drove men to pursue self-interest, and thus a system of government designed to have "ambition checked by ambition" set within strict constitutional limits might establish a stable government that did not endanger liberty. Realizing that "enlightened statesmen" would not always guide the nation, Madison embraced a checks-and-balance system of separate but overlapping and shared powers. Madison's concern to have a government with controlled and limited powers is seen throughout his writings, yet nowhere is it more evident than in *Federalist* No. 51: "You must first enable the government to control the governed; and in the next place, oblige it to control itself."[25]

By contrast, Alexander Hamilton was a forceful defender of executive power. He promoted a version of executive power different from Madison's dispersed and separate powers. While Madison believed that the new government's powers should be "few and defined,"[26] Hamilton wanted to infuse the executive with "energy." Hamilton advocated vigorous government and a strong presidency. As Hamilton wrote in *Federalist* No. 70, good government requires "energy," and he scornfully rejected the weak executive: "A feeble executive implies a feeble execution of the government. A feeble execution is but another phrase for a bad execution; and a government ill executed, whatever it may be in theory, must be, in practice, a bad government."[27] To Hamilton, a strong executive was an essential ingredient that defined good government. Again to cite *Federalist* No. 70, "Energy in the executive is a leading character in the definition of good government. It is essential to the protection of the community against foreign attacks."

Hamilton called for a strong president within a more centralized system of government. But such a system would undermine Madison's determination to check government power. The presidency, a unitary office headed by one man, would have no internal check. Because of this, Madison believed in a need for strong external checks—that is, a strong Congress and rule of law system. While Madison may have won the day at the Constitutional Convention, creating a presidency with limited powers, history has largely been on the side of Hamilton. The presidency has grown to more closely resemble the Hamiltonian model than was originally intended by the framers.

Left strictly to its own constitutional devices, the Madisonian presidency was a somewhat limited institution. A dilemma was thus created, especially in the modern period: How could a president bring Hamiltonian energy to this Madisonian system, for Jeffersonian ends? The framers did not make it easy for the government to act—that was decidedly not their intent—and they left the powers of the office somewhat vague, expecting George Washington to fill in the gaps. This created, in Edward S. Corwin's words, "an invitation to struggle" for control of power.[28]

Most of the president's powers are shared with a Congress that has greater enumerated constitutional powers yet less of an institutional capacity to act. Sharing powers with a Congress that only occasionally responds to presidential initiatives makes leadership difficult. A system of baroque cross-powers and checked powers created a constitutional mechanism that is designed to prohibit one branch from exercising too much power on its own. Opportunities to check power abound;

opportunities to exercise power are limited. The fluidity and fragmentation of power creates a situation in which "the government" is controlled not by a single person or place but by different people in different places (if it exists at all), often seeking different ends.

As you will see in subsequent chapters, the jury is still out on the intent of the framers. Executive power, to Adler, the Constitutionalist, is narrower than that understood by Melanie Marlowe, an advocate of the Unitary Executive theory, who sees a more expansive executive.

What the Framers Meant, in Their Words

To better understand what the framers of the Constitution intended, we turn to the single most authoritative source for their views: *The Federalists Papers*.[29] Written to the citizens of New York in an effort to persuade them to support the ratification of the new Constitution, *The Federalist Papers* explain, in detail, the meaning of the document. While references to the executive are scattered throughout the *Federalist Papers,* the most direct description of this office is found in *Federalist* Nos. 67 to 77, all written by Alexander Hamilton.

In *The Federalist Papers,* Hamilton envisions an energetic executive, yet not one above the law, above Congress, above the Constitution, or independent of the other branches. The whole of *The Federalist Papers* presents a shared model of governance. If any one branch has the most power, it is Congress (Article I), yet even Congress shares some powers with the other branches.

Hamilton assures the reader that this new president is nothing like a monarch. If not a monarch, what then? This new president would be limited in power and connected via shared and overlapping powers to the other branches of government, especially to the Congress. The chief executive in a constitutional republic would be subject to the rule of law and bound by the Constitution.

Hamilton continues to debunk the charge leveled by Anti-Federalist critics of the Constitution that the president in some way resembles the Crown by drawing an explicit comparison in *Federalist* No. 69:

> I proceed now to trace the real characters of the proposed executive, as they are marked out in the plan of the convention. . . . The first thing which strikes our attention is that the executive authority, with few exceptions, is to be vested in a single magistrate. This will scarcely, however, be considered as a point upon which any comparison can be grounded; for if, in this particular, there be a resemblance to the king of Great Britain, there is not less a resemblance to the Grand Seignior, to the khan of Tartary, to the Man of the Seven Mountains, or to the governor of New York.

Even the power of Commander-in Chief has a legislative "turn on" switch, without which the title is of limited authority: "The President is to be the 'commander-in-chief' of the army and navy of the United States, and of the militia of the several States, when called into the actual service of the United States."[30] And who does the calling? The Congress. And the Congress alone has the power to declare war.

The president also must follow the law, as he takes an oath "to take care that the laws be faithfully executed":

> In most of these particulars, the power of the President will resemble equally that of the king of Great Britain and of the governor of New York. The most material points of difference are these:—*First.* The President will have only the occasional command of such part of the militia of the nation as by legislative provision may be called into the actual service of the Union . . . the power of the President would be inferior to that of either the monarch or the governor. *Second.* The President is to be commander-in-chief of the army and navy of the United States. In this respect his authority would be nominally the same with that of the king of Great Britain, but in substance much inferior to it. It would amount to nothing more than the supreme command and direction of the military and naval forces, as first general and admiral of the Confederacy; while that of the British king extends to the *declaring* of war and to the *raising* and *regulating* of fleets and armies—all which, by the Constitution under consideration, would appertain to the legislature. . . . *Third.* The power of the President in respect to pardon, would extend to all cases, *except those of impeachment.* . . . *Fourth.* The President can only adjourn the national legislature in the single case of disagreement about the time of adjournment. The British monarch may prorogue or even dissolve the Parliament. . . . The President is to have power, with the advice and consent of the Senate, to make treaties, provided two thirds of the senators present concur. The king of Great Britain is the sole and absolute representative of the nation in all foreign transactions. He can of his own accord make treaties of peace, commerce, alliance, and of every other description.[31]

Hamilton then concludes as follows:

> Hence it appears that except as to the concurrent authority of the President in the article of treaties, it would be difficult to determine whether that magistrate would in the aggregate possess more or less power than the governor of New York. And it appears yet more unequivocally that there is no pretense for the parallel which has been attempted between him and the king of Great Britain.[32]

Next, Hamilton moves on to describe what is necessary to ensure good government. In *Federalist* No. 72, Hamilton envisions "energy in the executive" as a leading cause of good government. Yet, as we have seen, "energy" does not mean an autonomous, independent, or all-powerful president:

> There is an idea, which is not without its advocates, that a vigorous executive is inconsistent with the genius of republican government. . . . Energy in the executive is a leading character in the definition of good government. It is essential to the protection of the community against foreign attacks; it is not less essential to the steady administration of the laws; to the protection of property against those irregular and high-handed combinations which sometimes interrupt the ordinary course of justice; to the security of liberty against the enterprises and assaults of ambition, of faction, and of anarchy. Every man the least conversant in Roman history knows how often that republic was obliged to take refuge in the absolute power of a single man, under the formidable title of dictator, as well against the intrigues of ambitious individuals who aspired to the tyranny, and the seditions of whole classes of the community whose conduct threatened the existence of all government, as against the invasions of external enemies who menaced the conquest and destruction of Rome.

A "vigorous executive" with "energy" is Hamilton's goal. The words *vigorous* and *energy* do not translate into a president above the law, independent of Congress, or adrift from the moorings of the Constitution. A vigorous, energetic, republican executive may be a strong executive but not an absolutist executive. Hamilton continues to develop this theme, writing as follows:

> A feeble executive implies a feeble execution of the government. A feeble execution is but another phrase for a bad execution; and a government ill executed, whatever it may be in theory, must be, in practice, a bad government. Taking it for granted, therefore, that all men of sense will agree in the necessity of an energetic executive, it will only remain to inquire, what are the ingredients which constitute this energy? How far can they be combined with those other ingredients which constitute safety in the republic sense? And how far does this combination characterize the plan which has been reported by the convention?

This is where Hamilton more fully develops his "energy in the executive" theme. In giving the executive energy, Hamilton insists that this energetic executive constitutes "safety in the republican sense." He goes back to constitutionalism and republicanism as the sacred standard against which the energetic executive must ultimately be judged.

Hamilton asks us to consider two related themes, the *energetic executive* as well as the demands of *republican safety*: "The ingredients which constitute energy in the executive are unity; duration; an adequate provision for its support; and competent powers. The ingredients which constitute safety in the republican sense are a due dependence on the people, and a due responsibility."

For the remainder of *Federalist* No. 70, Hamilton discusses "unity" in the executive. The single executive, the source of unity, is defended as the best source of both effectiveness and republican responsibility: "That unity is conducive to energy will not be disputed. Decision, activity, secrecy, and dispatch will generally characterize the proceedings of any greater number; and in proportion as the number is increased, these qualities will be diminished."

And what happens when the executive and legislature wish to move in different directions?

But however inclined we might be to insist upon an unbounded complaisance in the Executive to the inclinations of the people, we can with no propriety contend for a like complaisance to the humors of the legislature. The latter may sometimes stand in opposition to the former, and at other times the people may be entirely neutral. In either supposition, it is certainly desirable that the Executive should be in a situation to dare to act his own opinion with vigor and decision.

The same rule which teaches the propriety of a partition between the various branches of power, teaches us likewise that this partition ought to be contrived as to render the one independent of the other. To what purpose separate the executive or the judiciary from the legislative, if both the executive and the judiciary are so constituted as to be at the absolute devotion of the legislative? Such a separation must be merely nominal, and incapable of producing the ends for which it was established. It is one thing to be subordinate to the law and another to be dependent of the legislative body. The first comports with, the last violates, the fundamental principles of good government; and, whatever may be the forms of the Constitution unites all power in the same hands. The tendency of the legislative authority to absorb every other has been fully displayed and illustrated by examples in some preceding numbers. In government purely republican, this tendency is almost irresistible. The representatives of the people, in a popular assembly, seem sometimes to fancy that they are the people themselves, and betray strong symptoms of impatience and disgust at the least sign of opposition from any other quarter; as if the exercise of its rights, by either the executive or judiciary, were a breach of their privilege and an outrage to their dignity. They often appear disposed to exert an imperious control over the other departments; and as they commonly have the people on their side, they always act with such momentum as to make it very difficult for the other members of the government to maintain the balance of the Constitution.

The president is not the servant of the legislature; he is the servant of the law. Separation yes, but not absolutely; shared power, yes, but not servitude. The president was to be neither pied piper nor puppet of the Congress. It is a delicate balance. The final line of this last quote insists on balance as the goal. No one branch rules or dominates another: shared, overlapping, separate, balanced.

Federalist Nos. 74 to 77 continue to develop the theme of power as it relates to energy in the executive and the protection of republican government. In *Federalist* No. 74, Hamilton writes as follows:

The President of the United States is to be "commander-in-chief of the army and navy of the United States, and of the militia of the several States *when called into the actual service* of the United States." The propriety of this provision is so evident in itself, and it is, at the same time, so consonant to the precedents of the State constitutions in general, that little need be said to explain or enforce it. Even those of them which have, in other respects, coupled the chief magistrate with a council, have for the most part concentrated the military authority in him alone. Of all the cares or concerns of government, the direction of war most peculiarly demands those qualities which distinguish the exercise of power by a single hand. The direction of war implies the direction of the common strength; and the power of directing and employing the common strength, forms a usual and essential part in the definition of the executive authority.

Federalist No. 77 concludes with Hamilton reiterating his commitment to an energetic executive yet one that operates within a republican web of controls:

We have now completed a survey of the structure and powers of the executive department, which, I have endeavored to show combines, as far as republican principles will admit, all the requisites to energy. The remaining inquiry is: Does it also combine the requisites to safety, in a republican sense, a due dependence on the people, a due responsibility? The answer to this question has been anticipated in the investigation of its other characteristics, and is satisfactorily deducible from these circumstances; from the election of the President once in four years by persons immediately chosen by the people for that purpose; and from his being at all times liable to impeachment, trial, dismissal from office, incapacity to serve in any other, and to forfeiture of life and estate by subsequent prosecution in the common course of law. But these precautions, great as they are, are not the only ones which the plan of the convention has provided in favor of the public security. In the only instances in which the abuse of the executive authority was materially to be feared, the Chief Magistrate of the United States would, by that plan, be subjected to the control of a branch of the legislative body. What more can an enlightened and reasonable people desire?

The Evolution of Presidential Power

If the Constitution invented the skeletal outline of the presidency, and George Washington operationalized an incomplete creation, history more fully formed this elastic and evolving institution. Over time, the presidency grew from chief clerk to chief executive to national leader to imperial presidency. Thus, in some ways, the presidency is less an outgrowth of constitutional design and more a reflection of ambitious men, demanding times, exploited opportunities, and changing economic and international circumstances.

The original design created opportunities for ambitious men, especially in times of necessity, to increase presidential power. The presidency—elastic, adaptable, chameleon-like—has been able to transform itself to meet what the times demanded, ambitious officeholders grabbed, the people wanted, and world events and American power dictated.

Some presidents have been strong, others weak. Some eras demand change, others defy it.[33] The presidency has been shaped by industrialization, urbanization, the Cold War, the war against terrorism, American superpower status, economic booms and busts, and wars and demands of capitalism. Presidents helped shape some of these changes and were victims and innocent bystanders of others. Great social movements, technological changes, newly emergent groups, and a host of other forces created opportunities and restraints on leadership. The story of the rise and fall of presidential power is a complex and perplexing one. It is a story of elasticity and adaptability, of leadership and clerkship, of strong and weak officeholders, of change and stasis.

If one could plot the changes in presidential power over time, the overall trend would be upward, toward greater power. Yet it would not be a straight line. There is an action–reaction cycle at work, a zigzagging of presidential power that goes up and down over time. Strong presidents who added to the scope of presidential power were followed by weaker presidents as Congress or the courts rose up to defend their authority from presidential encroachments. Washington was followed by the weaker Adams; Jefferson by Madison, Monroe, and another Adams; Jackson was followed by Van Buren, Harrison, and Tyler; Polk was followed by Taylor, Fillmore, Pierce, and Buchanan; Lincoln by Johnson and others; Teddy Roosevelt by Taft; Wilson by Harding, Coolidge and Hoover; FDR and Truman by Eisenhower; LBJ and Nixon by Ford and Carter; Reagan by George H. W. Bush.[34]

We are left with what political scientist Jeffrey K. Tulis refers to as the "two constitutional presidencies."[35] There is the Constitution as written and the Constitution as it has evolved, the former a limited constitutional office, the latter, a more expansive, popularly based institution. The second presidency was invented to overcome the alleged shortcomings (in presidential power) of the original Constitution. If the framers saw the separation of powers as Madison's blessing, modern presidents often tend to see it as Madison's curse, the thing to be overcome if one is to govern effectively.

Ideology, Ideas, and the Modern Presidency

There was a time when there was a debate in the United States over the size, scope, and power of the American presidency. Lamentably, that debate has gone underground. It is time to reinvigorate that debate in light of the changes in the presidency brought on by the war against terrorism.

In the 1920s, the United States had a presidency still somewhat limited in size, narrower in scope, and reduced in power. The U.S. was only just emerging as a world power, and given the demands placed upon the office as well as the more limited public expectations, the presidency could be smaller, less powerful, and less ubiquitous.[36] With the onset of the Great Depression of 1929, then World War II, then the Cold War, the need for a larger, more powerful presidency became apparent. A large, powerful institutional presidency was created.

The Depression added new responsibilities for economic and social welfare roles to the federal government. World War II mobilized the nation not only for war but for centralized authority, and the Cold War brought on the creation of a National Security State headed by a powerful (and often unaccountable) president.[37] This strong, anti-Communist foreign policy presidency was generally supported by both the left and right on the political spectrum.

And yet, not all were sanguine about the central role of the presidency and the growth of presidential power. Conservatives emerged as contrarians, warning that the presidency was becoming a Leviathan, powerful and out of control. This presidency threatened the fabric of representative government and posed a very real threat to the separation of powers and checks and balances that had so ably served the United States for so many years. Calling for less, not more government, conservatives seemed to be tilting at windmills in an era of big government.

Conservative scholars such as James Burnham, Willmoore Kendall, and Alfred De Grazia[38] may have seemed lonely voices in the wilderness, yet they were steadfast in warning of the dangers of expanded presidential power. William F. Buckley's *National Review* also came out against the rise of the presidency. And 1964 Republican presidential candidate Barry Goldwater harangued against centralized presidential authority and big government. But they were no match for the intoxicating lure of the presidency.

Liberals countered these conservative critics with two main arguments: presidential leadership was inevitable, and presidential leadership was good. It was inevitable because when the U.S. became the leader of the West, it required strong, centralized leadership to oppose Communism and provide global leadership. It was positive in that only a strong president could overcome the lethargy built into the checks and balance system and provide progressive leadership to a system mired in gridlock.

From the end of World War II through the mid-1960s, this liberal versus conservative argument animated U.S. politics. But by the late 1960s, opposition to the war in Vietnam (a presidential war) led many liberals to question the very core assumption of the heroic presidency model they had so vigorously been promoting.

If Vietnam served as a wake-up call to the dangers of unchecked presidential power, the Watergate scandal all but brought the presidency to its knees, but not before conservatives could catch a glimpse of how alluring presidential power could be. Richard Nixon attempted to employ an "administrative" approach to governing that, had he not been dragged down by the crimes of Watergate, demonstrated how conservative presidents could engage in an end-run around Congress and govern independent of the legislature. Some conservatives found this too tempting to resist.[39] (See Table 1–1 for the fluctuation in presidential power over time.)

The Johnson and Nixon presidencies spurred a presidency-bashing period in which liberals (and some conservatives) turned on the office, characterizing it as "imperial." For a time (the Ford and Carter years), liberals embraced a small presidency notion, and a series of president curbing bills, such as the War Powers Resolution, were passed.

After a brief respite from presidential power, a bizarre turnaround occurred. With the election of Ronald Reagan, conservatives vigorously embraced a very unconservative position: Why not use the powers of the big government and big presidency to achieve conservative ends? Animated by the person and agenda of Ronald Reagan and determined to impose a new order on American politics, conservatives became seduced by the lure of presidential power and began to embrace a liberal (i.e., big government) approach to achieve their conservative ends. Conservative think tankers such as Terry Eastland[40] began to argue that presidential power, rather than poison, was the best way to impose conservative principles on the American polity.

TABLE 1–1 Fluctuations of Modern Era of Presidential Power

Era	Precipitating Event	Result
1930s	Great Depression	Increased role of presidency in domestic/economic policy; rise of American Welfare State
1940s	World War II	Centralized presidential power for war
1950s	Cold War	Bipartisan support for presidential power to fight Communism
1960s	Great Society	Growth of presidency in domestic policy
1970s	Vietnam/Watergate	Reaction, retreat from imperial presidential power
1980s	Conservative Rebirth	Right embraces big government/big presidency
1990s	Reaction	Reaction and retreat from presidential power
2000s	September 11, 2001	War against terrorism and return of imperial presidency

During the Reagan years, many one-time conservatives were converted to big-government advocates, calling for the repeal of the 22nd Amendment (which limits the president to two terms), embracing an imperial presidency in foreign affairs, supporting a huge growth in the size of government (the military component), voting to raise the federal government debt ceiling, eschewing a commitment to balanced budgets, and supporting the regal trappings of the office.

Ronald Reagan ran as a conservative, employed the rhetoric of conservatism (e.g., "government is not the solution to our problem; government *is* the problem"), yet governed as a big government activist. As scholar Julian E. Zelizer has written:

> Like Nixon, President Ronald Reagan believed in the usefulness of the presidency for conservative objectives. Reagan learned that Congress would present major obstacles to his conservative agenda even when Republicans controlled the Senate between 1980 and 1986. In response, Reagan and his Cabinet aggressively relied on executive power as a way to achieve conservative objectives that otherwise would have fallen to defeat.[41]

By the end of the Reagan years, both the Democrats and Republicans, liberals and conservatives, were in large part big government and big presidency advocates. The conservatism of the New Deal era seemed a quaint relic of the past. The United States was *the* dominant hegemonic power of the West, and with the collapse of the Soviet empire, the United States became the world's sole superpower. A big, powerful presidency—one size fit all—became the darling of both political parties.

America's dominant position in the world, its vast responsibilities, massive military, and powerful economy all seemed to cry out for strong presidential leadership. If we were the big kids on the global block, we needed strong, centralized power to guide us in a treacherous world. The Soviet Union may have collapsed, yet there were other dangers lurking in the mud. And September 11, 2001, brought those dangers right into our homes.

The Presidency and 9/11

Americans awoke (literally as well as figuratively) to a new threat on the morning of September 11, 2001. Terrorists commandeered airplanes and—as seen on international television—flew them into the Twin Towers of the World Trade Center in New York City. They also flew a plane into the Pentagon in Washington, DC, and another crashed into a field near Shanksville, Pennsylvania.

This act of barbarism drew an immediate response. U.S. citizens demanded that the president act. We looked, almost instinctively, to the White House for reassurance, response, and revenge. Power and trust were invested in one man—the President of the United States. Yet, questions remained.

The debate over presidential power after 9/11 was fought largely between the *Presidentialist* camp (the Unitary Executive), whose members see an expansive presidency, and the *Constitutionalist* camp, whose members argue that the Constitution calls for a sharing of power by the president and Congress. After 9/11, the Presidentialists grew bolder and began to make claims for the presidency that to some seemed to run counter to the weight of historical and constitutional evidence.[42]

Emboldened by the terrorist attack against the United States, armed with overwhelming public support for an aggressive response, cognizant of the withering away of an independent congressional response, and unconcerned with the potential checking power of the courts, these Presidentalists ratcheted up their claims of presidential power and mobilized the government in support of their policies. Many of these Conservatives (or neo-Conservatives), who attacked the use of presidential power when in the hands of Democrats,[43] now called for unchecked presidential power in the hands of the conservative, George W. Bush.

In politics, so many advances are opportunity based. September 11 created an opportunity for conservative Presidentialists to seize power and pursue their political and policy objectives virtually unchecked. They were not shy about using this power. And their intellectual justification can be found in what is called "the Unitary Executive."

The Unitary Executive

If, as the Bush administration asserted, the war against terrorism will be a war without end, and if "necessity" trumps the Constitution, giving the president a vastly increased reservoir of power, it is imperative to come to grips with the potential threats the war powers pose to the constitutional republic. If used too hesitantly or unwisely, the security and future of the nation are put at risk; if used too aggressively or too expansively, the security of the constitutional republic is endangered.

The cache for the unitary executive grew primarily out of several law journal articles touting a new, originalist construction of the robust version of presidential power.[44] Yet, even many conservatives are skeptical of this newly discovered originalist construction of broad presidential power. [45] Dissecting the Unitary Executive doctrine, conservative columnist George F. Will refers to "this monarchical doctrine," writing as follows: "It is that whenever the nation is at war, the other two branches of government have a radically diminished pertinence to governance and the president determines what the pertinence shall be."[46] (See also Melanie Marlowe's chapter in this book.)

Initially, the Bush administration was powerful and popular. But as the results of the administration's actions in Iraq and elsewhere came home to roost and soured with the public, allies, and political opponents, the Bush presidency was compelled to move beyond its bold power assertions and present a political and intellectual justification of its unilateral actions.[47]

Many of the president's policies were highly controversial. On his own claimed authority, he established military tribunals (commissions); set questionable standards for determining "enemy combatants"; seemed to authorize torture; set up a detention center at Guantanamo Bay, Cuba; began a policy of "extraordinary renditions"; established an illegal National Security Agency eavesdropping program domestically; set up secret detention centers in Europe; denied U.S. citizens habeas corpus; and denied citizens access to attorneys, all on his own claimed wartime authority and without congressional approval. It was a breathtaking claim, as well as exercise of presidential prerogative.[48]

While his popularity hovered at the 80 percent range, the president felt emboldened by a clear mission and political capital that was unrivaled. Yet his power level did not last. As the war in Iraq soured; as examples of the torture of U.S. prisoners came to light; as memos defending torture and extralegal authority on behalf of the president were leaked to the press; as news of "extraordinary renditions" hit the airwaves; as the stories out of the U.S. detention center in Guantanamo Bay, Cuba, surfaced; as the shocking photos of Abu Ghraib were released; as the president's plans for military tribunals and denial of Geneva Convention rights became known; the administration was forced into a defensive posture. Could all these acts emanate solely from the executive branch? Did the president have that much unchecked power?

Critics went on the attack, arguing that the president's actions threatened the separation of powers, Rule of Law, the Constitution, and checks and balances. And while George W. Bush was not the first president to move beyond the law, his bold assertion that the Rule of Law did not bind a president in time of war marked a new, and critics charged dangerous, approach and was a grave challenge to the Constitution and the separation of powers.

Bush was comfortable exercising a swaggering style of leadership that was dubbed "the Un-Hidden Hand" leadership style. There was nothing subtle about this ostentatious approach. It was leadership by sledgehammer.[49] At first it worked. But over time, boldness proved insufficient. Critics demanded to know what were the underpinnings of the presidential boldness. The answer: a theory of power known as the Unitary Executive.[50]

The Unitary Executive is a model of presidential power that posits that "all" executive powers belong exclusively to the president.[51] In its most expansive form, the Unitary Executive sees presidential authority disembodied from the separation of powers and checks and balances, and thus it seems in contradiction to the original model of constitutionalism envisioned by the framers.[52] This monarchical conception of presidential power was posited by Richard M. Nixon when he said, "When the president does it, that means that it is not illegal."[53]

Modern-day Presidentialists see a Hobbesian world where war and violence are the norm, a world where governments are created to provide order in a disorderly world. And who is better positioned to provide order, direction, and centralized leadership than the president?

Conclusion

If indeed the presidency is contested territory, we must now have the debate over the scope and limits of presidential power, a debate that will determine the future of the office. A rich variety of options are before us. Do we wish to embrace the Libertarian alternative? The Constitutional option? A Conservative, Moderate, or Liberal approach? Is the Presidentialist model our best hope for the future?

A democracy requires that we choose. This book is an effort to jump-start the debate. We are today poised on a precipice. What we choose will shape the presidency for decades to come.

Ours is an 18th-century Constitution governing a 21st-century superpower. Just as we have outgrown the clothes we wore as a child, some argue that we have outgrown our Constitution. This is the argument implicitly made by the Justice Department's Office of Legal Council Lawyers during the Bush administration, and we must ask if this position, the Presidentalists' Unitary Executive position, is—or is not—legitimate. Or can the world's only superpower be guided by a Constitution written in an age when travel and communication were slow, weapons were of limited destructive capability, and the United States was a tiny, weak state?

In the war against terrorism, the size, scope, and power of the presidency expanded dramatically. There was a tectonic shift toward the executive. Is that inevitable and necessary, wise and justified, or do we wish to reclaim the rule of law, separation of powers, and checks and balances? The fault lines are still threatening us. Let the debate begin.

Notes

1. See Thomas E. Cronin and Michael A. Genovese, *The Paradoxes of the American Presidency*, 3rd ed. (New York: Oxford University Press, 2010).
2. Clinton Rossiter, *The American Presidency* (Baltimore: Johns Hopkins University Press, 1960), 59.
3. See Noah Webster, *Sketches of American Policy*, ed. Harry R. Warfel (New York: Scholars' Facsimiles & Reprints, 1937).
4. See Bernard Bailyn, *The Ideological Origins of the American Revolution* (Cambridge, MA: Harvard University Press, 1967), Chapter 4.
5. See Charles C. Thach Jr., *The Creation of the Presidency, 1775–1789: A Study in Constitutional History* (Baltimore: Johns Hopkins University Press, 1923).
6. Thomas E. Cronin, ed., *Inventing the American Presidency* (Lawrence: University Press of Kansas, 1989).
7. See Harvey C. Mansfield Jr., *Taming the Prince: The Ambivalence of Modern Executive Power* (New York: Free Press, 1989), Chapter 1.
8. "The Debates in the Federal Convention of 1787 Reported by James Madison: June 1," the Avalon Project at Yale Law School.
9. See also, John Yoo, *Crisis and Command* (New York: Kaplan, 2009); Steve G. Calabresi and Christopher S. Yoo, *The Unitary Executive* (New Haven, CT: Yale University Press, 2008).
10. James Madison, letter to George Washington, April 16, 1787, The Founders' Constitution, Volume 1, Chapter 8, Document 6, accessed May 14, 2006, http://press-pubs.uchicago.edu/founders/documents/v1ch8s6.html.
11. For further quotations, see Peter Irons, *War Powers: How the Imperial Presidency Hijacked the Constitution* (New York: Henry Holt, 2005), 11–27.
12. See Michael A. Genovese, *Presidential Prerogative: Imperial Power in an Age of Terrorism* (Palo Alto, CA: Stanford University Press, 2011).
13. "The Debates in the Federal Convention of 1787 Reported by James Madison: June 4," the Avalon Project at Yale Law School, accessed May 14, 2006, http://www.yale.edu/lawweb/avalon/debates/604.htm. Accessed May 14, 2006.
14. Ralph Ketcham, *Presidents Above Party* (Chapel Hill: University of North Carolina Press, 1984), 9.
15. Alan Wolfe, "Presidential Power and the Crisis of Modernization," *Democracy* 1, no. 2 (1981): 21.
16. Charles Beard and Mary Beard, *The Rise of American Civilization* (New York: Macmillan, 1933), 317.
17. For a historical review of the rise of presidential power, see Michael A. Genovese, *The Power of the American Presidency 1789–2000* (New York: Oxford University Press, 2000).
18. *Myers v. United States* 272 U.S. 52, 293, 1926.

19. Joseph Story, *Commentaries on the Constitution of the United States* (Minneapolis, MN: Filiquarian Publishing, 2010).

20. *Youngstown Sheet & Tube Co. v. Sawyer* 343 U.S. 579, 635, 1952.

21. See Michael A. Genovese, *The Power of the American Presidency, 1787–2000* (New York: Oxford University Press, 2000).

22. David E. Haight and Larry D. Johnston, eds., *The President: Role and Powers* (Chicago: Rand McNally, 1965), 1.

23. See William G. Howell, *Power Without Persuasion: The Politics of Direct Presidential Action* (Princeton, NJ: Princeton University Press, 2003).

24. See Richard Neustadt, *Presidential Power* (New York: Wiley, 1960).

25. James Madison, Alexander Hamilton, and John Jay, *Federalist* No. 51, in *The Federalist With Letters of "Brutus,"* ed. Terrence Ball (Cambridge, UK: Cambridge University Press, 2003), 252.

26. James Madison, *Federalist* No. 45, in *The Federalist with Letters of "Brutus,"* ed. Terrence Ball (Cambridge, U.K.: Cambridge University Press, 2003), 227.

27. Alexander Hamilton, *Federalist* No. 70, in *The Federalist with Letters of "Brutus,"* ed., Terrence Ball (Cambridge, U.K.: Cambridge University Press, 2003), 341.

28. Edward S. Corwin, *The President: Office and Powers, 1978–1984,* 5th ed. (New York: New York University Press, 1984), originally published in 1940. See also Joseph M. Bessette and Jeffery Tulis, *The Presidency in the Constitutional Order* (Baton Rouge: Louisiana State University Press, 1981); Louis Fisher, *The Constitution Between Friends* (New York: St. Martin's Press, 1978).

29. Alexander Hamilton, James Madison, and John Jay, *The Federalist Papers,* ed. Michael A. Genovese (New York: Palgrave Macmillan, 2010) *The Federalist Papers* are used as much as a political tool as a source of expert commentary. Readers should be especially sensitive to the uses toward which *The Federalist Papers* are sometimes directed.

30. *Federalist* No. 69.

31. *Federalist* No. 69.

32. *Federalist* No. 69.

33. Stephen Skowronek, *The Politics Presidents Make: Leadership From John Adams to Bill Clinton* (Cambridge, MA: Belknap, 1997).

34. Michael A. Genovese, *The Power of the American Presidency* (New York: Oxford University Press 2000).

35. Jeffrey K. Tulis, "The Two Constitutional Presidencies," in *The Presidency and the Political System,* ed. Michael Nelson (Washington, DC: CQ Press, 2010), 1–33.

36. See Michael A. Genovese, *The Power of the American Presidency, 1789–2000* (New York: Oxford University Press, 2000).

37. See Garry Wills, *Bomb Power: The Modern Presidency and the National Security State* (New York, Penguin, 2010).

38. James Burnham, *Congress and the American Tradition* (Piscataway, NJ: Transaction Publishers, 2003, originally published in 1959); Willmoore Kendall, "The Two Majorities," in *Midwest Journal of Politics* (Bloomington, IN: Midwest Political Science Association, 1960); and Alfred De Grazia, *Republic in Crisis* (Carmel, NY: Federal Legal Publications, 1965).

39. Jeffrey Hart, "The Presidency: Shifting Conservative Perspective?" *National Review*, November, 1974.

40. Terry Eastland, *Energy in the Executive: The Case for an Active Presidency* (New York: The Free Press, 1992).

41. Julian E. Zelizer, "The Conservative Embrace of Presidential Power," *Boston University Law Review* 88, no. 2 (2008):500.

42. For a critique, see Robert J. Spitzer, "The Unitary Executive and the Commander-in-Chief," in *Saving the Constitution From Lawyers* (Cambridge, UK: Cambridge University Press, 2008), 90–128.

43. See John Yoo's attack against President Clinton's use of presidential power in John C. Yoo, "The Imperial President Abroad," in *The Rule of Law in the Wake of Clinton,* ed. Roger Pilon (Washington, DC: The Cato Institute, 2000).

44. Michael Stokes Paulsen, "The Constitution of Necessity," *Notre Dame Law Review* 79 (2004, July): 1257; see also, Steven G. Calabresi and Kevin H. Rhodes, "The Structural Constitution: Unitary Executive, Plural Judiciary," *Harvard Law Review* 105 (1992): 1153.

45. Harold H. Bruff, *Bad Advice: Bush's Lawyers in the War on Terror* (Lawrence: University Press of Kansas, 2009).

46. George F. Will, "No Checks, Many Imbalances," *The Washington Post,* editorial, February 16, 2006, A27.

47. Louis Fisher, "The Unitary Executive: Ideology Verses the Constitution" (paper presented at the annual meeting of the American Political Science Association, Philadelphia, PA, 2006).

48. James P. Pfiffner, *Power Play: The Bush Presidency and the Constitution* (Washington, DC: Brookings, 2008); Louis Fisher, *The Constitution and 9/11* (Lawrence: University Press of Kansas, 2008).

49. See Betty Glad and Chris J. Dolan, eds., *Striking First* (New York: Palgrave Macmillan, 2005).

50. The source of the president's justifications for the exercise of the extraordinary powers can be seen in a series of memos, most of which were written by members of the Office of Legal Counsel. See John C. Yoo, "The President's Constitutional Authority to Conduct Military Operations Against Terrorists and Nations Supporting Them," Memorandum Opinion for the Deputy Counsel to the President, September 25, 2001; Jay S. Bybee, Assistant Attorney General, U.S. Department of Justice, "Memorandum for Alberto R. Gonzales." On December 30, 2004, the Justice Department issued a new memorandum, which repudiated the administration's August 2002 memorandum rejecting the earlier, narrow view of torture; Working Group Report on Detainee Interrogations in the Global War on Terrorism; Assessment of Legal, Historical, Policy, and Operational Considerations," April 4, 2003, accessed March 25, 2011, http://www.defenselink.mil/news/Jun2004/d20040622doc8.pdf. For all Bush Administration legal memos, see *The Torcher Papers: The Road to Abu Ghraib,* Kren J. Greenberg and Joshua L. Dratel, eds. (Cambridge, UK: Cambridge University Press, 2005).

51. See Steven G. Calabresi and Kevin H. Rhodes, "The Structural Constitution: Unitary Executive, Plural Judiciary," *Harvard Law Review* 105 (1992): 1153-1216; Steven G. Calabresi and Christopher S. Yoo, *A History of the Unitary Executive: Executive Branch Practice From 1789–2004* (New Haven, CT: Yale University Press, forthcoming).

52. Christopher S. Yoo, Steven G. Calabresi, and Anthony J. Colangelo, "The Unitary Executive in the Modern Era, 1945–2004," *Iowa Law Review* 90 (2004): 601; Christopher S. Yoo, Steven G. Calabresi, and Lawrence D. Nee, "The Unitary Executive During the Third Half-Century, 1889–1945," *Notre Dame Law Review* 80 (2004): 1; Steven G. Calabresi and Christopher Yoo, "The Unitary Executive During the Second Half-Century," *Harvard Journal of Law and Public Policy* 26 (2003): 668; Steven G. Calabresi and Christopher S. Yoo, "The Unitary Executive During the First Half-Century," *Case Western Reserve Law Review* 47 (1997): 1451; Steven G. Calabresi and Saikrishna B. Prakash, "The President's Power to Execute the Laws," *The Yale Law Journal* 104 (1994): 541.

53. See Frederick A. O. Schwarz Jr. and Aziz Z. Haq, *Unchecked and Unbalanced: Presidential Power in a Time of Terror* (New York: The New Press, 2007), Introduction.

CHAPTER 1

Conservatives and the Presidency

Ryan J. Barilleaux

I AM A CONSERVATIVE. I believe that "established laws, customs, and traditions provide continuity and stability in guiding society."[1] As an American conservative, I believe that the United States possesses a political tradition that should be preserved through citizen support and careful statecraft. The president plays a leading role in protecting the American tradition, and the presidency serves the nation poorly when it ignores that tradition or acts in ways that will undermine it. As a conservative, I want a president who can be strong enough to serve the nation's defense and security needs, but who respects our tradition of constitutional balance and limited government. Achieving that kind of presidency requires reform.

What do conservatives mean by reform? The answer lies in understanding the distinction—important to conservatives—between reform and change: Conservatives favor reforms that preserve the principles and traditions that are key to promoting continuity and stability in society, but they oppose those changes aimed at implementing someone's vision for remaking society and politics. This distinction has led conservatives to resist "progressive" plans for social change through the power of the central government, such as Lyndon Johnson's Great Society or President Obama's remaking of the American health care system. But it has also led conservatives to favor great political reforms such as the adoption of the Constitution, as well as specific policies such as Ronald Reagan's tax cuts and budget priorities (toward defense and away from domestic programs) to check the growth of the welfare state and enhance the nation's security.

When it comes to considering the American presidency, conservatives want reform rather than merely change. We want a presidency that will be strong in those areas where the federal government ought to be strong—specifically, defense and national security—but more restrained in those areas—most of domestic policy—where state and local government and/or private enterprise ought to take the lead. As we shall see, conservative ideas about reforming the presidency distinguish it from other perspectives because they seek a careful balance that is consistent with the American political tradition.

What a Conservative Believes

As the eminent conservative thinker Russell Kirk once put it, conservatism is more a "state of mind" about life than an ideology, and it usually defends the status quo because conservatives believe that change should arise from experience, history, and tradition rather than rationalist schemes for remaking society.[2] While there are different varieties of conservatism (each with a different emphasis on the most important values), they are generally united by agreement on several core principles.

Since conservatives value continuity and stability and favor "established laws, customs, and traditions," they see themselves not as cosmopolitan citizens of the world but as heirs to the particular culture and institutions of their own society. American conservatives value the legacy of what is generally called "Western civilization" or the "Mediterranean tradition,"[3] but they believe that their own special heritage is what can be called the "American tradition."

The American tradition is marked first by recognizing that the U.S. Constitution (rightly interpreted) and the common law heritage serve as the proper basis of our "established laws" and should be changed cautiously and gradually. The Constitution should not be taken lightly or conveniently reinterpreted to fit the ideas or interests of the moment, and neither political leaders nor judges should assume that they can read their own ideas into the nation's fundamental law because that will allow them to achieve the political results they desire. Conservatism holds that both the letter and spirit of the Constitution must be observed.

Second, conservatives believe that the "customs and traditions" of the American people should be respected and preserved by the government, not undermined. These customs and traditions include the following elements: 1) protection of orthodox and traditional religious values; 2) a nationalistic and patriotic spirit; 3) limited government, especially at the federal level; 4) skepticism about statism and utopian schemes for social reform; 5) an individualist spirit that focuses both on one's duties to the community and on traditional liberties; 6) a preference for free economic markets (tempered by respect for community values); and 7) a desire for gradual change from existing institutions in order to safeguard "continuity and stability" in society.[4]

Because conservatism is about safeguarding established and valuable laws and traditions, conservatives often oppose change that will lead to conditions that are worse than what already exists. This fact was captured succinctly in William F. Buckley's famous comment that a key task for conservatives is to "stand athwart history yelling Stop. . . . "[5] Conservatives do not merely favor the status quo; their desire to protect valuable principles means that they often oppose proposals for change because they see that change is often not for the better. But conservatives do favor reforms that will promote or help to restore the principles they hold dear. For American conservatives, this commitment to true reform implies a concern for the proper working of the constitutional system. As we shall see, conservatives have devoted considerable attention to the issue of presidential power in the modern age, because of the central role that the presidency has come to play in the federal government since the days of Franklin Roosevelt, and because of the close association between the presidency and the expansion of the federal government since the New Deal. This concern has led conservatives to oppose, and then to embrace, and lately to oppose again, the "enlargement of the presidency"[6] that has characterized the office for nearly a century.[7]

The Problem

For conservatives, the central problem of American government is that the federal government has grown too large, both in size and scope. Bigness alone is one problem (which even many liberals agree is a problem), but it is the breathtaking sweep of federal responsibilities that conservatives oppose. The central government has expanded far beyond the idea of limited government and robust federalism, and it often pursues schemes of social reform that are somewhat utopian in nature, seeking to remake American society according to the vision of progressive political elites.

A key element of this growth is the enlargement of the presidency, which has become the central figure in big government. Determining whether the presidency drove the process or it was driven by the overall growth of government is something of a chicken-egg problem, but the essential point for conservatives is that the presidency is now the focus of what is supposed to be a separated system, and this focus encourages presidents to continually expand the powers of the office in order to meet enormous expectations of what government should achieve.

The presidencies of George W. Bush and Barack Obama illustrate this problem. While conservatives applauded Mr. Bush's commitment to national security and his determination to protect citizens from another terrorist attack, they were disappointed by Bush's overall approach to government. Not only did he assert presidential power in security matters but in nearly all areas of power, and his policies of "big government conservatism" broadened the sweep of federal power (e.g., the No Child Left Behind legislation). Many conservatives, including Jack Goldsmith (formerly an official in the Bush Justice Department), Charles Kessler (a conservative writer and scholar), and others, found serious flaws in Bush's policies and conduct of the presidency.[8] Conservatives have likewise found much to criticize in the Obama presidency, from his policies aimed at expanding the federal government to his embrace of George Bush's most comprehensive claims of unilateral power in dealing with terrorism. Regardless of whether these broad executive powers are wielded by liberals or conservatives, they make the president the motive force of the American political system in a manner that diminishes the appropriate role of Congress (which is reduced to second-guessing presidential actions) and teaches citizens to view the chief executive as a kind of benevolent despot and seek political salvation in the person of a presidential candidate.

This president-centered political system leads politicians to practice what Henry Fairlie called the "politics of expectation."[9] Analyzing the political appeal of John and Robert Kennedy, Fairlie discerned in them a style of politics that led their supporters to expect remarkable things from the presidency, from the federal government, and from politics itself. Jack and Bobby built their political personae on carefully wrought images of themselves as leaders who could bring their followers into some vaguely defined promised land. They taught their supporters to expect more from government than it can deliver, and several presidents of the half-century since then have done likewise. When President Obama ran for the office in 2008, his campaign promised remarkable changes if he was elected, not only in public policy but in the very nature of politics and in how Washington works. It is not surprising that many independent voters who were drawn to him in 2008 should be disappointed, even embittered, in 2009 when they learned that he neither changed Washington nor even acted much differently from other politicians. But the desire for salvation by the president remains a fixture of our politics.

How did the presidency come to be the focus of the American political system? It was not designed to be the central figure that it is today, nor was it inevitable that it should become so. Rather, the presidency was transformed into the engine of big government and has been embraced by the broad mainstream of Americans. Liberals and many conservatives alike are now presidentialists, although they are often unsatisfied with the consequences of president-centered government.

Presidential Orthodoxy

At the Federal Convention of 1787, the delegates wrestled over the shape and powers of the executive. Alexander Hamilton favored a strong central government under the leadership of a vigorous chief executive. James Madison, among others, favored a greater balance of powers between the three branches of government. The product of these deliberations was the loosely drawn Article II of the Constitution, which lays the foundation of the presidency but leaves considerable room for interpretation and evolution.[10] But this new chief executive would be embedded in a separated system, the operations of which would keep the president from becoming a Caesar.

Federalist 57 explained that the promise of the Constitution lay not in the virtues of any one part of the new regime but in "the genius of the whole system."[11] We might consider this "holistic" model of the Constitution as the original orthodoxy on the American system. Its strength lay in ambition counteracting ambition, with each branch playing a role in preserving constitutionalism and promoting the larger public interest. Indeed, scholars such as John Agresto and Jeffrey Tulis have demonstrated that the system of separation of powers was designed to operate this way, with the outcome being something greater than might be achieved under legislative dominance or executive tyranny. As Jeffrey Tulis has explained, "Powers were separated and structures of each branch differentiated in order to equip each branch to perform different tasks. Each branch would be superior (although not the sole power) in its own sphere and in its own way. The purpose of separation of powers was to make effective government more likely."[12]

Conservatives long adhered to this orthodoxy. Each branch had different functions and each contributed to effective government in its own way. During the period of the traditional presidency (i.e., before Franklin Roosevelt permanently altered the role of the chief executive), presidents performed the duties of their office according to two "rules" of behavior: the *Rule of Restraint* and the *Rule of Necessity*.[13]

The Rule of Restraint characterized what was expected of the president in ordinary times. According to this "rule," the president was expected to restrain himself (they were all men) in a manner befitting the chief executive of a republic, in which great power was vested in the people's representatives in Congress. Indeed, it was considered inappropriate for presidential candidates to campaign vigorously for office—that would suggest a dangerous Caesar-like grasping for power—and to pretend that they were being summoned to office by their fellow citizens. The president did not make regular pronouncements on bills before Congress, propose a budget or a legislative program, or hold news conferences. The president need not be passive, but he had to hold his power in check. This "rule" helps to explain why so many occupants of the traditional presidency were forgettable figures or eminent statesmen whose tenure in the White House was not the high point of their career (Adams, Madison, Grant, Taft, and others).

When urgent times demanded action, however, the president responded to a different "rule." the Rule of Necessity. According to this rule, the president was expected to do whatever was necessary to protect the national interest. By this rule, presidents waged war—even a civil war—issued proclamations and orders, vetoed bills, and dominated politics in their time. This "rule" explains the presidencies of Jackson, Polk, Lincoln, and Theodore Roosevelt; each of these men was faced with what he saw as times that demanded action.

From Orthodoxy to Heresy

In the 20th century, the orthodox understanding of the Constitution was replaced by the heresy of *constitutional instrumentalism,* that is, the view that the system is legitimate only to the extent that it serves the correct goals. The roots of this position can be found in Woodrow Wilson's reinterpretation of the Constitution and the presidency.[14] Wilson saw the Constitution's separation of powers as the chief obstacle to effective government. He wanted to overcome the limits of checks and balances (as he saw it) by strengthening the president's role as party leader. This would help to break down the "parchment barriers" between the branches. In contrast to the orthodox position that the representative qualities of the government were embodied in Congress, Wilson asserted that only the president could be the true representative of the people. Only the president represented a national constituency. Wilson thus rejected the orthodox understanding as a barrier to promoting the effective, progressive government that he wanted to implement.

Wilson conducted his presidency in a manner consistent with these ideas, but he was unable to transform the public's view of the office. His successor in the White House, Warren Harding, campaigned for office pledging a "return to normalcy," which, among other things, implied a return to the traditional presidency. It was Franklin Roosevelt who permanently altered the role of the presidency in the government and the life of the nation, making assertive leadership the norm for what came to be known as the "modern presidency."

In doing so, Roosevelt rewrote the "rules" of presidential behavior. He replaced the rules of Restraint and Necessity with the *Rule of Responsibility,* which held that it was the president's responsibility to discern what policies and actions were needed to protect and preserve the nation's prosperity and security and to work to develop and implement those policies.[15] According to this new way of thinking, Congress should follow the lead of the president, who was the leader of his party, of the large and active executive branch, of public opinion, and of growing American military power. One key measure of presidential power in this period was the "boxscore," that is, the chief executive's rate of success in convincing Congress to go along with his legislative recommendations. Franklin Delano Roosevelt (FDR) and Lyndon Baines Johnson (LBJ) epitomized the modern presidency, because (at least for a time) each was able to present to Congress a sweeping program of domestic legislation and win its passage. Indeed, Johnson was portrayed in one editorial cartoon as a concert pianist mastering his instrument (labeled "Congress"), out of which flowed the names of laws and programs proposed by the Johnson Administration. The modern presidency was marked by vigorous use of power, with an emphasis on legislation.

By the 1960s, constitutional instrumentalism had taken hold as the new orthodoxy. Alonso Hamby has noted that FDR's success in the New Deal enshrined liberalism as the new mainstream for American politics.[16] But no one made the point better than Thomas Cronin, who captured the effect of instrumentalism on the presidency in his description of the "textbook presidency" of the 1960s: "With the New Deal presidency in mind, these textbooks portrayed the president instructing the nation as a national teacher and guiding the nation as national preacher. Presidents, they said, should expand the role of the federal government to cope with the increasing nationwide demands for social justice and a prosperous economy. . . . "[17]

Even Ronald Reagan, the first truly conservative president in decades, could do little to alter this new orthodoxy. His policies shifted priorities in federal spending, reduced some of the regulatory state that had grown up in previous decades, and took a more assertive approach to the Cold War and foreign policy than had prevailed for several administrations, but he did not undo the New Deal-Great Society architecture to any significant degree. Nor, for all his admiration of Calvin Coolidge and other modest presidents, did he move the presidency from the center of the political system. Conservatives admire Reagan as president, but they realize that he could not repeal the political history of the 20th century; rather, he "stood athwart history yelling Stop" in order to prevent further movement along the path carved by FDR and LBJ.

Constitutional instrumentalism was originally the heresy proclaimed by liberals. For a long time, conservatives clung to the orthodox notion that it was important how particular policy goals were achieved and that a presidicentric system undermined the constitutional system itself. In the middle decades of the 20th century, the result of the clash between liberal and conservative views of the Constitution was a series of policy battles over the liberal agenda. Conservatives, often unable to deflect pressure for liberal programs and initiatives, relied on arguments about process (states' rights, the powers of Congress, or interpretation of constitutional provisions such as the Commerce Clause) to attack proposals from the left.

While arming themselves for these battles, liberals and conservatives alike often embraced a second heresy: *institutional partisanship*. To defend and promote the ends they favored, each side expressed preference for one institution of government over the other.

Most liberals followed Wilson in proclaiming that the presidency was superior, because it was the only national office. This position, expressed by the young Arthur Schlesinger Jr. and others, is the view reflected in Cronin's "textbook presidency." Liberals argued that Congress (which, in the old joke, was the opposite of progress) ought to do what the president wanted because only the chief executive knew what the nation wanted and needed. John Kennedy, for example, essentially took this position, as Theodore Lowi has pointed out: in two major statements made in 1962, Kennedy called on Congress to delegate to the president power over taxes and spending, and he argued that policy problems of modern times are too complex for the legislature and should be left to the executive to resolve.[18]

Until the 1970s, conservatives upheld Congress as the organ of deliberation and resistance to presidential aggrandizement. Prominent among these thinkers were James Burnham and Willmoore Kendall. Burnham, in his 1959 book, *Congress and the American Tradition,* edged toward the position that the very survival of free government in the United States depended on Congress.[19] In his widely read essay on "The Two Majorities" (1960), Kendall saw both Congress and the presidency as representing legitimate (but distinct) majorities of the people. Nevertheless, Kendall expressed a clear preference for Congress as the superior institution of free government, because its members were closer to the actual lives of citizens in their real communities.[20] Among politicians, conservatives such as Ohio senators Robert Taft and John Bricker favored restraining presidential power, by constitutional amendment if necessary. These and other conservatives wanted presidents to defer to the magisterial will of Congress, which stood for liberty and other virtues.

There are two problems inherent in each variety of institutional partisanship. First, institutional partisanship does damage to a constitutional system based on "the genius of the whole system." Taking sides with one branch or another is tempting, especially for a country in which being a sports fan involves loyalties stronger than religion, ideology, or marital fidelity. But the ultimate logic of institutional partisanship suggests that strengthening one branch at the expense of another will actually improve the system. In the 1950s, some conservatives proposed the Bricker Amendment to restrain the president's power to make international agreements, while a decade later LBJ proposed four-year term for representatives, in order to tie the House more closely to the presidency. In short, partisanship leads to bad ideas for guaranteeing permanent dominion by one branch over the others.

Second, after choosing one branch over another, it is not such a long step to switch sides in the war between the branches. Having abandoned the idea that the whole is greater than the sum of its parts, what is there to hold someone to one branch over another? In the midcentury war of the branches, the choice of sides by conservatives and liberals was frequently determined more by necessity than by principle. FDR had made the presidency the great engine of liberalism, so the division on which institution the left and the right would support was obvious.

What happens, however, when the tables are turned? What does one do when conservatives control the White House and liberals are entrenched on Capitol Hill? The answer is simple: switch sides. Something of a reversal took place in the 1970s and 1980s, as liberal Democrats learned to speak the language of deliberation, patience, and legislation, while Reaganite conservatives began to speak of the need for "energy in the executive." But the switch was not complete, for the liberals had supported presidential power too long to give it up entirely. They had come to accept the importance of Congress, which the conservatives still respected as well, but both liberals and conservatives had become presidentialists.

Many conservatives began heading this way during the Nixon presidency. Indeed, Jeffrey Hart, a conservative intellectual and Dartmouth professor, went so far as to suggest in 1974 that conservatives support an "imperial presidency." In an influential essay for *National Review* published in 1974, Hart argued that conservatives abandon (at least temporarily) their long-standing resistance to Caesarism while a strong conservative president employed his power to undo the works of liberalism and confront the liberals in Congress. Hart embraced institutional partisanship because he believed it would advance the conservative agenda he supported.[21]

The final shift occurred during the Reagan years, when many conservatives began to spout arguments about executive prerogatives and power that were reminiscent of FDR's New Dealers. In the period since then, both liberals and conservatives have been disciples of presidential power; although, when out of the White House, each has found the incumbent president (of the opposite party) to be going too far in the assertion of executive prerogatives. Consider the reactions to the last three presidents: conservatives criticized various actions by Bill Clinton as excessive—such as his unilateral designation of large natural areas as protected wilderness and national monuments—but the Republican-controlled 104th Congress also tried to give him a line-item veto; liberals denounced George W. Bush's use of signing statements, indefinite detention of terrorism suspects, and other unilateral actions, but the leading Democratic candidates for president in 2008 did not disavow these powers; and now, Barack Obama, once a critic of George W. Bush, has embraced most of the unilateral exercises of power undertaken by his predecessor.

What Happened to Constitutional Conservatism?

The consequence of these developments is that many conservatives—George W. Bush and Dick Cheney, for example—have embraced a too-powerful presidency in pursuit of particular policies or outcomes. Just as liberals have followed Wilson in supporting a stronger presidency and federal government in order to achieve certain ends, so many conservatives have put expansive presidential power above the "genius of the whole system"—that is constitutional orthodoxy. With liberals and conservatives both acting as presidential partisans, we have seen the decline of the constitutional ethic in American politics.

The constitutional ethic is a principle that holds that the means for conducting our politics and government is as important as the policy ends we want to achieve. Conservatives were once the guardians of the constitutional ethic—and still should be—but some conservative thinkers and politicians have wandered away from this orthodox view, pursuing policy goals by more expeditious means. Against their better judgment, many conservatives supported the excesses of the George W. Bush presidency. Doug Bandow, a conservative writer and former Reagan Administration official, made this point before Bush had even finished his first term:

> The president and his aides have given imperiousness new meaning. Officials are apparently incapable of acknowledging that their pre-war assertions about Iraq's WMD capabilities were incorrect; indeed, they resent that the president is being questioned about his administration's claims before the war. They are unwilling to accept a role for Congress in deciding how much aid money to spend. . . . Some of Bush's supporters have been even worse, charging critics with a lack of patriotism. Not to genuflect at

the president's every decision is treason. Liberals should identify with the Bush record. He is increasing the size and power of the U.S. government both at home and abroad. He has expanded social engineering from the American nation to the entire globe. He is lavish with dollars on both domestic and foreign programs. For this the Left hates him?[22]

Not surprisingly, many of these same defenders of President Bush revived their commitment to limited government when Barack Obama took office, just as many liberal critics of Bush have become fairly muted in the face of Mr. Obama's adoption of most of Bush's claims to executive power. Constitutional conservatism should not be a principle that is applied only to liberal presidents but to all chief executives and to the entire system.

The Solution

Is there a conservative solution to the problem of a metastasized federal government and an overgrown presidency? There is, although any good conservative will warn that the solution must not do more harm than the problem it is intended to correct. Reform of the presidency and our political system is in order, but it will be difficult to achieve in the face of political realities.

Conservatives are committed to principle, but they also pride themselves on being realists. While they may wish that certain policy changes, Supreme Court decisions, or presidential actions of the 20th century had not altered the role of the federal government and the place of the presidency, they also recognize that these changes did occur and that the nation will not return to an earlier era. But that realization does not mean that these reforms should not be contemplated or attempted.

I advocate that we consider two strategies for reform. The first is to adopt institutional reform that would address the problems identified earlier. These reforms would be politically difficult to achieve, however, so they represent an agenda for what I would do to reform the presidency if I had the power to do so. They also illustrate the point that conservatives are not just defenders of the status quo. The second strategy is one that involves a change in attitude, thought, and behavior on the part of presidents and Congress, but not institutional change. In some ways, changing minds is more difficult than changing institutions, but this sort of reform does not involve the difficult process of structural change.

Institutional Reform

If the central problem conservatives identify is that the federal government has grown too large, encompasses too many responsibilities, and centers on an overgrown presidency, the solution is to develop a set of institutional reforms that will restrain the presidency and the federal government in a manner that is consistent with the genius of the constitutional system. This does not imply a wholesale repeal of the New Deal and Great Society, even if certain liberal policies and programs ought to be altered or dismantled (but that is a topic for another essay). Rather, what our nation needs are reforms that will help to restore the sort of limited and balanced government the Constitution was designed to produce.

Reforming Nominations. Reform begins with presidential selection. A key part of the enlargement of the presidency and the politics of expectations comes from a selection system that requires candidates to enter into a series of plebiscites (we call them primaries) and endure months of campaigning (during which endless promises are made: "If I am elected . . .") in order to seek the presidency. In consequence, only those with boundless ambition, little regard for personal dignity or privacy, and a willingness to devote up to two years to full-time campaigning seek the office. It also reinforces the enlarged role of the presidency and the outsized expectations that Americans have about what presidents can or ought to do.

The best reform of the selection process would be one that makes each party's national convention a real decision-making body once again and not just a rubber stamp of the results of primaries and caucuses. Representative decision making is consistent with the spirit of the constitutional system and would move us away from the plebiscitary primary system.

Several ideas have been proposed for achieving this reform, each involving a different means for delegate selection and various mixes of elected officials and delegates selected in primaries or caucuses.[23] One plan, proposed by Jeanne Kirkpatrick (a practicing political scientist and veteran of Democratic presidential campaign politics before she became Ronald Reagan's United Nations Ambassador), would eliminate primaries altogether. Kirkpatrick described the idea: "I propose . . . that the nominating process of each party shall consist of its elected public officials and party leaders—its congressmen, senators, governors, state party chair and cochairs, mayors of major cities, and possibly members of the national committees. I propose that there be no presidential primaries at all."[24] Kirkpatrick's plan would help reconnect presidential candidates with their parties' leaders and would avoid the plebiscitary nature of the primaries. Convention delegates (today's "superdelegates") would be motivated to select presidential nominees who could attract voters and lead the party on to victory.

Of course, there would be charges that this system is less democratic than the current system of primaries and caucuses. But the idea that the current system, in which very few eligible voters participate (primary turnout is usually well below 20 percent of eligible adults; caucus turnout is typically in the single digits), somehow serves as a model of "democratic" decision making is unconvincing. Most observers (not just conservatives) agree that the nomination process takes too long, costs too much, gives outsized influence to certain key states (mostly Iowa and New Hampshire), and raises expectations about what candidates will be able to accomplish if elected. Holding conventions made up of elected officials and party leaders would replace the current nomination mess with a process that promotes representation and strengthens parties.

Revitalizing Checks and Balances. Conservatives long supported the constitutional orthodoxy of limited and balanced government, but our constitutional arrangements have been distorted by events and changes that have taken place since the beginning of the 20th century. What we need are reforms that will facilitate limited government and the functioning of the checks-and-balances system. Specifically, these reforms include returning the Senate to the states and imposing term limits on Congress and the presidency.

The original Constitution made the Senate a body to represent the states, and senators were elected by state legislatures. The Senate thus acted as a check on the growth of the federal government, and thus in one respect, on the enlargement of presidential power. Todd Zywicki, who has studied the history and effects of the 17th Amendment (mandating direct election of senators), has concluded that "the long term size of the federal government remained fairly stable and relatively small in scale during the pre-Seventeenth Amendment era. Although the federal government grew substantially in size in response to particular crises, most notably wars, it returned to its long-term stable pattern following the abatement of the crisis. The 'ratchet effect' of federal intervention persisting after the dissipation of the crisis which purportedly spawned it, was absent from American history until 1913."[25]

Zywicki has demonstrated that, contrary to the claims of those supporting direct election of senators, the prereform Senate actually served the public interest: "In general, the activities of the federal government prior to the Seventeenth Amendment were confined to the provision of 'public goods,' such as defense and international relations. Redistributive activity to special-interest groups was virtually nonexistent at the federal level."[26] The 17th Amendment fueled the expansion of the federal government and promoted the sort of special-interest influence that liberals bemoan: "Changing the method by which the Senate was elected undermined the check that bicameralism provided against special interest legislation. Thus, not only was there steady growth in the size of the federal government in the 1920s, but this growth was driven by special interest legislation."[27]

Related to this reform is the imposition of term limits on federal elected officers. Limiting the terms of members of Congress would increase rotation in office, but Zywicki and others have argued that such limits would have a beneficial effect on government policy. Not only has the tenure of both representatives and senators lengthened considerably since the early 20th century, but long service in Congress tends to create a political class disconnected from the nation it governs. As conservative writer George Will has argued, "Term limits would increase the likelihood that people who come to Congress would anticipate returning to careers in the private sector and therefore would, as they legislate, think about what it is like to live under the laws they make."[28]

What do these reforms have to do with the presidency? They both affect the way Congress operates and relates to the executive. Returning the Senate to the states would help to restore checks and balances and put a brake on presidential power, whether directly or by limiting federal power. It is a reform that would not alter the power of the institution or the "genius of the whole system," but it would alter the way in which the Senate participates in the constitutional system. This would have a salutary effect on congressional monitoring of government power. As for term limits, Zywicki argues that "term limits will actually increase churning within the legislature, upsetting legislative coalitions and making it difficult to create legislative 'contracts' among legislators. Term limits would also have the obvious effect of reducing the durability of legislative contracts between legislators and special interests."[29]

Special interests, the bane of all reformers left and right, benefit more from big government—in which the intricacies of laws and programs affect the tangible interests of groups who lobby the legislature—than from limited government.

What about limiting the presidency? The 22nd Amendment codified the two-term tradition, but an idea that has surfaced repeatedly through our national history would limit the president to a single six-year term. This proposal—endorsed most recently by Larry Sabato[30] but also embraced by several presidents and others over the years—has been advanced for a number of reasons. Some of its advocates claim that it will insulate the chief executive from partisan and political pressures and enable the president to govern solely in the national interest.[31] This is nonsense, but that does not mean that limiting the president's tenure in office cannot be beneficial.

A single presidential term of six years would not alter the powers of the office or its political nature, nor would it insulate a president from polls or partisan pressures. But limiting the president to a single term would serve to de-emphasize the presidency. A key factor in the enlargement of the presidency was the transformation of the norm of presidential restraint to a norm of president-centered government. Along with that norm came the idea of presidential indispensability, symbolized in part by FDR's election to a third and then a fourth term. Limiting the president to a single term returns us to the idea that the presidency is not the center of the system and that it is a limited office. A single term does not inhibit the president from responding to crises, particularly in the area of national security, but in limiting presidential tenure, it blunts the notion of indispensability.

Limiting Government and Enhancing Federalism. Other reforms are also in order. The combination of a balanced-budget amendment to the Constitution, an "unfunded mandates" amendment, and an item veto for the president, would all serve to promote limited government.

Zywicki makes the case that requiring a balanced budget and prohibiting unfunded mandates would be beneficial correctives to big government tied to powerful interests:

> Running a budget deficit enables politicians to transfer wealth from unrepresented future generations to powerful contemporary interest groups. A constitutional amendment requiring a balanced budget, there-fore, corrects this imbalance in the political process which forces unrepre-sented future generations to bear the burden of current expenditures through the higher taxes which they will have to pay to retire the debt. . . . The ability of the federal government to impose unfunded mandates creates massive agency problems with respect to federal actors, as they are able to take credit for addressing whatever problem the mandate is sup-posed to address while imposing the costs on state and local actors.[32]

Again, what is the link to the presidency? It is in the way in which the Rule of Responsibility created the "textbook presidency" that Cronin described, one tied to the expansion of the federal government. Like members of Congress, presidents use deficit spending and unfunded mandates to claim credit for programs without taking responsibility for their costs. George W. Bush earned the ire of many con-servatives for his No Child Left Behind legislation, because it both expanded fed-eral control over public education and imposed the cost for the act on states and local schools (which is why many conservatives do not consider Bush a conservative president). The discipline of a balanced-budget amendment and no unfunded mandates would limit the incentive for the president to promote expensive and expansive programs without a realistic discussion of their costs.

An item veto for the president, tied to these other reforms, would make it clear that the president has a duty to monitor spending. Widely used at the state level, the item veto has been demonstrated to be an effective tool for fiscal discipline. Conservatives have long sought to give that power to the president, and the 104th Congress attempted to achieve it through legislation, but the Supreme Court struck down that approach as unconstitutional. We need a "fiscal discipline" amendment that would incorporate a balanced budget, an item veto, and a prohi-bition against unfunded mandate.

The cumulative effect of these institutional reforms would be to rein in the presidency by altering the presidential incentive structure. The presidency today is occupied by an individual chosen by a lengthy and arduous process that resembles

a series of plebiscites. The process encourages candidates to make expansive promises and encourages voters to seek salvation by getting just the right person in the
White House. Once in office, the president is surrounded by expectations that
encourage the incumbent to promote and protect big government that shifts costs
and burdens on future generations and states and local governments. Presidents are
also encouraged to do big things rather than to provide the stabilizing influence
that the founders of the Constitution sought in creating an executive to counterbal-
ance the legislature.

Of course, it is unlikely that these reforms will be adopted at any time in the
near future, because any idea that appears less "democratic" will be denounced as
elitist (abolishing primaries, returning the Senate to the states), and because discipline is less attractive than largesse (as in the matter of spending and mandates).
That is why, whether or not these institutional reforms are adopted, a reform in the
ethics of presidential conduct is in order.

The Constitutional Ethic

A truly conservative perspective on the presidency is one that holds to the fundamental principles and values of the Constitution. The presidency (and Congress
and the courts and all citizens) needs to be conducted according to the constitutional ethic.

The constitutional ethic holds that the means are as important as the ends. For
Americans, and especially for American conservatives, this means that presidents
should conduct themselves in a manner that is consistent with the letter and the spirit
of the Constitution. This ethic implies several things about presidential conduct:

1) Grounding presidential action in the Constitution: The expansive presidency
has often been justified by vague claims to power based on "the Constitution and
laws" of the United States, with little explanation or clarification of the real source
of such claims. George W. Bush, for example, made sweeping claims on the basis
of the "Unitary Executive," a constitutional principle that Bush employed as a
weapon to justify nearly any exercise of executive power he cared to make. Barack
Obama, while not employing the terminology of the Unitary Executive, has also
made broad claims. This approach to presidential authority is inconsistent with the
constitutional ethic, but it is increasingly common.

Throughout the history of the Republic, presidents have engaged in expansive
exercises of power through a dynamic that I have described elsewhere as venture
constitutionalism.[33] Venture constitutionalism is a form of constitutional risk-
taking, by which a chief executive asserts legitimacy for actions that do not conform to the settled understanding of the president's constitutional authority. In the
president's view, a successful claim of venture constitutionalism expands executive

authority and moves the chief executive closer to meeting his responsibilities (and interests); if unsuccessful, the president can blame others for interfering with his attempts to serve the public interest, protect the institution, or whatever. Not all forays into venture constitutionalism are wrong (e.g., Lincoln's actions to save the Union), but in the age of the Rule of Responsibility, presidents have been encouraged to resort to such assertions in order to meet the enormous responsibilities imposed by president-centered government.

The constitutional ethic requires that the president ground exercises of authority clearly in the Constitution and the laws and that the president be prepared to explain and defend any attempt to broaden uses of power both in terms of the actual need and the constitutional principle at stake. Yes, Lincoln expanded presidential power, but he did so only to conduct the war and was both willing and able to justify his actions. The spirit that ought to guide presidential conduct is that of William Howard Taft, who maintained that presidential power needed to be grounded on—directly or by clear inference—the Constitution and law.[34] A president who seeks such grounding need not be passive, but he can and should be restrained. Taft himself took actions to assert executive authority—for example, issuing an executive order to require departments to submit their budget requests to him as well as to Congress—but he justified them as reasonable interpretations of his constitutional powers.

Not only should the president ground his actions in this way, but Congress must insist that expansive uses of executive power be justified. If the legislature were to do so in a deliberate fashion, it would go a long way toward creating a conversation between the branches on constitutional ethics. Grounded presidential action implies more restrained presidential conduct, which in turn implies that the presidency not seek to always be at the center of the American political system. Charles Jones has reminded us that ours is a separated system[35]; the problem is that presidents (abetted by Congress, the media, punditocracy, and the public) act as if ours is a presidential system.

2) Consulting Congress: While there are certainly situations in which the president needs to act decisively and expeditiously, it is both constitutionally ethical and good politics for the chief executive to consult Congress in areas where the national interest is involved. Take, for example, George W. Bush's 2005 approval of domestic surveillance by the National Security Agency. That action contravened an existing statute and created a furor that could have been avoided. As George Will pointed out in reference to the decision, it was appropriate for the president to consult Congress and consultation would have strengthened the administration's position: "After all, on Sept. 14, 2001, Congress had unanimously declared that 'the president has authority under the Constitution to take action to deter and prevent acts of international terrorism,' and it had authorized 'all

necessary and appropriate force' against those involved in Sept. 11 or threatening future attacks."[36]

In a similar fashion, George H. W. Bush resisted consulting Congress on the first Persian Gulf War. He went to great lengths to seek authorization of the war from the United Nations Security Council and to build an international coalition, but he avoided consulting Congress until the legislature acted on its own. In the end, both the House and Senate supported him by an overwhelming margin.

Even if the president has authority to act, if there is not an element of urgency that prevents doing so, consulting Congress adheres to the spirit of the Constitution. During the Taiwan Straits Crisis (1954–1955), Dwight Eisenhower sought congressional endorsement of his policy of support for Taiwan against threats from the People's Republic of China. The result was the Formosa Resolution (January 28, 1955), which recognized the president's authority to use force to defend Taiwan. This resolution passed even as members of Congress stated that they believed the president already possessed the authority to act without legislative endorsement.[37] Eisenhower's hand in the crisis was strengthened by the explicit support of Congress.

3) Respecting Congress and the law: Recent presidents have sought autonomy from Congress by acting unilaterally. There are times when such actions are necessary: in a crisis or in the face of congressional overreach. But presidents have also gone out of their way to have their way through unilateralism when they could not get it otherwise. Consider both cases.

On one hand, there are times when the president must act unilaterally. Crises are times when swift and decisive action is required; unilateral action may be all that is possible. There are also times when presidents have had to respond to legislative overreach: Presidents Eisenhower and Ford were each presented with legislation that contained provisions by which Congress sought to act in an unconstitutional fashion (e.g., interfering with the president's appointment power, establishing a congressional veto); each responded by noting in a signing statement that the provision would be ignored or interpreted so as to avoid constitutional problems. The president was reminding Congress of its obligation to the law.

But recent presidents have also employed signing statements as devices for accomplishing through fiat what they could not achieve in the legislative process. Signing statements violate the constitutional ethic when they are used to circumvent the legitimate power of Congress. Signing statements became particularly controversial under George W. Bush, but they were also employed by Barack Obama until criticism led the White House to announce that the Obama Administration would no longer issue signing statements. But the administration also revealed that the Justice Department's Office of Legal Counsel would issue memoranda that would have the same effect as signing statements.[38] These memoranda would be even more insidious than signing statements, however, because they are not publicly recorded, as are the statements they replace.

The president shows disrespect for Congress and the law when the chief executive acts in this manner. Respect does not mean surrendering to Congress on all fronts, but it does mean employing unilateral power carefully, not as a convenience or as a device for excluding the legislature from its legitimate role in making policy. It is also appropriate—and constitutionally ethical—for the president to remind Congress of its obligations and limitations under the Constitution.

4) Respecting the institution of the presidency: The constitutional ethic also requires that the occupant of the White House show respect for the office. This means that presidents who bring shame or dishonor on the presidency ought not to hang on to office; the office and its constitutional status are larger than the fortunes of one politician.

This principle means it was appropriate for Richard Nixon to resign the presidency in 1974 when it became apparent that he had participated in an attempt to cover up the Watergate break-in and related activities. Had Nixon committed a crime that met constitutional grounds for impeachment? It really does not matter: He had dishonored the office and lost the moral basis for continuing as president.

Likewise, Bill Clinton should have resigned the presidency in 1998 when it became apparent that he had brought shame on his office by engaging in an extramarital affair with a White House intern. His actions in that scandal, including lying to a grand jury, may or may not have risen to the threshold of "high crimes and misdemeanors" required for impeachment, but they certainly demeaned the presidency. For that offense, the constitutionally ethical action would have been for Clinton to resign.

Impact and Conclusion

If the institutional reforms outlined earlier were adopted, the presidency would not suddenly be stripped of its powers. The consequence would be a more restrained presidency in a more limited government, which is what conservatives supported in the more orthodox constitutionalism of an earlier era. But even if these reforms are not adopted, applying the constitutional ethic will help the president carry on in a manner more consistent with the sort of balanced government that the framers of the Constitution sought to create.

Conservatives want a restrained presidency in a system of limited government. As long as an enlarged presidency seeks limitless autonomy in a big government that is too expansive and too expensive, conservatives will be unhappy. The irony is that nearly everyone else will be dissatisfied as well.

Notes

1. Charles W. Dunn and David Woodward, *American Conservatism From Burke to Bush* (Lanham, MD: Madison Books, 1991), 43.
2. Russell Kirk, *The Conservative Mind,* 7th ed. (Chicago: Regnery Books, 1986), 13–20.
3. Eric Vogelein, *The New Science of Politics* (Chicago: University of Chicago Press, 1952), 188.
4. Adapted from Dunn and Woodward.
5. William F. Buckley, "Publisher's Statement," *National Review,* November 19, 1955, 5.
6. Rexford G. Tugwell, *The Enlargement of the Presidency* (Garden City, NY: Doubleday, 1960).
7. The term "enlargement of the presidency" is taken from Tugwell.
8. See, for example, Jack Goldsmith, *The Terror Presidency* (New York: W.W. Norton, 2007); Charles R. Kessler, editorials and essays in *The Claremont Review,* including "Bush's Philosophy," *The Claremont Review* (Fall 2005), accessed August 11, 2010, http://www.claremont.org/publications/crb/id.847/article_detail.asp and "The War President," *The Claremont Review* (Spring 2004), accessed August 11, 2010, http://www.claremont.org/publications/crb/id.940/article_detail.asp; and Doug Bandow, "Righteous Anger: The Conservative Case Against George W. Bush," *The American Conservative* (December 1, 2003), accessed August 11, 2010, http://www.amconmag.com/article/2003/dec/01/00008/. Bush was especially controversial among conservatives, who approved of some of his policies and applauded his selections for the Supreme Court, but who opposed his "big-government" domestic policies and were divided on his war in Iraq.
9. Henry Fairlie, *The Kennedy Promise* (Garden City, NY: Doubleday, 1973).
10. Clinton Rossiter, *1787: The Grand Convention* (New York: Macmillan, 1966). See also Forrest McDonald, *Novus Ordo Seclorum* (Lawrence: University Press of Kansas, 1985).
11. *The Federalist No. 57,* accessed August 11, 2010, http://www.constitution.org/fed/federa57.htm.
12. Jeffrey Tulis, "The Two Constitutional Presidencies," in *The Presidency and the Political System,* 3rd ed., ed. Michael Nelson (Washington, DC: CQ Press, 1990), 95.
13. Discussion of the "rules" of presidential behavior adapted from Tugwell. See also Ryan J. Barilleaux, *The Post-Modern Presidency* (New York: Praeger, 1988), especially Chapter 3.
14. This discussion is adapted from Ryan J. Barilleaux, "Liberals, Conservatives, and the Presidency," *Congress & the Presidency* 20 (March 1993): 75–82.
15. Adapted from Tugwell, 1960.
16. Alonzo Hamby, *Liberalism and Its Challengers* (New York: Oxford University Press, 1992), Chapter 1.
17. Thomas Cronin, *The State of the Presidency* (Boston: Little Brown, 1980), 78.
18. Theodore J. Lowi, *The End of Liberalism,* 2nd ed. (New York: W.W. Norton, 1979), 274–275.
19. James Burnham, *Congress and the American Tradition* (Chicago: Regnery Books, 1959).
20. Willmoore Kendall, "The Two Majorities," *Midwest Journal of Political Science* 4 (November 1960): 317–345.

21. Jeffrey Hart, "The Presidency: Shifting Conservative Perspectives?" *National Review* (November 22, 1974): 1351-1355.

22. Bandow, "Righteous Anger."

23. For a discussion of several proposals, see James Ceasar, *Reforming the Reforms* (Cambridge, MA: Ballinger, 1982), Chapter 5.

24. Jeanne Kirkpatrick and Michael Malbin, *The Presidential Nominating Process: Can It Be Improved?* (Washington, DC: American Enterprise Institute, 1980), 16–17.

25. Todd Zywicki, "Beyond the Shell and Husk of History: The History of the Seventeenth Amendment and Its Implications for Current Reform Proposals," *Cleveland State University Law Review* 45 (1997): 174.

26. Zywicki, 1997, 179.

27. Zywicki, 1997, 179.

28. George F. Will, *Restoration: Congress, Term Limits and the Recovery of Deliberative Democracy* (New York: Free Press, 1992), 200.

29. Zywicki, 1997, 179.

30. Larry Sabato, *A More Perfect Constitution* (New York: Walker & Co., 2007).

31. For a review of the arguments for and against this proposal, see Bruce Buchanan, *The Citizen's Presidency* (Washington, DC: CQ Press, 1987), Chapter 7.

32. Zywicki, 1997, 230–231.

33. For an extended discussion of venture constitutionalism and its consequences, see Ryan J. Barilleaux, "Venture Constitutionalism and the Enlargement of the Presidency," in *Executing the Constitution,* ed. Christopher S. Kelley (Albany, NY: SUNY Press, 2006), 37–52.

34. William Howard Taft, *Our Chief Magistrate and His Powers* (New York: Columbia University Press, 1916). Taft's views are often misrepresented by citing very brief excerpts from this book. Reading the whole book makes it clear that Taft's understanding of presidential power, while more limited than that of Teddy or Franklin Roosevelt, was not of a do-nothing passive executive that he is often made out to be.

35. Charles O. Jones, *The Presidency in a Separated System* (Washington, DC: Brookings Institution Press, 1994).

36. George F. Will, "Why Didn't He Ask Congress?," *The Washington Post,* December 20, 2005, accessed August 16, 2010, http://www.washingtonpost.com/wp-dyn/content/article/2005/12/19/AR2005121900975.html.

37. For a discussion of this case, see Ryan J. Barilleaux, *The President and Foreign Affairs* (New York: Praeger, 1985), 33–48.

38. Charlie Savage, "Obama Takes New Route to Opposing Parts of Laws," *The New York Times,* January 8, 2010, accessed August 16, 2010, http://www.nytimes.com/2010/01/09/us/politics/09signing.html.

CHAPTER 2

Moderates on the American Presidency

Thomas E. Cronin and *Michael A. Genovese*

Who We Are, What We Believe

We are moderates.

It isn't always easy being a moderate. We sometimes envy our more ideologically centered colleagues. They typically have stronger, more certain, or even more rhetorically compelling views.

Moderates live a bit more in gray territory. Thus we got suspicious when George W. Bush talked in "good versus evil" rhetoric, or when Barack Obama claimed he was going to completely change how Washington did business and, moreover, that he and his team "would change the world."

Life isn't that simple. Living life in the gray means we often see the world in more-or-less terms, not in the black and white.

Like the framers of our Constitution, we have a mixed view of human nature. We do not believe that humans are perfectible, thus we are suspicious of utopians. We do not believe that humans are all base and corrupt, thus we are equally suspicious of dystopian scenarios. We tend to believe humans are capable of selfless acts, yet we can also be selfish and greedy, and we often give in to temptation. While capable of great selfless acts of generosity, we are also capable of vicious acts of cruelty. Because of this, whenever we empower government to act, we always insist on checks and balances.

We do not see a brutal state of nature (a Hobbesian world), yet it is a world of some danger. Yes, there are people out there who mean us harm, and we have to be ready to use force where necessary. Yet, force must be the last not the first resort. Prudence and judgment, along with hope and caution, should guide our relations with the world. We do not see the creation of a perfect world as possible, but we see the need to work for a more peaceful one.

Moderates believe in politics, in bargaining and compromise, in "power listening" instead of "sound-bite shouting" at one another, in sitting down and discussing differences and working through them. We bemoan the decline of civility as our politics have become more polarized. We believe in disagreeing without being disagreeable. And we celebrate the founders and most of the system they created. Like the framers, we believe in representative democracy, just not too much democracy. We like reasonable checks and balances. We think the Declaration of Independence and the Constitution serve us pretty well and that we ought to try to live up to them a bit more. We firmly believe in the artful practice of politics and pragmatic agreement-building based on common shared values and aspirations. Yes, all that can be slow and frustrating, yet efficiency isn't always the wisest course. It's better to take our time and make the right decision, rather than a hasty decision, one we will regret later. We are more persuaded by hope than by fear, and yet, we know hope can be ill founded.

In general, we'd like our president and Congress to enrich both liberty and equality in America, to make tough decisions that will lead us to reasonable, balanced budgets, make America safer, and create even more equality of opportunity for every American. We don't expect miracles but we do expect progress.

We moderates are Madisonian, and if we have a motto it is from *Federalist 51* where Madison wrote the following:[1]

> If men were angels, no government would be necessary. If angels were to govern man, neither external nor internal controls on government would be necessary. In framing a government which is to be administered by men over men the great difficulty lies in this, you must first enable the government to control the governed and in the next place oblige it to control itself. A dependence on the people is no doubt the primary control on the government. But experience hath taught mankind the necessity for auxiliary precautions.

Moderates are sympathetic to the constitutionalist perspective (see David Gray Adler's chapter in this book), yet they fear that it might become a straitjacket (or as pragmatists warn, our Constitution cannot be "a suicide pact"[2]), especially if applied too literally in an emergency. Thus, we are aspirational constitutionalists, yet operational pragmatists.

Being moderate does not mean we are always in the center, yet we often are. It is not about "splitting the difference." We believe that as a nation, we are all in this together, and we should share the burdens as well as the benefits. We loathe the warfare of the politics of personal destruction so prevalent on some cable television shows and slash-and-burn talk radio. We believe in limited but energetic government. We believe government that is too big or too small is a danger. The former is a danger to our liberty, the latter a danger to our needs and security. We believe freedom is not license and that it comes with responsibilities. We tend to believe that both negative freedom (freedom *from*) and positive freedom (freedom *to*) have a place in the American scheme.[3]

Our leaders are imperfect, our constitutional system is imperfect, and our citizens are imperfect followers. Thus, we seek better leaders, better institutions, and better citizens. Better, not perfect. Our expectations, like our politics, do not seek or expect perfection. We want to take reasonable steps in the right direction, knowing that flawed humans are prone to error.

Moderates believe we need effective leaders in all our branches as well as in and out of government. We are not in favor of a strong presidency at the expense of strength in the Congress or in the courts. Indeed, strong presidents need strength in the leadership of Congress.[4]

Moderates don't believe we will often have great leaders in the White House. That happens every once in a while and usually happens when circumstances shape events and a president can successfully persuade and work with supportive legislators and the public.

Moderates generally accept the complicated separation of power and constitutional principles we have inherited yet believe that every generation has to improvise and adjust some aspects of our system to meet the challenges of new times.

Leadership is hard to exercise in the absence of a community with shared values and shared political interests. Leadership can be exercised, to be sure, when a Pearl Harbor or 9/11 attack occurs. Yet on matters such as entitlement reform and climate change (global warming), national leadership is more difficult to exercise. In such times our system seems cumbersome.

Leaders need followers—in large numbers. As we discuss, Congress represents, sometimes too effectively, the rich diversity of political, social, and economic interests in the nation.

Some fear that in promoting moderation one is simply reinforcing the status quo. After all, weren't the great social and moral movements to end slavery or to advance civil rights essentially the work of agitators, rebels, and mavericks? Would not moderation have stifled, even destroyed such movements? No. Moderates weigh, evaluate, and consider the pleas of the passionate dissenters, populists, and reformers. We reject many of their demands. Yet, we think constitutionally elected leaders need to listen carefully and sometimes reformulate, reframe, or at the very least appreciate these messages. This is precisely what occurred in the civil rights drive of the 1950s and 1960s. Passionate voices pleaded for a remedy to the injustice of racial discrimination. Martin Luther King Jr. and others made their case and we listened, were persuaded, and then lent our support to that movement. For such movements to succeed, the moderate middle must be persuaded. This allows for change while keeping society grounded in consensus politics. To change, the center must be persuaded.[5]

If Martin Luther King Jr. woke us up to the moral imperative, it took centrist leaders, like John Kennedy and Lyndon Johnson, to help bring the nation to demand change. They were able to "galvanize but not polarize,"[6] and the great middle pushed for change without caving in to the demands of extremists.

The Challenge

The presidency has often suffered from presidents who seemed ill prepared to navigate the choppy waters of our complex and often frustrating system of government. It takes a special person to perform well in an office embedded in a separation of powers system that often seems an antileadership system. After all, there are many roadblocks. We contend there are few things fundamentally defective with the American system. We often lack either effective leaders or willing followers (and sometimes both) to help bring about progress.

It is difficult (except in a crisis) for presidents to ask the people to make sacrifices for the common good, to move beyond self-interest.

There are a variety of good reasons why presidents rarely perform up to public expectation. Some of the blame rests with individual presidents who lack sufficient political skill or discipline. Part of the blame rests with the structural design of the American constitutional system that separates and fragments power. There are a variety of other permanent and temporary roadblocks that inhibit presidential leadership.

The American presidency, public misperceptions to the contrary, is often a limited office with less power than the public believes is true. Each president faces exacting responsibilities and high (often far too high) public expectations with limited political resources. Presidents also act in our political culture, which prizes liberty considerably more than equality. It should not surprise us that disappointment in the presidential performance is frequent.

Often the result is political gridlock and public cynicism. Historically, this problem is not new. In other eras, our presidents have faced gridlock and political fragmentation. But in recent years, this paralysis has taken on a new tone of urgency.

With the demise of the Soviet empire, the dramatic changes taking place in the post-1989 world, the rise of globalism, the weakening of political consensus at home, and the demands of the war on terrorism, the need for effective leadership and presidential persuasiveness is even higher than in the past.

What is wrong with the presidency? It is tempting to say, "Nothing that a good FDR can't fix." Franklin D. Roosevelt had the political skill and temperament ideally suited to the task of being president. He had a lot of what we today call *emotional and contextual intelligence* and political savvy. Yet, we cannot expect every president to be FDR, thus we need also to find institutional and systemic features that might make for a better functioning presidency.

The American presidential–congressional separation of powers system has now been in place for more than 223 years. This system was not, at the time of its invention, a copy of any previous system, nor, with a few exceptions such as Costa Rica, has it been successfully replicated in more than a few major nations.[7]

Americans regularly bemoan the polarization of American political discourse and are frustrated by the frequency of gridlock or the slowness in the adoption of progressive policies. Yet exceedingly few Americans fault the constitutional procedures they inherited from the founders. Only an occasional reformer or maverick scholar advocates that the United States should adopt a parliamentary system.[8]

Most Americans cherish the system as it is, because it has become part of the fabric of American democracy, because it is the only system they really understand, and also because it has not only lasted but allowed the peaceful transfer of power to occur on numerous occasions.

Forty-three individuals have served as president and about ten of them are now celebrated as American heroes or icons—especially Abraham Lincoln, Franklin Roosevelt, George Washington, Thomas Jefferson, Theodore Roosevelt, John F. Kennedy, and Woodrow Wilson. Some enthusiastically add Andrew Jackson, Harry Truman, and Ronald Reagan to the list.[9]

On 21 occasions, such as on January 20, 2009, Americans have witnessed the peaceful transfer of presidential power from one political party to a challenging opposition political party.

No presidential or congressional election has ever been postponed, even in times of war or dire economic circumstances. This reality, along with the record of peaceful transfers of power among individuals and parties, is a remarkable feature of American political life, and it is among the reasons most Americans, even though they may give decidedly mixed evaluations of Congress or individual presidents, generally value their Constitution's presidential–congressional separation of powers system.

Several generals have served as president, yet Americans have not had to worry about military takeovers or even military intrusion in American politics. This too is a remarkable achievement, especially in contrast to presidential systems in Latin America.

Nor has regionalism played a major enduring role in American politics, with the one large exception of the Civil War. Four of our first six presidents did come from one state, Virginia, but presidents have now come from a great many states and all the distinctive regions of the country except the Northwest and Rocky Mountain West, which, until recently, were not well populated.

If gridlock, paralysis, strident partisanship, and ideological polarization give the appearance that our government is broken, one might rightly inquire: What would a moderate do? First, we cannot simply fix the presidency and expect all to be well. Ours is a deeply connected system; a web of interrelationships comprises our separation of powers system. Seeing—even fixing—the presidency in isolation of the other elements of government is a recipe for continued failure.

Moderate Senator Evan Bayh (D-Indiana), who in 2010 announced that he would not seek reelection, citing the mess on Capitol Hill as his chief reason, offers useful "small" steps that might help make Congress more functional. As a way to soften the strident partisanship, Bayh suggests that the Senate, for example, get together once each month for a nonpolitical lunch as a way to improve the civility in Congress. He also suggests small improvements in campaign financing, ways to make the filibuster less of a partisan weapon (he suggests setting the filibuster stopping vote at 55 instead of 60), plus he believes the following:

> The most ideologically devoted elements in both parties must accept that not every compromise is a sign of betrayal or an indication of moral lassitude. When too many of our citizens take an all-or-nothing approach, we should not be surprised when nothing is the result.

> Our most strident partisans must learn to occasionally sacrifice short-term tactical political advantage for the sake of the nation. Otherwise, Congress will remain stuck in an endless cycle of recrimination and revenge. The minority seeks to frustrate the majority, and when the majority is displaced it returns the favor. Power is constantly sought through the use of means which render its effective use, once acquired, impossible.[10]

The public is not without guilt. As long as we demand contradictory things from our government (e.g., lower taxes and more services), as long as we see ourselves at war with fellow citizens with whom we disagree, we will remain a divided nation. And a divided nation is hard to govern. In a democracy, we must be willing to bargain, and compromise, and not see every conflict as a "to the death" combat.

Turning now to problematic aspects of the presidency, we contend the United States has been reasonably well served by its presidential–congressional system. Yet no system is perfect and the U.S. system, with its constitutional procedures, has debatable flaws or drawbacks, six of which we discuss here:

1. The Gridlock Question
2. The Accountability Question
3. The Electoral College Problem

4. The Length and Expense of Presidential Campaigns
5. The Vice Presidency Problem
6. An Inability to Prevent a Widening Inequality Gap

1. The Gridlock Question

In the literature considering the advantages and disadvantages of "presidentialism," authors invariably suggest that one of the potentially glaring pitfalls of the nonparliamentary system is the sustained gridlock and dysfunctional tension between separately elected presidents and the national legislators.[11]

Most everyone agrees that the American governing arrangements encourage struggle and a certain amount of competitive contention. Yet, they also require collaboration among the policymaking branches. The architects of the American Constitution viewed the separation of powers not as a weakness but as a source of strength, as a way to ensure deliberation and agreement-building, and, equally important, as a way to prevent tyranny.

The American founders were convinced that though legislative and executive power had to be entrusted somewhere, no one person or institution could be entirely trusted with such power. Thus they devised a cunning system of checks and balances so there could be no rash action, no impulsive rush to judgment, no monarchical chief executive, and no legislative tyranny of the majority. The result of all this is that we sometimes have a "nobody's-in-charge system," or as President John F. Kennedy famously said after being in the White House for two years, that what surprised him most about being president was "how hard it was to get things done."

President Barack Obama's excruciating yet ultimately successful bid to reform health care insurance in the United States is an example of just how difficult it is to achieve reform in our slow, cumbersome system. The system, stacked against change, is difficult to move, and efforts at presidential leadership often fail.

In this, the United States stands in contrast to parliamentary systems such as those in Great Britain, Canada, Japan, or Germany. Rather than having a separation of powers as the U.S. does, parliamentary systems have a fusion of power. Prime ministers are responsible to, yet also generally have considerable power over, the majority party or the majority coalition, and they are thereby granted—especially on domestic and economic matters—more legislative power than a U.S. president possesses. Fusing the executive and legislative powers together can create more power and greater accountability. Whether things go well or ill, voters in such a system know who is responsible.

The politics of shared power as it is in the United States necessitates the development of agreement between a president and Congress. The model, or the theory of governance, on which the American system was founded is based on consensus and coalition building. Consensus means agreement about *ends;* coalitions are *means* by which the ends are achieved. Since power is fragmented and dispersed, something (crises or emergencies) or someone (usually a president) has to pull the disparate parts of the system together.

While the popular expectation in this modern era holds that the American president is the "chief legislator" who guides the Congress in much of its lawmaking activity, the reality is often different. The decentralized character of power in Congress, the multiple access and veto points within the congressional process, the rise in importance of the filibuster power in the U.S. Senate, the independence and the frequent weakness of the legislative leadership all conspire against easy presidential victories.

An added factor in recent times has been the restraining reality of a disturbingly large national debt and worrisome trade imbalances. These two realities have handicapped Republican as well as Democratic presidents from winning passage for initiatives that have higher price tags, increased taxes, and accelerating deficits associated with them.

When do presidents enjoy success in getting legislative initiatives adopted? Presidents and political eras are so variable that this question is hard to answer.[12]

Yet looking back over the past hundred years, activist presidents such as Wilson, FDR, LBJ, and Reagan were most successful during their first two years. Roosevelt's "honeymoon" extended well into his second two years both because his party won additional votes in the midterm elections of 1934 (which only rarely occurs—it also happened in 1998 and 2002) and because of the dire emergency of the Great Depression.

Presidents also generally gain greater leverage with Congress in the aftermath of emergencies such as the Depression of the early 1930s, the assassination of President Kennedy, and the terrorist attack on the United States in September of 2001.

Do higher presidential public opinion ratings or prestige or likeability factors empower a president in dealing with Congress? The evidence here is mixed. It is generally believed that presidential popularity translates into overcoming gridlock, but this depends on which party controls Congress, what policies a president is advocating, and at what point in the president's tenure it is.

John Kennedy was a popular president and his party, albeit divided, controlled Congress. But his legislative record was not impressive.[13] Bill Clinton enjoyed considerable popularity in his second term, especially during America's technology boom, yet his legislative record was also limited.

What happens when one party controls the White House and the other party controls one or both chambers of the Congress? Here again the record is mixed. Several scholars find that so-called "divided government" has not measurably altered the capacity of the U.S. government from passing important legislation and approving needed foreign policy initiatives.[14] Thus the famous national interstate highway system won passage in the mid-1950s and an important tax reform act passed in 1986. Here are some enduring realities about gridlock in American national politics:

1. Progressive legislation, such as social security, civil rights, voting rights, Medicare, tax reform, and health insurance coverage, often takes a long time to "incubate" or develop in the United States.
2. Congress generally plays a key role in incubating the national policy agenda—especially on domestic and economic policies.[15]
3. Rarely do presidential elections produce policy mandates for an incoming or a reelected president, yet presidents such as Lyndon B. Johnson or Ronald Reagan did gain political capital because they won healthy election victories in 1964 and 1980. In contrast, presidents who won narrow election victories as did John F. Kennedy in 1960 and George W. Bush in 2000 have a tougher time winning adoption of major legislation in Congress. In a good many presidential elections, the mandate, if there is one at all, is primarily a mandate to retire the ineffective incumbent or temporarily punish the incumbent's party. This was the case in 1968, 1976, and 1980, and it was probably one of the main reasons for Barack Obama's victory in 2008.
4. Presidents have greater success in working with Congress in their first few years than later in their presidential tenure. Every president earns a certain amount of political capital, yet this gets depleted over time.
5. The challenge in a separated powers or revolving gridlock system involves presidents and leading members of Congress engaged in often painstaking deliberation to find a working consensus that can override the twin supermajority obstacles of the Senate's filibuster (which effectively now requires 60 votes to cut off) and the presidential veto that requires a two-thirds vote in each chamber to override. The strength of the filibuster is that a president and his party now need 60 votes in the Senate to overcome stalemate. The strength of the presidential veto means the opposition party must rally a decided supermajority to get its way.
6. Gridlock occurs because of these supermajority procedures and because there is often a lack of consensus among both members of the public and their members in Congress.

A few liberals, such as James MacGregor Burns and James L. Sundquist, have long sought to reshape the presidential–congressional system more along the lines of a parliamentary system. They deplore the deadlock of democracy our system so often produces and are especially critical that majority sentiment, at least as they see it, is thwarted from being translated into desired public policies. Here is how Sundquist defines the gridlock challenge for the American system:

> Insofar as the system of multiple vetoes is embedded in the Constitution, it represents the determination of the statesmen assembled in Philadelphia, reacting to the rule of George III, to design a structure of government with powers so scattered that no domestically bred tyrant could hope to seize them all. In that aim the Founding Fathers succeeded wholly.
>
> The United States has never had to expend much worry from the threat of tyranny. But if the powers of government are so dispersed that they cannot be assembled by would-be dictators to serve subversive purposes, by the same token they cannot be readily assembled by democratic majorities either, to use for good and constructive ends. There lies the basic trouble.[16]

Sundquist and Burns would have us elect members of the House of Representatives to four-year terms and believe we should cast one vote that would select president and members of Congress on the same ticket to ensure that a unified accountable party would take office.

But the vast majority of political scientists and political leaders in the United States prefer the existing system, even with its tensions and periodic gridlock. They like the old adage that constitutional democracy and Madisonian checks and balances provide a political system for people who are not too sure they are right.

Much as even moderates in America are embarrassed that it took so long to gain passage for the right to vote for women and African Americans and environmental protections to be implemented, moderates in both our major parties believe that ours is a policymaking system that requires deliberation, coalition-building, patience, and struggle over the long haul. "In a democracy like the United States," Brady and Volden write, "policy is worked out through elections, debate over policy changes, further elections, and finally the passage of policy changes."[17]

The alternative of a parliamentary system in America is rarely debated and is not seriously considered. Americans willingly live with the untidiness of the country's separation of powers system and view the sometimes painfully slow policymaking process as the price we must pay to protect against both the tyranny of a wayward executive and the tyranny of a narrow-based majority that would hastily impose its views on the rest of the country.

One final point should be added here. While liberals or progressives complain that our separation of powers system has made it very difficult for progressive legislation to become enacted—or it has at least slowed down and weakened such policies—conservatives have also seen their legislative objectives thwarted by the same system. Thus, George W. Bush's scheme to "privatize" social security and numerous proposed conservative amendments to the U.S. Constitution (for a balanced budget, an item veto, or for banning flag burning or abortion) have similarly failed to be enacted.

The enduring reality is that one person's "gridlock" is another person's safeguard, check, or protection against "wrongheaded" policies. Thus, conservatives often like to say that while liberals and some moderates complain that gridlock is an American problem, others see it as an American achievement.

2. The Accountability Question

Protection from attack is a prime obligation for leaders in every nation. Thus it was that the American constitutional framers specified commander-in-chief authority when war is authorized. The framers explicitly gave the U.S. Congress the responsibility and power to declare as well as fund a war. But they plainly gave presidents the power to manage the military operations.

Abraham Lincoln, Woodrow Wilson, Franklin Roosevelt, Harry Truman, and a few more recent presidents have assumed broad executive powers as they sought to protect American security. But the history of presidential use, and sometimes misuses, of the war power has become problematic, especially as it has enlarged the presidency and made it less accountable to Congress and the people.

The presidential election of 2008, some people believed, would bring a different kind of president—one dedicated to reversing the trend of a new imperial presidency. But, as historian Garry Wills notes, "The momentum of accumulating powers in the executive is not easily reversed, checked, or even slowed." Wills explains:

> It was not created by the Bush administration. The whole history of America since World War II caused an inertial transfer of powers toward the executive branch. The monopoly on the use of nuclear weaponry, the cult of the commander in chief, the worldwide network of military bases to maintain nuclear alert and supremacy, the secret intelligence agencies, the entire national security state, the classification and the clearance systems, the expansion of state secrets, the withholding of evidence and information, the permanent emergency that has melded World War II with the cold war and the cold war with the "war on terror"—all these make a vast and intricate structure that may not yield to effort at dismantling it.[18]

He is right. In the larger comparative context, wars invariably challenge any nation's existing checks and balances—even in nations such as the United States with written constitutions and where personal rights are a settled part of the political and social culture.

Constitutional democracies have never succeeded in constructing a perfect system for keeping executives accountable. Still, while perfection is impossible, progress in this area should be our goal.

Writers on the American presidency regularly note that we need Hamiltonian energy in the presidency to make our Madisonian system of separation of powers and checks and balances work in order to advance the Jeffersonian, Lincolnian, and Rooseveltian goals of freedom, equality, and social justice. But an energetic presidency is far different from an imperial presidency.

Too many recent presidents have acted unilaterally and without collaborating with Congress. Some presidents have acted in defiance of Congress and the law.

Presidential scholars in the United States are generally in agreement that presidents who use and stretch their "hard" formal powers but neglect their informal "softer" powers of persuasion and education will eventually lose both the Congress and the American people. This is exactly what has happened with a series of presidents, including Lyndon Johnson, Richard Nixon, and George W. Bush.

The lesson is pretty clear: Presidents cannot, in the long run, win the support of Congress and the American people if they lie to them, engage in unprecedented secrecy, and bypass cherished principles of shared governance and constitutionalism.

Effective presidents need to celebrate politics, political dialogue, and political bargaining with leaders in the Congress. A "truly strong president," historian Arthur M. Schlesinger Jr. reminded us, "is not the one who relies on power to command but the one who recognizes his responsibility and opportunity, to enlighten and persuade."[19]

In an age of international terrorism, both the United States and other constitutional democracies will need an effective, powerful presidency (or national executive), one that may occasionally bend but not break the Constitution. But we do not want presidents who believe they are above the law and disembodied from the system of checks and balances that have served so well to control state power. Americans recognize the need for a powerful presidency yet insist that it remain a constitutional presidency.

Are there rules that can guide us in our effort to attain a strong but accountable presidency in this age of nuclear proliferation and always possible terrorism? While no firm, rigid rules can be stringently enforced, here are several features of accountability that might apply:[20]

- In a major war or crisis, presidential power should expand to meet the demands of the time.
- Added or enhanced presidential power, however, should never be viewed as a "blank check" for the president.

- All presidential acts during an emergency are reviewable by Congress and the courts.
- Constitutional rights shall be fully enforced. To paraphrase two noted U.S. Supreme Court rulings (in 2008 and 1866, respectively), the laws and Constitution are intended to remain in force in extraordinary as well as normal times, and they are the law for rulers as well as the people, equally in war and in peace, and cover with the shield of its protection all classes of men, at all times, and under all circumstances.
- When presidents believe they need to move beyond the law, they must consult with and get congressional approval (perhaps by a joint specially prearranged committee of both houses of Congress) prior to acting.

3. The Electoral College Problem

The U.S. electoral college system was adopted for a variety of complicated political bargaining reasons at the Constitutional Convention in 1787, and ever since, it has been one of the most heatedly debated aspects of the American presidential system. Between 60 and 75 percent of Americans regularly say they support replacing this way of electing American presidents.

This is not the place to explain how the anachronistic electoral college system works. But let us point to three of its notable deficiencies.

First, with the electoral college method, a president can be elected who has fewer popular votes than an opponent, as was the case in 1824 when John Quincy Adams, with 31 percent of the vote, defeated Andrew Jackson, with 41 percent of the popular vote. This happened also in 1876 when Rutherford B. Hayes, with just 48 percent of the vote, won over Samuel J. Tilden, with about 51 percent of the popular vote, and in 1888 when Benjamin Harrison, with nearly 48 percent, won over Grover Cleveland, with almost 49 percent of the popular vote. George W. Bush had 500,000 fewer votes than did former Vice President Al Gore, yet he still became president because he won more electoral votes.

Rarely mentioned yet of interest is the fact that in all four of these cases, the Democratic candidate lost to the more conservative (in the last three occasions the Republican) candidate.

There is yet another unusual and profoundly undemocratic aspect to the electoral college. In the event that no candidate secures a majority of electoral votes, the decision as to who becomes president is given to the U.S. House of Representatives. This happened in 1800 and 1824 and was a possibility in other elections such as 1968 and 2000.

In these House elections, the delegation from each state casts a single vote. If a delegation is evenly divided, this state forfeits its vote. Consecutive ballots are taken until a candidate wins a majority (26) of the state delegations. Note that states with only one member of Congress representing just 600,000 or so constituents are in this instance equal to large states such as California, Texas, and New York. Such a voting scheme has no legitimacy in this modern era.

Another flaw of the electoral college process and its related state procedures is that in 48 of the 50 states, the presidential candidate who wins the plurality of votes is allowed to win *all* of that state's electoral votes. One side effect of this is that it discourages voters in the minority party from voting. Thus Republicans in Massachusetts or in New York and Democrats in Utah or Texas lack at least one of the incentives to go out and cast their vote because they know in advance that their vote will not matter. Thus these procedures discourage voter participation, one of the central principles of a civil society and civic culture.

Fortunately, America has not exported the electoral college elsewhere. Most presidential systems have relied on a direct, popular, one-person one-vote system of electing presidents. A variety of proposals have been put forward to improve upon the American system of presidential elections, including a congressional district system (essentially already being used in the states of Maine and Nebraska) and various proportional representation or "single transferable vote" systems, where voters signify their second and third choices on their ballot, thus combining a "first heat" and "runoff" election into a single transaction. In addition, there are some ingenious hybrid proposals that would retain the federal state by state election count yet allocate a "national bonus vote" to the popular national vote winner so as to ensure the national winner wins and the loser loses.[21]

Americans, for reasons that are not altogether clear, have never had a first-rate national dialogue about correcting this archaic, complex, ambiguous, undemocratic, and flawed system of electing presidents. Several of the proposed remedies would help make the American democracy live up to its oft-proclaimed democratic ideals and pretensions, but many Americans worry about the negative side effects of these reforms for federalism, voter fraud, and the perpetuation of the familiar two-party system.

4. The Length and Expense of Presidential Campaigns

Unlike in parliamentary systems where national elections are announced, conducted, and completed in a matter of several weeks, presidential campaigns in the United States now last for at least two years.

Americans love their country, celebrate democratic ideals, and generally prize the American presidency, but they are dismayed about the length and cost of the presidential elections. People see the selection process as an often self-defeating system, more like a demolition derby, a process of eliminating good people rather than encouraging talented candidates to run for the White House.

Scholars and journalists worry, with some justification, that the qualities needed to win the presidency are not necessarily the same as those needed to govern the nation and serve as a statesman.

Long gone are the days when party leaders could select their presidential candidate. Nowadays, because of a proliferation of 30 or more states with primaries and about a dozen or so states that hold local party caucuses, a candidate who is especially well financed and can devote himself or herself to two years of exacting nationwide full-time campaigning has a clear advantage over those who can't raise the funds or who are tied to administration or legislative leadership responsibilities.

The "entry cost" for merely getting into the race is well over several hundred million dollars. This discourages a lot of promising candidates. Making matters worse, the national media in the United States inevitably give major attention to those who are already well known or who demonstrate that they can raise uncommon sums of money.

The process of raising huge sums of campaign contributions is a compromising and sometimes corrupting one. The burden and necessity of having to raise millions for a presidential race explains why some otherwise attractive candidates decide against running. It is also at the heart of why some people are disaffected by the American political process. People rightly ask this: When does a large political contribution become a bribe? When does aggressive campaign soliciting become equivalent to a shakedown or a conspiracy to extort funds? Said one candidate who twice ran for the presidency, "It's a curse. It's the most disgusting, demeaning, disenchanting, debilitating experience in a politician's life."

In 2008, the Obama campaign alone spent well over a billion dollars on the race to win the White House.

Policy issues seem to be less important in many U.S. elections because of the tendency for both parties to offer candidates who take moderate policy stands to appeal to independents and new voters. Both major party candidates do extensive polling and closely echo the popular sentiment. Clear-cut policy stands are infrequent as candidates devote more attention to their concerns about general goals and the performance of the incumbent.

Candidates who can frame issues and present a compelling personal narrative, project relaxed sincerity as well as competence, and draw in the voters emotionally, usually have the best chance of winning.

The Obama 2008 campaign combined issue initiatives, such as wanting to get out of Iraq and health insurance coverage for all, with conspicuous emotional or general appeals about hope and change. In the end, the 2008 election was, more than anything else, a mandate to retire President George W. Bush and at least temporarily punish his political party.

One of the other disappointing aspects of presidential campaigns in the United States is that voters, especially in "swing" battleground states, are relentlessly bombarded with negative ads. And in the smear attacks, accuracy is often the first casualty.

Outside interest groups on both the right and the left too often spread false accusations about the leading candidates and their advisers. This is most assuredly not new in American politics nor is it peculiarly American, but in the age of the Internet and instant communication forms—blogs, twitter, and websites that are difficult to verify—life has become more difficult for candidates and even more confusing for voters.

5. The Vice Presidency Problem

One of our conspicuous constitutional mistakes was the invention of the vice presidency. It is one of our oldest problems. To the founding constitutional fathers it was mostly an afterthought. Few people of great ability seek the office and we have had some unqualified vice presidents, such as Nixon's Spiro Agnew and George H. W. Bush's J. Danforth Quayle.

Several recent vice presidents have been given much greater access and have functioned as important senior advisers to the presidents they served, but these efforts to infuse more importance into the office fail to remedy the constitutional mistake of having created this hallowed and politically lame institution.[22]

Nine vice presidents have become president because of death or, in Nixon's special case, a forced departure.

The constitutional problem here is that vice presidents have minimal political legitimacy. They are selected at the national party convention solely by the party's presidential nominee. And they are not infrequently selected in a frenzied, hurried, heat of the moment, last minute, decision-making process. This is due in part to the fact that many possible vice presidential nominees don't want the job. Critics point out, for example, that Barack Obama spent more time selecting the White House dog than his rival John McCain spent selecting Governor Sarah Palin as his vice presidential running mate in 2008. To be sure, the party convention "blesses" the presidential nominee's choice, yet this confers little or no political legitimacy.

Vice presidents are constitutionally designated as presidents and presiding officers of the U.S. Senate and given the right to cast a Senate vote in the case of a tie. These days, vice presidents rarely preside over the Senate and are now considered almost exclusively a member of the executive branch. Vice presidents, however, do occasionally cast a tie-breaking vote.

But many people question the legitimacy and the desirability of vice presidents casting any type of vote. They do not represent states or districts or constituents. Who are they voting for? And why are they, advisers to the president, even allowed in that altogether separate branch?

The more important and larger issue regards the possibility of the vice president taking over the presidency because of death, disability, resignation, or impeachment. Exceedingly few voters consider this possibility when they vote for president. Vice presidents get into office almost entirely by accident. It's a package deal.

There have been repeated calls for abolishing the vice presidency, yet this is not likely to happen. If it were to happen, one possible solution to the so-called succession problem would be to have each president designate in advance a senior cabinet officer such as secretary of state or attorney general who would serve as acting president for a hundred days, during which time the major parties could hold conventions and a national replacement election could be held to elect a popularly, democratically elected president who would have earned the political and constitutional legitimacy to govern until the next presidential election.

We should emphasize here that few Americans view this as a problem. Americans blindly accept the vice presidency because it is such a long-standing part of our constitutional procedures. Moreover, they also accept it as something of a "national security blanket" for those unfortunate occasions when a sitting president is no longer available to steer the ship of state. People think the mere fact that this office is in the Constitution and that some wise political architects long ago put it there conveys to it enough legitimacy that we shouldn't bother much about it.

6. An Inability to Prevent a Widening Inequality Gap

Another challenge for the American political system in recent decades has been the inability of its political leaders to lessen inequality in America. We proudly celebrate the rights to life, liberty, and the pursuit of happiness. But the pursuit of happiness is severely constrained for those who live in the bottom quartile in the United States.

Over the last generation, more and more of the economic rewards and "happiness" associated with economic growth have plainly gone to the rich and super-rich. Most other Americans have seen a diminution of their economic assets and opportunities.

Wealthy Americans enjoy a far greater influence on how public policies such as tax policy and regulatory policies are shaped in Washington, DC.[23]

And rich Americans are noticeably less supportive of measures to provide economic security for others and the redistribution of economic rewards to their less privileged countrymen.

> They are more supportive of free trade and deregulation. They are less supportive of Medicare and Social Security. They are more supportive of tax cuts, especially cuts in taxes on dividends and capital gains. They are markedly less supportive of health insurance expansions financed by an

increase in taxes—in fact, income is a better predictor on this vital issue than party affiliation. Unlike poorer Americans, however, wealthier Americans can back their positions up with serious money. As money has become more and more prominent, our politics has become more and more like the parable in Matthew 13: "For whosoever hath, to him shall be given, and he shall have more abundance."[24]

The argument is regularly made that the inequality gap in America is primarily the result of globalization, the outsourcing of manufacturing, and the decline of unions. These doubtless contribute to this challenge, but it is the public policies, especially on taxes and welfare, made in Washington, DC, that are the main contributors to the increased inequality in the country. And the way our elections are run and the way in which influence is exercised both within and on our presidential–congressional system is a central factor in the policies that regularly get enacted.

A Note About Presidential and Congressional Terms

The U.S. system provides for a fixed four-year presidential term with reeligibility for one additional term of four years. The two-term limit was established by the 22nd amendment to the Constitution in 1951. This amendment was adopted in 1951 and is still debated in academic circles. But the American people have largely accepted and indeed approve of this two-term limit.

Advocates of repeal say this two-term limit unduly restricts the American citizen's right to decide who will be their leader. If the people want to vote for someone, especially an experienced veteran in the White House, there should be no rule telling them they don't have that choice.

Critics also bemoan that every president's sun now begins to set the day a president's second term begins—the so-called "lame duck" syndrome. We have, critics contend, dealt the modern presidency a major blow by depriving second-term presidents the political weapon of their availability for another term, which keeps both political supporters and rivals guessing.

Advocates of retaining the 22nd Amendment (and on this question, this chapter's authors are in disagreement) say eight years is plenty. The notion of rotation in office is healthy and desirable, especially in a robust democracy.

Eight years, supporters of the two-term limit believe, is ample time to introduce a party's best policy ideas and to try to bring about necessary policy improvements and changes. And if these changes are valid and valued, they will be mostly honored and continued by the next administration.

Most Americans reject the idea that any political leader is indispensable. The late Charles de Gaulle of France used to quip that the cemeteries of the world are full of people who once viewed themselves as indispensable.

The two-term limit for presidents provides that an honored citizen can serve eight years in this powerful position, yet it protects the country from potential excesses or abuses of power that could come from prolonged tenure.

Finally, a long-term presidency—say of 12 or 15 years—would be able to "pack" the Supreme Court as well as the whole federal judiciary. Ridding themselves of a permanent executive was precisely why Americans fought in the American Revolution. Moreover, for a variety of understandable reasons, the U.S. presidency has become a far more powerful branch of government than was ever imagined by the framers of the U.S. Constitution. Most of these developments or realities cannot be reversed. But the 22nd Amendment can serve as an additional, practical "auxiliary precaution" in James Madison's sense of checks and balances.

U.S. senators have a six-year renewable term of office, and on average, they serve for about thirteen or fourteen years. Few advocate changing their six-year terms. Yet there are a number of scholars who criticize the wholly undemocratic character of the U.S. Senate, which, of course, is based on the notion of two senators per state and not at all based on population.[25] But this is not something that can be changed (unless we amend the Amending Clause), because the U.S. Constitution prohibits amending this situation (in Article 5 of the U.S. Constitution).

Then there is the issue of the short two-year renewable terms for members of the U.S. House of Representatives. Reformers would lengthen these terms to four years in order for those who come in with a new president or who get elected with a reelected president to work and negotiate on legislation for a whole presidential term.

The two-year term is criticized by many as overly short, although others defend it as a central means to allow the voice of the public to be regularly heard in Washington.

The current system of two-year House terms, six-year Senate terms, and four-year presidential terms makes it challenging for these separate branches to legislate together. Here is how one thoughtful student in the American legislative process sees it:

> The current electoral cycle, therefore, exacerbates the potential for institutional conflict and creates an atmosphere conducive to stalemate in the policy making process. It is the presence of mid-term elections that shortens the period available in the president's four-year term for program development and enactment, forcing administrations to move their agendas early and fast perhaps without giving their initiatives the optimal level of substantive review. The existing electoral routine strengthens no part of the policy making system . . . [and] it does not allow participants in either branch to strengthen their role in the production and enactment of policy initiatives.[26]

Public opinion survey data is generally split on the proposed idea to lengthen House terms to four years, though one relatively recent poll reports 50 percent support for lengthening these terms to three years compared to 46 percent who would oppose such reform.[27]

In sum, the fixed lengths of terms for presidents and members of Congress are unlikely to be changed in the near future. One reason for this is that many, and perhaps most voters, would see this as taking away a voter's right to protest and "send a message" to Washington every two years. In effect, many people would perceive this "reform" as a congressional power grab and a weakening of their ability to keep government accountable.

On the General Strengths of the American Presidential–Congressional System

All the drawbacks discussed here have not prevented effective presidents—working with Congress—from acting to enact important policy advances and major foreign policy decisions.

The key in almost every case is that a competent president who helped make the American system work figured out what was needed to be done and then collaborated with the Congress and persuaded the American people about the desirability of the proposed action.

"When the country is not sure what ought to be done," wrote Arthur M. Schlesinger Jr., "it may be that delay, debate, and further consideration are not a bad idea. And if our leadership is sure what to do, it must educate the rest—and that is not a bad idea either."[28]

In a large, diverse, and now ethnically complicated nation like the United States, policy changes do not generally get approved quickly. The United States is still a relatively conservative nation, especially when it comes to protecting private property, personal liberty, and the so-called "private sector." Welfare policies and business regulations all get subjected to heated debate. Privileged interests invariably protect their privileges, usually with success.

Progressive measures such as a minimum wage, health care, collective bargaining, consumer and environmental protection regulation, and Medicare do sometimes eventually get enacted. Yet Americans are ideologically distrustful of government, which can be a healthy thing.[29] Still, it is an enduring reality of American politics that when any new program is proposed that calls for expanding governmental power and raising taxes, Americans at least initially display ideological predisposition to oppose it just as Bostonians dramatically opposed British taxes on tea in the 1770s.

New, and especially progressive, policies invariably have to go through or get "processed" in a series of stages or acts prior to their gaining acceptance by candidates for Congress and the presidency. One of the authors has elsewhere elaborated on these stages and acts.[30]

Political change can be seen as a three-act process. We view presidents, cabinet members, and most members of Congress as Act III leaders who enter the debate after reforms are proposed, pushed, and promoted by other Act I and Act II activists. They often get criticized as simply fixers, bargainers, transactional brokers, or even opportunists. This portrait is usually overdrawn, yet a core of truth remains. Act III types not only are brokers but have to be bargainers and agreement-makers in order to make the separation of powers and federal system work. The American political system has so much built-in conflict, so many representatives of competing class and diverse business and labor sector constituencies, and so many checks and balances, that compromise at the highest levels is inevitable.

A refined appreciation of how the American presidential–congressional separation of powers system works recognizes that most national office-holding leaders operate in the Act II and a half to Act III range. They are necessarily dependent on other types of leaders to generate the policy inventions and the popular advocacy movements that help the nation to renew and change itself. We become better and more realistic judges of presidents and congressional leaders if we appreciate the considerable degree to which national leadership is dispersed and that much of the needed leadership—at least on many occasions—is less leadership from the top down but percolates up from local and state governments, from research institutes and "think tanks," from citizen activists, from university or corporate research centers, and from entrepreneurial, nongovernmental agents.

Yet the history of the last 65 years or so suggests that presidents are more successful than most people believe in either enacting their primary policy goals or at least helping to advance their ideas in productive discussions so that at a later time they will be embraced.

Let us list a number of major programs that came about because of fruitful presidential–congressional collaboration—some of which came about during periods of divided government:

- The Harry Truman era Marshall Plan and the G.I. Bill
- The Eisenhower era Interstate Highway System
- The Johnson era Civil and Voting Rights Acts and Medicare
- The Nixon era China Initiative
- The Carter era Camp David Accords
- The Reagan era Tax Reform Act of 1986
- The Clinton era North American Free Trade Agreement
- The Bush–Obama era Economic Stimulus Initiatives
- The Obama era Health Care Initiative

President Truman had to work with Republicans in control of Congress at a critical time in our foreign policy. He was often successful because of critical alliances he formed with Republicans, such as Senator Arthur Vandenberg.

President Eisenhower, whose general style was to move more cautiously and only after public opinion and Congress were on board, proved successful on certain issues such as the monumental interstate highway system because he forged strategic alliances with leaders in the Congress, such as Speaker Sam Rayburn and U.S. Senator Lyndon Johnson.

President Lyndon Johnson was ultimately able to win important, if too long delayed, civil rights legislation because he eventually won the support of leading Republican senators, such as Everett Dirksen and Thomas Kuchel.

Richard Nixon's historic trip to China in early 1972 needed the support of leading Democrats in Congress and full, formal diplomatic relations with China would not be completed until Democrat Jimmy Carter was in the White House in 1978.

President Jimmy Carter enjoyed success with various Middle East talks and summits, yet he was able to initiate and pursue such negotiations only with support from Republican leaders in Congress.

A historic landmark tax reform package won bipartisan support in 1986 because Democrats like Speaker Tip O'Neill, House leader Dan Rostenkowski, and U.S. Senator Bill Bradley were able to collaborate with President Ronald Reagan in a period of divided government.

Democratic President Bill Clinton inherited most of the North American Free Trade proposed legislation from his Republican predecessor George H. W. Bush and needed substantial Republican votes in both chambers of Congress to put this initiative into action.

Both George W. Bush and Barack Obama collaborated in 2008 to fashion various economic stimulus investments to respond to the Great Recession of 2008 and 2009. Bush needed Democratic support in 2008 and Obama, who had majorities in both Houses, reached out for Republican support and yet received no Republican votes in the House and only three in the Senate.

President Barack Obama was able to pass health insurance reform, yet he did so with no House Republicans voting for the bill. This "zero support" was unprecedented in modern times.

All of this is to emphasize that presidents and Congress need each other and that legislating together, while never easy, can and does take place on a regular basis. It is true that more gets done in what we call the presidential "honeymoon" period of the first 18 months or so of a presidency—as was true under Wilson, FDR, LBJ, and Reagan. Presidents are sometimes advantaged when they can claim an election "mandate" and especially if their party gained a significant number of new seats in Congress. This surely happened, for example, in 1932, 1934, and 1964. Presidents can also be helped by emergency crisis situations (thus the slogan, "a crisis should never be wasted"), such as a depression, a Pearl Harbor attack, a terrorist attack such as 9/11/2001, or a major recession. It is after times such as this that legislation, such as the Social Security Act or the U.S. Patriot Act, gets enacted.

The enormous growth of the role of government in the United States and the markedly enlarged role the United States has played in the post–World War II international era have obviously enlarged the visibility, responsibility, and role of American presidents in world affairs. There are a lot of obvious reasons why Congress has at times failed to exercise some of its constitutional prerogatives during this period. Congress sometimes seems either a broken branch or an overly obstructionist branch. But most Americans believe that the American political system works best when it has a strong presidency, a strong Congress, and an equally strong and independent Supreme Court. Americans might occasionally lament the gridlock and stalemate aspects of our system, yet, on balance, they admire the ingenious system of mostly constructive competitiveness our framers designed 223 years ago.

A strong presidency is the product of internal and external events that cannot be reversed. But no one believes that "strength" in the presidency alone should be equated with "greatness" or even "goodness." We share the apt and poignant perspective by the late political historian Clinton Rossiter:

> A strong President is a bad President, a curse upon the land, unless his means are constitutional and his ends democratic, unless he acts in ways that are fair, dignified, and familiar, and pushes policies to which a "persistent and undoubted" majority of the people [and we would add Congress] has given support.

> We honor the great Presidents of the past not for their strength, but for the fact that they used it wisely to build a better America. And in honoring them we recognize that their kind of presidency is one of our chief bulwarks against decline and chaos.[31]

The Road Ahead

Thus, we say two cheers for the distinctively American presidential–congressional separation of powers system. It is an imperfect institution, embedded in an imperfect system, headed by imperfect people who govern in an imperfect world. It is a slow, often messy system that often gets sidetracked by privileged interests or ideological posers, and yet, as Winston Churchill said in 1947, "Democracy is the worst form of government except for all those other forms that have been tried from time to time."[32]

Is anything *really* fundamentally wrong with the presidency? Yes, we have had some less politically skilled chief executives (e.g., Carter) and some demon-driven presidents (Nixon), some character-flawed magistrates (Clinton) and some faith-based overreachers (George W. Bush). But we have also had some intelligent (Obama), politically skilled (FDR), straight-shooting (Truman), prudent

(Eisenhower, George H. W. Bush), and decent (Ford, Carter, and Reagan) men serve in the White House. The task is to *make the presidential–congressional system work better.* To do that, presidents need skill, temperament, experience, judgment, and empathy. And the Congress needs party leaders who are motivated on big issues to find common ground. And the system, with a few structural modifications, less political polarization, better citizen engagement, some modest institutional reforms, and luck, can be made to work better.

We need a president grounded in the fundamental principles of the framers, heading an office that can meet the challenge of the modern era and is prepared to lead effectively in the 21st century.

We believe that the baroque system of checks and balances works best when presidential leadership animates and drives the system yet works collaboratively with congressional leaders of both parties. At its best, a president can be a leader, a teacher, a guide, and a mobilizer on behalf of all Americans. Yet, the office that nourishes responsible leadership is also capable of abuse. Some gridlock is built into the system; this is the legitimate price we pay for a responsible government.

How do we (a) transform our 18th-century Constitution into a guiding document capable of serving a 21st-century superpower and (b) support presidential power and leadership yet control and constitutionalize it? Can the presidency be made both powerful *and* accountable? Will this require major surgery or merely political improvisation?

The United States *needs* presidential leadership. The only way to reduce the need for a strong presidency is to reduce America's role in the world, retreat from global leadership, reduce the size of government, and free the economy of regulations and controls. This will not happen.

The presidency is thus necessary yet always potentially dangerous. We can't live without it, yet living with it may threaten constitutionalism and our traditional notions of a republic. How do we resolve this dilemma?

Aristotle, in his *Nicomachean Ethics,* tried to guide the enlightened statesman toward effective leadership and stewardship in his discussion of *phronesis.* Loosely translated, phronesis means knowledge put into appropriate action for a good cause. It is the exercise of reason and good judgment, and sound logic, as applied to a complex world, recognizing the limits and possibilities at hand and arriving at a constructive course of action that is most likely to lead to a morally and politically good result. The verb *phronein* means intelligent awareness, and the noun *phronesis* means practical prudence or sound deliberation resulting in correct suppositions about a good end. Wisdom, prudence, good judgment, morally appropriate ends— these are the factors that bring phronesis to light. It is moral discernment applied to complex human affairs, prudence in action, goal maximization directed toward socially good ends, the effort to convert morally and socially sound ideals into policy, and it is what defines effective leadership.

Phronesis goes beyond prudence; it is prudent judgment directed into action to achieve a good result. It is *judgment* and *action*.[33] As political scientist James Bill writes, "Phronesis recognizes a certain balance between the cognitive and the emotional. It brings reason and passion together in empathy." Further, "to exercise phronesis is not only to match means with a policy goal. Phronesis also means to deliberate and act in a way that maintains means, ends, and the conduct of policy in balanced tension." In this way, phronesis is the art of the statesman and an "explicit recognition of moral as well as pragmatic dimensions of effective action." The leader who possesses the skills to govern effectively has competence, judgment, and a sense of justice. He or she has the necessary skills to govern effectively and the ethical compass to govern wisely.

James Bill sees former presidential adviser George Ball as a modern example of phronesis in action. Others might nominate General Brent Scowcroft, James A. Baker, or Richard Holbrooke as prudent policy leaders. Aristotle had his eye on the great Athenian lawgiver, Pericles. To Aristotle, Pericles had the ability to see what was good and to further translate that vision into feasible policies designed to achieve those worthy and attainable goals. Pericles served the public interest even as he tried to shape it. He sought justice in an unjust world, and he had the skills to translate his vision into policy. If you are looking for presidents who might fit this model, look to George Washington, Abraham Lincoln, and Franklin D. Roosevelt. In general, they did the right things for the right reasons, toward the right ends.

Skill matters. And what skills must the effective leader possess? Machiavelli answered this question with an analogy. The skilled leader must be both the *lion* and the *fox*. The lion was strong, a great fighter; it instilled fear in its rivals. But the lion lacked cunning, wisdom, and the ability to fool an adversary. Thus, the fox was the skilled manipulator who by cunning, guile, and deception was able to misdirect an adversary. While the fox is not a master in battle, it is skilled in the art of deception and wise in the choice of tactics. The effective leader combines the skills of the lion and the fox. As Machiavelli states in Chapter XVIII of *The Prince,* "As a prince is forced to know how to act like a beast, he must learn from the fox and the lion. Those who simply act like lions are wrong."[34] Here we inevitably think of the mistakes of George W. Bush over the war in Iraq, where he strutted and acted like the lion, yet where he was also sometimes ill advised and ill prepared to use his full arsenal of tools to deal with the problem at hand. In the end, he was so intent on playing the lion—even when playing the fox might have been wise—that he walked into a mess that could have been and should have been avoided.

The Impact

The changes suggested, some modest, others a bit more profound, would, we argue, have the effect of making the presidency more effective, more democratically accountable, better able to work *within* the separation of powers system, less of a threat to our Constitution, and better able to serve the nation.

Successful presidents serve the nation. Yet, to what ends? The framers of the republic had a clear answer to that question. To the framers, the answer was embedded in the Preamble to the Constitution:

> We the people of the United States, in Order to form a more
> perfect Union, establish Justice, insure domestic Tranquility,
> provide for the common defense, promote the general Welfare,
> and secure the Blessings of Liberty to ourselves and our
> Posterity, do ordain and establish this Constitution for the
> United States of America.

So, in order to form a *more perfect union,* the new government was to establish *justice,* insure domestic *tranquility,* provide for *defense,* promote general *welfare,* and secure *liberty,* and not just for ourselves, but for our *posterity* as well. That is what our government intended to do.

That is still the moderates' political agenda.

Effective presidential leadership is power for a purpose. The presidents we elevate to Mount Rushmore status expanded democracy and economic opportunity, opened doors to the excluded, spoke and worked for our highest values, and stood up against evil and ignorance. Yes, they made deals, bargained and compromised, settling for the politically possible rather than the perfect solution. Yet they moved us toward admirable goals. Clinton Rossiter, writing of FDR, noted that he "rarely lost sight of a truth that most politicians have yet to perceive: that politics is only a game, and a shabby game at that, if it is not directed to larger and nobler ends."[35]

Conclusion

The presidency often seems an impossible or near impossible job. It has humbled most of its occupants.

Presidential leadership can on occasion animate the American system. Without it, only rarely are we able to overcome the roadblocks and conservatism built into the system. We know that presidential leadership is often frustrated by an 18th-century Constitution, written for a small, relatively isolated, militarily weak and economically underdeveloped nation. Today, we are decidedly a world leader. Yet, we are still governed by that 18th-century Constitution. How can an 18th-century Constitution govern *the* world's greatest power in the 21st century? Creative presidential leadership, together with creative congressional will and creative social movements and societal leadership, will sometimes supply the answer.

But it must be creative leadership within a democratic or republican context, bound by as well as supported by an attentive and active public. Leadership can often be sandwiched by equally dangerous alternatives found in the saying "Pity the leader caught between unloving critics and uncritical lovers."[36]

In considering reform of our presidential–congressional system, we should keep in mind the Latin adage *aegrescit medendo* (the remedy may be worse than the disease). Pursue reform, yet be aware of the unintended consequences of reform. This should humble us as we consider dramatically changing the system of government that has served us so well for so long.

You cannot divorce power from purpose. True leadership, effective leadership, uses power for morally high purpose. In his book, *Transforming Leadership,* James MacGregor Burns writes:

> The clues to the mystery of leadership lie in a potent equation: embattled values grounded in real wants, invigorated by conflict, empower leaders and activated followers to fashion deep and comprehensive change in the lives of people. The acid test of this empowerment is whether the change is lasting or whether it is temporary and even reversible. Deep and durable change, guided and measured by values, is the ultimate purpose of transforming leadership, and constitutes both its practical impact and its moral justification.[37]

Notes

1. Michael A. Genovese, ed., *Hamilton, Madison, and Jay: The Federalist Papers* (New York: Palgrave MacMillan, 2009).

2. See Richard A. Posner, *Not a Suicide Pact: The Constitution in a Time of National Emergency* (New York: Oxford University Press, 2006).

3. See Ted Halstead and Michael Lind, *The Radical Center: The Future of American Politics* (Harpswell, ME: Anchor, 2002); Donald I. Warren, *The Radical Center: Middle Americans and the Politics of Alienation* (South Bend, IN: University of Notre Dame Press, 1976); Mark Satin, *Radical Middle: The Politics We Need Now* (New York: Basic Books, 2004).

4. See Louis Fisher, *On Appreciating Congress* (Boulder, CO: Paradigm, 2010).

5. See Erik W. Doxtader, "Characters in the Middle of Public Life: Consensus, Dissent, and Ethos," *Philosophy and Rhetoric* 33 (2000): 336–369; Arthur M. Schlesinger Jr., *The Vital Center: The Politics of Freedom* (Cambridge, MA: Riverside Press, 1949); Anthony Downs, *An Economic Theory of Democracy* (New York: HarperCollins, 1957); and Antonio de Velasco, *Centerist Rhetoric* (Lanham, MD: Lexington Books, 2010).

6. See Thomas E. Cronin, *On the Presidency* (Boulder, CO: Paradigm, 2009); Bruce Miroff, *Icons of Democracy* (Lawrence: University Press of Kansas, 2000).

7. Still about three dozen nations have had "presidential" systems, though only about a dozen of these are major nations. And even in these dozen, the stability of leadership in several of them has witnessed decidedly "rocky" periods, for example in Chile,

Nigeria, Philippines, and Venezuela. A smaller nation, Honduras, is the most recent presidential nation where a president was forced out by the military in collaboration with other establishment actors.

8. The most famous "reformer" proposing a move toward a parliamentary system in America was a young political scientist named Woodrow Wilson, who changed his views on the subject as he grew older. See Thomas W. Wilson, "Cabinet Government in the United States," *The International Review,* 3rd ed. no. 5 (August 1879): 146–163.

9. For further discussion of how Americans judge and rate their presidents, see Thomas E. Cronin and Michael A. Genovese, *The Paradoxes of the American Presidency,* 3rd ed. (New York: Oxford University Press, 2010), Chapter 2.

10. Evan Bayh, "Why I'm Leaving the Senate," *The New York Times,* Week in Review, February 21, 2010, 9

11. See especially Juan J. Linz, "The Perils of Presidentialism," *Journal of Democracy* (Winter, 1990): 51–69. See also Arend Lijphart, ed., *Parliamentary Versus Presidential Government* (New York: Oxford University Press, 1992).

12. See the helpful research of Charles Jones, *The Presidency in a Separated System* (Washington, DC: The Brookings Institution, 1994). See also Matthew N. Beckman, *Pushing the Agenda: Presidential Leadership in U.S. Lawmaking, 1953–2004* (New York: Cambridge University Press, 2010).

13. Cronin has discussed his case in detail in "President John F. Kennedy: Act III Politician," Chapter 4 in Thomas E. Cronin, *On the Presidency* (Boulder, CO: Paradigm, 2009), 83–118.

14. See especially David R. Mayhew, *Divided We Govern: Party Control, Lawmaking, and Investigation, 1946–1990* (New Haven, CT: Yale University Press, 1991). See also Jones, *Presidency in a Separated System.*

15. See the useful history of liberal legislation in James L. Sundquist, *Politics and Policy: The Eisenhower, Kennedy and Johnson Years* (Washington, DC: The Brookings Institution, 1968).

16. James Sundquist, "Four More Years: Is Deadlock the only Prospect?" *Public Administration Review* (May/June, 1973): 280–281, and his *Constitutional Reform and Effective Government* (Washington, DC: Brookings, 1986). See also James MacGregor Burns, *The Power to Lead: The Crisis of the American Presidency* (New York: Simon & Schuster, 1984).

17. David W. Brady and Craig Volden, *Revolving Gridlock,* 2nd ed. (Boulder, CO: Westview, 2006), 209. See also Marcus E. Ethridge, *The Case for Gridlock: Democracy, Organized Power, and the Legal Foundation of American Government* (New York: Lexington Books, 2010).

18. Garry Wills, "Entangled Giant," *The New York Review of Books* (October 8, 2009): 4; See also Garry Wills, *Bomb Power: The Modern Presidency and the National Security State* (New York: Penguin Press, 2010).

19. Schlesinger, quoted in Thomas E. Cronin, *On the Presidency* (Boulder, CO: Paradigm, 2009), 140. See also Joseph S. Nye, *The Powers of Leadership* (Oxford University Press, 2006).

20. These are expanded from Thomas E. Cronin and Michael A. Genovese, *The Paradoxes of the American Presidency,* 3rd ed. (New York: Oxford University Press, 2010), 301.

21. See George Edwards, *Why the Electoral College Is Bad for America* (New Haven, CT: Yale University Press, 2004); Cronin and Genovese, *The Paradoxes of the American Presidency*, 3rd ed. (New York: Oxford University Press, 2010), Chapter 3.
22. See Cronin and Genovese, *The Paradoxes of the American Presidency*, 3rd ed. (New York: Oxford University Press, 2010), Chapter 8. Both political scientist Clinton Rossiter and historian Arthur M. Schlesinger Jr. have, at earlier times, concluded that the mandate for a vice president is a serious flaw in our Constitution.
23. See Larry M. Bartels, *Unequal Democracy: The Political Economy of the New Gilded Age* (New York: Russell Sage Foundation, 2008); see also Benjamin I. Page and Lawrence R. Jacobs, *Class War?: What Americans Really Think About Economic Inequality* (Chicago: University of Chicago Press, 2009); Martin Gilens, "Inequality and Democratic Responsiveness," *Public Opinion Quarterly* 5 (2005): 778–796.
24. Jacob S. Hacker and Paul Pierson, *Winner-Take-All Politics: How Washington Made the Rich Richer—And Turned Its Back on the Middle Class* (New York: Simon & Schuster, 2010), 151.
25. See, for example, Sanford Levinson's provocative *Our Undemocratic Constitution: Where the Constitution Goes Wrong* (New York: Oxford University Press, 2006).
26. Mark A. Peterson, *Legislating Together: The White House and Capitol Hill From Eisenhower to Reagan* (Cambridge, MA: Harvard University Press, 1990), 291.
27. See Larry J. Sabato, *A More Perfect Constitution: Why The Constitution Must Be Revised* (New York: Walker and Co., 2008), 192.
28. Schlesinger, originally in *The Wall Street Journal* (1982); also in Arend Lijphart, ed., *Parliamentary Versus Presidential Government.*
29. Garry Wills, *A Necessary Evil: A History of American Distrust of Government* (New York: Simon & Schuster, 2002).
30. Thomas E. Cronin, *On the Presidency* (Boulder, CO: Paradigm, 2009) 64–71.
31. Clinton Rossiter, *The American Presidency*, rev. ed. (New York: Harcourt Brace, 1960), 257.
32. Winston Churchill, Speech to the British House of Commons, November 11, 1947.
33. See James A. Bill's excellent biography of George Ball for an example of phronesis in practice, *George Ball* (New Haven, CT: Yale University Press, 1997), 204–205.
34. Niccollo Machiavelli, *The Prince and Other Writings,* trans. Wayne A. Rebhorn (New York: Barnes & Noble Classics, 2003).
35. Clinton Rossiter, *The American Presidency* (Baltimore, MD: John Hopkins University Press, 1987), 149.
36. John Gardner, *On Leadership* (New York: Free Press, 1990), 135.
37. James MacGregor Burns, *Transforming Leadership* (New York: Grove, 2003), 213.

Portions of this chapter were earlier delivered by Thomas E. Cronin as an address in Seoul, Korea, in October 2009, at The Korean National Academy of Sciences, on *Presidential vs. Parliamentary Government.*

CHAPTER 3

Liberals and the Presidency

Robert J. Spitzer

LIBERALISM AND THE AMERICAN PRESIDENCY are not necessarily a natural match. Classical liberalism, as it was understood at the time of America's founding as an independent nation, viewed government with suspicion. Freedom from government control and the elevation of personal liberty reflected liberalism's animating spirit, along with the embrace of economic *laissez faire* (literally, to leave alone) and minimal government. Closely related was a firm belief in a tolerant and open society and the Jeffersonian belief that the wisdom of the public could be relied upon more than that of an active government.[1] This "Whiggish" liberalism "tended to see society as beneficent and government as malevolent."[2]

Core liberal values remained mostly constant, but as society evolved, the liberal view of government power changed. In the 18th century, the only democratic nations were small ones; the idea of a nation the size of the United States successfully establishing a stable, viable republic seemed almost beyond imagining.[3] Yet the nation, already sprawling at the end of the 18th century, became far larger, and it also not only retained, but expanded, its democratic impulses. By the end of the 19th century, the largely rural nation that Thomas Jefferson knew had become an industrial and geographic giant, with power over society increasingly exercised by huge corporations—big oil, steel, mining, the railroads, among others—that exploited their work force, and the resources of the nation, without heed to anything other than profits. Liberals didn't abandon the belief in capitalism (although others did), but they also realized that only one force could rein in corporate excesses to protect the public. That force was an activist government. Activism itself came to be embodied in one office: the American presidency.

What a Liberal Believes

Writing in 1945, a young historian wrote an award-winning biography of President Andrew Jackson in which he summarized the liberal view of the presidency this way: "Jeffersonianism required Hamiltonian means to achieve its ends."[4] Arthur

M. Schlesinger Jr., himself the son of a noted historian, would come to embody the liberal view of the presidency—both its virtues and its sins. Although Jefferson and Alexander Hamilton were bitter foes during most of their careers, and they differed in their views of the presidency,[5] Schlesinger's formula combined Jefferson's egalitarian spirit with Hamilton's tireless advocacy of a vigorous executive to produce a liberal activism that would advance the public interest through aggressive and constructive presidential leadership.

The prototype of the liberal activist presidency was strongly advanced by the earlier writings of a British scholar of American politics, Harold J. Laski. Writing well beyond analysis of a single president, and on the eve of World War II, Laski set out a kind of blueprint for liberal presidential activism by contrasting that branch with the branch considered by the Constitution's founders to be the first branch of government, Congress. Presidents should not be limited by Congress, Laski asserted in his book, for "the Congress is not a body capable of constructive leadership; the functions it performs most effectively are those of criticism and investigation rather than responsibility for the direction of affairs."[6] Governance in the 20th century, according to Laski, "requires a strong executive"[7] to lead Congress and the nation, as Franklin Roosevelt had done in the decade prior to Laski's writing. The president, Laski concluded, "must be given the power commensurate to the function he has to perform. . . . If he is to be a great president, let us be clear that it must be given."[8]

Laski's call for strong, decisive presidents in need of ever more power would become the mantra of most presidency analysts for the next three decades, and this would also find great favor in the public mind.[9] Yet it had no greater champion than political scientist Clinton Rossiter, whose 1956 book, *The American Presidency*, would be the most widely read on the subject for over a decade. Rossiter pulled no punches. He agreed with Laski that Congress was barely capable of effective governance, that the president was not only indispensable to constructive leadership, but that strong, decisive, activist presidents were the very definition of good and effective governance. At the outset of his book, Rossiter confessed "my own feeling of veneration, if not exactly reverence, for the authority and dignity of the Presidency."[10] While he invokes constitutional limitations, he simultaneously seems to jettison them, preferring instead a president of boundless vision, action, and leadership—of "power and glory"[11]—unencumbered by conventional checks and balances. The Napoleonic overtones to some of Rossiter's writing about America's elected executive seemed to escape general notice.

The larger lesson was a simple one: the greatest and most successful presidents in American history were those who were most active in exercising powers: Washington, Jefferson, Lincoln, Theodore Roosevelt, Wilson, and especially the four-term Franklin Roosevelt, whose administration spanned the formative years of the most influential presidency writers of the mid-20th century. These presidents were mostly, but not only, Democrats, but all shared a liberal spirit (Washington perhaps less than the others) that used government power for mostly noble ends: to establish the American government, explore the continent, end slavery, bust the trusts, establish national parks, regulate banking, stem the Great Depression, defeat fascism, and provide a social safety net. Presidential activism yielded greatness. Greater activism, perforce, meant even better governance. Great presidents were muscular presidents who exercised great power on behalf of the people, to whom presidents were accountable. Or so the narrative went.

The Problem

I have taught Introduction to American Government for over 30 years. Every semester, I pose a question to my students when we get to the topic of the American presidency. After establishing that the chief trait of the presidency is its progressive acquisition of greater and greater power, I pose this question: What will eventually happen if more and more and more power accrues to the presidency? Students always know the answer: Eventually, we arrive at dictatorship. For what is a dictator, after all, but an executive who holds most or all of the power of government? Despite their perfunctory bows to the separation of powers, the liberal presidentialists functioned as though oblivious to this obvious political truism; they were seduced by their own narrative, and they were eventually forced to confront the consequence of ever-escalating presidential power unencumbered by significant congressional or other Madisonian checks, beginning in the late 1960s. (It is no small irony that Rossiter foresaw this very prospect in his first book, *Constitutional Dictatorship*.[12]) Two sets of factors gave liberals this rude awakening: the misdeeds of some active presidents and the conservative embrace of activism, beginning in the 1980s.

Presidents Behaving Badly

The presidencies of Lyndon Johnson and Richard Nixon demonstrated that presidential activism could produce perverse results. Johnson's presidency began in the terrible tragedy of John F. Kennedy's assassination; yet that premature end turned a page to a less glamorous, but arguably more effective, liberal Democratic president. Using the full resources of his office and his prodigious personal skills, Johnson orchestrated and implemented his Great Society, extending voting and other rights to African Americans, expanding the government's social safety net, and using the powers of office to advance many other traditionally liberal objectives. At the same time, however, Johnson engineered the escalation of fighting in the Vietnam War, first hiding his intentions, then misleading the public about the course of the war. Liberals ultimately grew deeply disenchanted with "Johnson's war," and many felt that he had abused his power to draw the country ever more deeply into a costly (both in money and human treasure), unjust, and misbegotten conflict.

The election of Johnson's successor, Richard Nixon, turned the presidency over to a conservative but pragmatic Republican. Liberals held out few illusions that Nixon would use his office in any manner similar to Johnson, but his pragmatic approach to governance suggested a more centrist presidency. Yet Nixon was not only an activist in office but something more: He came to view the powers of his office as synonymous with his personal wishes. The Watergate scandal came to epitomize an out-of-control presidency where, as Nixon said in an interview after he was forced from office, "when the president does it, that means that it is not illegal."[13] There, in succinct expression, was the liberal presidentialists' nightmare. Nixon's expansive view of the powers of office pushed aside the Constitution and the law because it justified a series of felonies and abuse of the power of office. Only the looming threat of impeachment forced the first resignation of a sitting president in American history.

These two presidencies prompted many *mea culpas* from the liberal presidentialists. Most notable was that of Arthur Schlesinger. After years of writing that extolled the activism of Jackson, Franklin Roosevelt, and Kennedy, Schlesinger penned a new book, the title of which came to epitomize what was now viewed as an out-of-control presidency: *The Imperial Presidency.* As Schlesinger confessed, "Historians and political scientists, this writer among them, contributed to the rise of the presidential mystique."[14] To say the least. Presidential reality had smacked liberal presidentialists in the face.[15] Maybe James Madison really was on to something when he wrote in Federalist 51 that "ambition must be made to counteract ambition."[16]

This liberal "reality check" emphasized a related mistake: liberal presidentialists, and to a great degree the American ethos, had lost the key distinction between the empirical measurement of something and feelings about what was politically good. Historians and others took great interest in the relative rankings and evaluations of presidents throughout history—who were the "greats," the "near-greats," and the "failures"? This exercise became a regular feature of polling since historian Arthur Schlesinger Sr. took the first such poll in 1948. This fixation with presidential rankings and greatness blurred the divide between activism and success, a distinction that only reemerged with the misguided "activism" of the Nixon presidency.[17] Sobered reanalysis of presidents initially criticized for their lack of activism revealed that effective presidents weren't necessarily the most active[18] and presidential activism itself was by no means an unmitigated good.[19]

Conservative Presidents Embrace Activism

The traditional conservative view of presidential power, as it existed in most of the 20th century, viewed strong, activist presidents with suspicion. As President

William Howard Taft wrote early in the 20th century, after his presidency, "The President can exercise no power which cannot be fairly and reasonably traced to some specific grant of power or justly implied and included within such express grant as proper and necessary to its exercise."[20] Other, more contemporary writings argued on behalf of a more restrained, and narrowly constitutional, interpretation of presidential powers.[21] But this Whiggish/conservative tradition emphasizing limited presidential power was swept aside by the presidency of Ronald Reagan. Partly as a response to what was viewed by some as an abrogation of presidential powers in the 1970s by a resurgent Congress, Reagan's election in 1980 brought into office a new conservatism that planted feet in two seemingly contradictory camps: constitutional originalism and activist presidentialism. The chief architects of this new activist conservatism were lawyers working in the Reagan Justice Department and in a newly founded organization of conservative lawyers, the Federalist Society.[22] Together, these groups produced a new theory of presidential power, the Unitary theory, which argues that the framers envisioned and created expansive executive power.

Presidential liberals now no longer had a monopoly over presidential activism. Yet liberals' philosophical differences with activist conservatives consisted of two parts. The first was a difference in public policy. Liberals supported liberal policies, whereas conservatives supported conservative policies. That was fair enough. The second difference was more significant. Liberal presidentialists generally recognized the historical consensus that presidential power as found in the Constitution was relatively limited (as was the vision of most founders), but the document's architecture was sufficiently vague that it allowed for the possibility of greater presidential power, a pattern that unfolded primarily in the 20th century. Further, this rise of strong presidentialism was viewed as both necessary and good, coinciding as it did with the growth of the modern American republic. Conservatives hewing to the Unitary theory argued that the founders intended to grant presidents vast power, that this power had been somehow misunderstood, hemmed in, and whittled away over the decades, so that conservative presidents staking out substantial power claims, like Reagan and George W. Bush, were only reclaiming for their office constitutional powers that had properly belonged to the institution all along.[23]

This activist conservative (as distinct from Whiggish conservatism) narrative suffered from four problems: First, this "originalist" interpretation of expansive presidential powers fit poorly with nearly all the evidence of what the founders understood, how they constructed presidential powers in 1787, and how those who ran the country in its early decades (and who had created the modern Constitution) actually behaved; in fact, constitutional originalism leads to legislative dominance, not coequal branches, and certainly not to presidential preeminence.[24] Second, the notion that presidents had, on the whole, lost powers from the end of the 18th century to the present contradicted the bedrock understanding that the presidential institution has (in fits and starts) grown in powers significantly and dramatically in the last two centuries.[25] Third, the intellectual provenance of the Unitary theory as constitutional theory was inherently suspect, as its architects claimed to discover an entirely new theory that had been somehow missed in nearly 200 years of intense and prolific constitutional scrutiny.[26] Fourth, the intellectual foundation for the Unitary theory rested on a political motivation: to construct a conservative justification for presidential activism that maintained fidelity to constitutional originalism, the secular religion of the modern conservative movement.[27] In short, liberal presidentialists could have no quarrel with conservatives who now sought to use the powers of the presidency to advance conservative political and policy objectives, just as liberal presidents had done in the past and, presumably, would continue to do in the future. But they did and do quarrel with a tendentious theory constructed solely to provide political cover for actions that, in at least some instances, skirted the outer edge of both the law and the Constitution, especially in areas like foreign policy and war powers.[28]

Liberal Presidentialism After Watergate

Liberal presidentialism was a sobered presidentialism after the Johnson–Nixon period. During the heyday of the New Deal coalition (1932–1968), liberal Democrats advanced their political and policy goals with activist presidents leading the way. But the post-1968 era was primarily an era of divided government, where neither party ever held the kind of decisive majorities that typified most earlier eras in American politics. Even Ronald Reagan, who won election twice by the largest margins of any president during this period of time, could not win one-party control of Congress, as the Democrats retained control of the House of Representatives during his entire presidency and won the Senate back from the Republicans in the midterm elections of 1986. In this era of relative deadlock and close party competition, neither party could muster decisive majorities; both parties became more adept at thwarting the initiatives of the other, and the ability of presidents to exercise the kind of decisive leadership of bygone times seemed greatly reduced.

In recent decades, the presidents who exhibited the greatest degree of in-office activism were conservative Republicans Ronald Reagan and George W. Bush; Bush indeed became the first president to attempt implementation of the Unitary theory of executive power. Yet the verdict of most liberal presidentialists, as well as of many conservatives, was that the second Bush's presidency, not unlike Nixon's, was presidential activism gone awry. Democrat Bill Clinton achieved much in his eight years, but he was largely thwarted when it came to the enactment of sweeping policy change, including his signature policy goal, health care reform. Barack Obama's presidency may, by its end, come to be judged on an activist par with Reagan and Bush (although from a liberal rather than conservative direction), but liberals have already expressed considerable dismay at Obama's relatively centrist and consensus-oriented style of governance, even taking into account enactment of the Democrats' cornerstone policy goal: the health care reform package of 2010.

The Solution

What, then, is the solution to the flaws of liberal presidentialism? Each of the chapters in this book may be taken as a possible solution to the flaws of the others. While each offers an important and valuable perspective on the American presidency, liberal presidentialism provides, I argue here, the most realistic, viable, and constructive alternative to the puzzle of presidential power.

Let me first address the question of activism, both as a matter of Constitution and of politics. Constitutionally, most founders, with a few exceptions (notably Hamilton), did not establish, embrace, or even envision anything like the activist presidency that emerged in the 20th century, and the Constitution's Article II surely did not create by design such an activist presidency, despite the unitarians' argument to the contrary. The constitutionalists and the traditional conservatives are correct in their conclusion that the Constitution created a relatively limited executive. On the other hand, they underestimate the significance of the fact that Article II was written with deliberate ambiguity founded, at least in part, in uncertainty, so presidential activism, per se, does not violate the words (or arguably, the spirit) of Article II. In addition, it cannot be true that the three-branch relationship established by the Constitution was viewed as rigid and immutable. Change was and is possible within that dynamic. Because the country began with legislative supremacy does not mean that this would, or should, forever be the norm within the constitutional system. Thus, the originalists also underestimate the regime-changing impact of American political development and change on the American polity,[29] which takes us to the politics of liberal presidential activism.

One need not embrace the tenets of political liberalism to accept the necessity of presidential activism in modern American governance. President Obama was criticized from many quarters for the $787 billion bank bailout bill he pushed through Congress in 2009 to stave off financial collapse. But some of his critics had already forgotten that Obama's predecessor, George W. Bush, pushed through Congress a similarly gigantic bailout bill in 2008 for the very same reason—to stave off a literal financial collapse of epic proportions. Such aggressive action to intervene in the economy would have been unthinkable before the 1930s. While a conservative Republican like Bush and a liberal Democrat like Obama would disagree over government involvement in many policy areas, the parameters within which government action is generally accepted have moved profoundly since the founding period and the 19th century. And while such action involves Congress as well as the presidency, presidential leadership is instrumental to the functioning of the modern American state. No amount of wishing by originalists or libertarians can turn back that clock.

What, then, of *liberal* presidential activism? One may, of course, turn to the standard liberal–conservative debate over policy objectives, but this is not the place for that debate. If liberal presidentialism can defend activist presidentialism, then it can have no quarrel with the legitimacy of conservative presidential activism. On the other hand, the record of liberal presidentialism is, by and large, not only defensible, but admirable.

One must, however, separate means and ends. In the pre-Watergate era, liberal presidentialists concerned themselves little with means if the ends seemed just. Yet that is a flaw that cannot and should not stand.

The liberal presidentialist naiveté about law and the Constitution that suffused so much activist presidency cheerleading before the 1970s must be jettisoned, in favor of renewed separation of powers rigor. Presidential activism of any ideological stripe must be clearly bounded by the rule of law and established constitutional principles. Even if Congress is no longer the center of American governance, it still maintains the panoply of express and implied powers set out in Article I and ultimate authority over the most important powers of governance: control over money and control over the use of force. Modern presidents have exercised vastly greater authority in these areas, partly because Congress has willingly given powers over to the executive, as in the case of budgeting,[30] partly because of congressional acquiescence and a generally sympathetic judiciary[31] and partly because of aggressive presidential aggrandizement, as in the case of war powers.[32] But liberal activism can and should only function in a democracy within the clear confines of the separation of powers. To illustrate the line that must be drawn between presidential activism and extraconstitutional adventurism, I turn to two different sets of examples—two cases from Franklin Roosevelt's presidency and the contemporary controversy over presidential signing statements.

Two Roosevelt Cases

Consider two controversial actions by the paragon of liberal activism, Franklin Roosevelt. In 1937, after winning a smashing reelection victory the previous year, Roosevelt proposed to Congress a bill that would have increased the size of the Supreme Court (and the lower federal courts) by adding a new seat for each sitting justice over the age of 70 who did not choose to retire. In his March 9 radio address to the nation to explain and defend the bill, Roosevelt gave two specific reasons for his proposal: to encourage the Court to be "speedier and, therefore, less costly," and to "save our national Constitution from hardening of the judicial arteries,"[33] meaning to infuse the judiciary with younger people. FDR's speech also included a litany of complaints against the third branch, chiefly that it had consistently thwarted New Deal programs, and this indeed was what he hoped to change. But Roosevelt's so-called "court packing" plan foundered and failed.[34] It even lost the support in Congress of many of his stalwart advocates, owing to the belief that Roosevelt had gone too far and that he was meddling improperly with another branch of government. Most would agree that Roosevelt's move was a costly political mistake. Yet the proposal—a request to Congress that it make the change through the normal legislative process—was perfectly proper, if politically misbegotten. The size of the Supreme Court, and the number and composition of the lower federal courts, is constitutionally determined by Congress, and FDR acted with legal propriety to make the request. It was a political overstep, but not a legal or constitutional one, from an activist president who misread the politics of the moment.

By comparison, consider Roosevelt's increasingly aggressive military actions in the North Atlantic in the months before America formally entered World War II. By 1940, the wars in Europe and Asia were going badly for America's allies. Isolationist sentiment was still strong in the United States, and Roosevelt publicly expressed great caution about becoming involved in that conflict, even as he knew that the United States had to eventually act to thwart Nazi Germany and Imperial Japan. The fall of France and the German invasion of the Soviet Union cast an ever-darker shadow over Europe. While Roosevelt wished to help Britain more aggressively, he felt constrained by domestic politics and resistance in Congress. Responding to the French's last-gasp appeal for large-scale American military help as German troops overran the country, Roosevelt replied, "Only the Congress can make such commitments."[35] Yet Roosevelt did covertly up the ante, and by the summer of 1941, the United States was in a de facto war in the North Atlantic, at Roosevelt's initiation, and with the urging of Britain. American ships were not only passing intelligence to British warships to help them sink Nazi submarines, but Roosevelt had issued "shoot-on-sight" orders to American air and naval forces to initiate attacks against German and Italian vessels in international waters.[36] America's formal entry into the war did not occur until December 8, 1941, the day after the Japanese attack on Pearl Harbor.

Given the magnitude of the fascist threat to America and the world and the justness of that cause, it is difficult in hindsight to level vehement criticism against Roosevelt for his actions. Unlike his successors, and to his credit, Roosevelt never claimed any inherent or unilateral power to begin a military conflict by his sole decision. Nevertheless, his decisions in the summer of 1941 exceeded his constitutional powers, and in that respect, they represented a serious abrogation of constitutional powers. The court-packing scheme was within constitutional bounds; the de facto shooting war in the North Atlantic was outside of those bounds.

A different example is provided by an old presidential action that has recently roiled constitutional and interbranch waters: presidential use of signing statements.

Signing Statements

In its essence, a signing statement is utterly unexceptional. It is a statement issued by the president at the time of a bill signing that offers comment on the new law.

Signing statements may simply praise the new legislation being signed by the president. They may also be used for political exhortations or excoriations. They may express reservations about portions of the new law, offer interpretations regarding the meaning or implementation of aspects of the statute, or, in extreme form, pronounce a reinterpretation of the law's language or meaning that may itself run the gamut from ambiguous to crystal clear.

As with much of what modern presidents do, the Constitution provides no authorization for such issuances (although the Constitution does require presidents who veto legislation to return vetoed bills to Congress along with the president's "Objections," which has always been taken to mean a written explanatory message[37]). In principle, a simple statement by the president offering comment on the bill being signed seems an eminently reasonable action on the president's part. The earliest such statement is traced to President James Monroe, who issued a statement in 1819 about a bill he had signed into law a month earlier pertaining to a reduction in the size of the army that stipulated how the president was to select military officers. In his statement, Monroe noted that such decisions belonged to the president, not Congress. Even so, he did not challenge the law's validity or constitutionality.[38]

Presidential signing statements during the balance of the 19th century were rare; rarer still were statements questioning the legality or constitutionality of the bills being signed. By one count, from Monroe until 1945, presidents raised constitutional objections in signing statements in fewer than 20 instances. From Presidents Truman through Nixon, signing statements increased in use, but those raising constitutional objections composed only about three to six percent of these.[39] Presidents Ford and Carter developed signing statements as coherent political tools to advance policy and power objectives, including a few signing statements that announced presidential intentions to ignore provisions of law considered to be unconstitutional or to exert executive prerogatives.[40]

But two qualitative changes then occurred. The first was during the Reagan presidency,[41] when the frequency of signing statements based on constitutional, power-related claims by the president increased dramatically.[42] The increase was part of a coordinated administration strategy, spearheaded by Attorney General Edwin Meese's Justice Department, to imbue signing statements with legal weight sufficient to influence legislative intent. In fact, lawyer Steven Calabresi (a cofounder of the conservative legal organization, the Federalist Society) claimed credit for first suggesting the idea of elevating signing statements to Meese.[43] To that end, Meese succeeded in persuading Westlaw Publishing to include signing statements in the Legislative History section of the authoritative record of legislative history, *U.S. Code, Congressional and Administrative News,*[44] even though the president is not a legislator, and the signing statement always comes after the legislative process (where legislative intent is expressed) is concluded. This development in the Reagan administration, in turn, was part of the development of the Unitary theory of executive power discussed earlier.

The second major change occurred during the second Bush presidency, when the administration, spearheaded by Vice President Dick Cheney, sought a full-bore implementation of the Unitary theory.[45] Part of that effort included extravagant use of signing statements that, in both quantitative and qualitative respects, ratcheted up the significance of these statements. As a legislative matter, the number of bills with attached signing statements during the Bush years was actually fewer than his immediate predecessors; however, the number of *provisions* challenged in Bush signing statements took a quantum leap. All previous presidents combined issued a total of about 600 signing statement provisions. In his eight years in office, Bush issued nearly 1,200 such statement provisions.[46] In turn, this effort served a larger presidential power metapurpose, described as an effort "to create a kind of body of precedent . . . to bolster presidential claims to authority or to limit Congress so that, after a time, what are in fact broad claims to power appear to be more or less routine legal formulae that may begin to be seen like little more than boilerplate language not worthy of careful attention" to undergird "a systematic effort to define presidential authority in terms of the broad conception of the prerogative . . . under the unitary executive theory."[47]

This truncated tale of signing statements well illustrates the paradox of presidential power. Signing statements in simple form are both reasonable and unexceptional. Initially used rarely, even apologetically by presidents,[48] they gradually became a presidential tool to prod the outer boundaries of statutory meaning. One can readily accept the argument of signing statement supporters that their use by presidents to defend their constitutional powers, offer constitutional interpretation of statutory language, and more effectively oversee the executive branch is justifiable,[49] at least in part, yet also note that this power has been seriously, even egregiously abused by presidents. Two cases illustrate.

On December 23, 2004, President Bush issued a signing statement when he signed into law the Intelligence Authorization Act for Fiscal Year 2005 (Public Law 108–487). That law included a provision barring U.S. troops in Colombia from participating in combat against rebels there except for self-defense, and it capped the troop presence at 800. Bush's signing statement included a statement that the executive branch would "construe the[se] restrictions . . . as advisory in nature. . . ."[50] Bush's signing statement for this bill, if taken at its word, changes the language of the law by substituting crystal-clear legal requirements with "advisory" statements—that is, meaning that the president did not consider himself bound by the plain and authoritative language of the law—the law that became law because he chose to affix his signature to it.

In 2006, Congress passed the Postal Accountability and Enhancement Act (Public Law 109–435), which confirmed a longstanding legal standard that mail could only be opened by the Postal Service without a warrant if it posed an "immediate threat to life or limb or an immediate and substantial danger to property."[51] Yet in his December 25, 2006, signing statement for this bill, President Bush said that he was construing this provision to allow "searches in exigent circumstances, such as to protect human life and safety."[52] As Senator Susan Collins (R-ME) noted on the Senate floor, this signing statement changed the law by expanding the definition of allowable warrantless mail opening *beyond* the protection of life and limb to "exigent circumstances." In other words, Bush's statement claims to insert this additional, more expansive meaning into the law he had signed, based on nothing more than his desire to do it.

Presidents surely have interpretive latitude, especially when legislative language is vague and therefore open to interpretation. This is nothing new. As the Whiggish President Taft noted after his presidency, "Let any one make the laws of the country, if I can construe them."[53]

But these two instances of presidential interpretation (in the midst of literally hundreds of other, similar signing statements) cannot be dismissed as an interpretive disagreement. What presidents may not do, even though Bush and a few of his predecessors have done so, is to rewrite legislation through signing statements in what some have called a de facto item veto.[54] The president has no power to rewrite a bill presented for signature, yet some signing statements, including the ones just described, do so. Nestled in Bush's 1,200 signing statement provisions are many such unilateral assertions.[55] This is a clear instance of presidential activism that has eclipsed legal and constitutional standards. As political scientist James Pfiffner concludes, "Bush's systematic and expansive use of signing statements constitutes a direct threat to the separation of powers system in the United States."[56] In Pfiffner's view, some of Bush's signing statements—that is, those that expressly state a refusal to treat clearly expressed law as law—represent a power "once asserted by kings,"[57] meaning the power to suspend the law.

The aggressive and even tendentious constitutional power claims of the Unitary theory have not only provoked criticisms from presidential liberals who otherwise support presidential activism, but they have also opened rifts with the conservative community, including conservatives who supported the conservative activism of the Reagan era, partly because of the thin claims to originalism on which the unitary view rest. Columnist and Unitary theory critic George Will, for example, noted with originalist skepticism, "Only one delegate [at the Constitutional Convention] . . . favored vesting presidents with an unfettered power to make war."[58] Former Reagan administration lawyer Bruce Fein has been a harsh critic of Bush administration unitary power claims, including abuse of executive privilege (which Fein dubbed "executive nonsense"), violation of the Foreign Intelligence Surveillance Act (FISA), and Bush's suspension of habeas corpus for detainees.[59] Former Bush federal attorney David Iglesias referred to Bush's power claims related to executive privilege as "executive privilege on steroids" and "executive carte blanche."[60] Joseph Baldacchino, president of the National Humanities Institute, referred to the "failures" of the Bush administration, singling out the administration's "warrantless searches and spying [and] the concentration of power in the executive branch at the expense of Congress, the courts and the states. . . ."[61] Writing in *The American Conservative,* Claes Ryn wrote with disdain about "the so-called 'unitary' executive—the notion of the pre-eminence of the president, who is to be as little constrained as possible by checks and balances and the rule of law. Their goal is wholly at odds with the constitutionalism of the framers."[62] The Cato Institute's Gene Healy is the author of a book that warns of "America's Dangerous Devotion to Executive Power" on its front cover. Healy dubs the Bush unitary view "Unitarian Heresies" and offers a lengthy analysis that undercuts the tenets of the unitary view; it is especially critical of Bush lawyer and University of California at Berkeley law professor John Yoo, primary author of the administration's torture memos and arch proponent of a nearly unlimited war power for the president.[63]

The features of unitary presidentialism, like the use of signing statements just described, render it dangerous to presidential activism, and therefore to American governance, precisely because it rejects traditional interbranch checks in many areas of presidential action, specifically in claims that Congress may exert no influence whatsoever over the president's control of the "unitary executive" (the mantra-like phrase referring to control of the executive branch that is invoked to express this view), and in claims that neither the Congress nor the courts may interfere with presidential decision making regarding foreign policy and national security matters.[64] Of all recent presidents, the second Bush presidency demonstrated itself to be the one most desperately in need of James Madison.

The solution to the problem of the presidential excesses described here I offer in the form of a simple mathematical equation:

$$(\text{Jeffersonian values} + \text{Hamiltonian vigor}) \div \text{Madisonian structuralism}$$

In words, this formula prescribes a presidentialism that includes traditional liberal values in the Jeffersonian tradition, combined with continued vigorous presidential activism (and here I reference Hamilton's beliefs, not the cartoonish caricatures of Hamilton's views that too often make their way into contemporary analyses of presidential power), but all "divided by," or tempered by, renewed and vigorous adherence to Madison's devotion to limited and blended powers, meaningful mutual checks, legislative primacy, and the constant reminder that ambition must be made to counteract ambition—most especially, presidential ambition. One may legitimately pose the question of whether, in the era of presidential governance, the separation of powers is "obsolete."[65] I argue here that the correct and necessary answer to this question is "no," as long as allowance is made for the tremendous evolutionary changes now manifested in the modern American state. Legislative supremacy envisioned and practiced early in the country's history is, I argue, no longer viable as a model for modern American governance. Yet that does not mean that the only alternative is the unitary executive.

Impact

The consequence of a constitutionally bounded liberal presidentialism is an executive office that continues to play the activist role that the nation and the rest of the government not only prefer but require. Like it or not, the modern American Republic, dating from the 20th century (and especially since the New Deal era) to the present, is a very different regime from that of 1789. It is, as Theodore Lowi noted, a regime that "can be characterized as *presidential government.*"[66] Even if the modern system typified by strong presidential leadership could not have been anticipated by the founders, their blueprint for American governance, organized around the separation of powers/checks and balances system, still offers the best remedy for retaining and maintaining constitutional governance and a strong but bounded presidency. The metaflaw of presidentialists before the Nixon era was that their tribute to constitutional structures was largely perfunctory. The role of vigorous and dynamic constitutional checks must indeed be real.[67] Stated another way, an activist presidency is a necessary, but not sufficient, condition for modern American governance. Whiggish presidents are an artifact of the past, as is old-style legislative supremacy; Americans will never again elect a president who campaigns, much less governs, on a platform of old-fashioned presidential restraint. While one may quibble with the wisdom of abandoning the Whig model of the presidency entirely, the quibble is purely academic. The Whig presidency is dead.

Conclusion

Thomas Jefferson penned this prescient prediction in a letter to James Madison in 1789: "The tyranny of the legislatures is the most formidable dread at present, and will be for many years. That of the executive will come in its turn; but it will be at a remote period."[68] Jefferson was dead on in two important respects: first, that legislative power would prevail at first in governance, but that over time, executive power would then be prevalent, and second, that the exercise of power was itself a kind of "dread."

Yet if governmental power was a "dread," it was a necessary dread or "necessary evil."[69] After all, Jefferson himself would press his power as president to acquire the Louisiana Purchase, doubling the land mass of the United States, among other aggressive actions. While Jefferson shared doubts about his own actions, he also wrote in 1807 that "on great occasions every good officer must be ready to risk himself in going beyond the strict line of the law, when the public preservation requires it; his motive will be a justification."[70]

Jefferson had this right, but to offer this admission is to accept neither the Schlesinger-Rossiter liberal naiveté about the unbounded virtue of presidential activism nor the specious, grandiose constitutionalism of the Unitary Executive theory. The Constitution is neither irrelevant nor sole and sufficient to understand

and explain presidential power, for the Constitution simply does not have all the answers to the riddle of executive power. This fact alone points to the flaws of certitude and generality that typify originalism as constitutional doctrine. In addition, the arc of presidential power from past to present is rooted in, but cannot be adequately explained by, Article II powers alone. Yet that does not mean that the Constitution's Article II is a Rorschach ink blot, the meaning of which is to be interpreted in any manner by whoever happens to be viewing it. All theories are not equally tenable; not every constitutional debate consists of two equally valid and legitimate opposing points of view. Text and historical evidence provide some answers. On the other hand, some questions simply cannot be answered. The grand irony for the unitarians is that an originalist reading of the Constitution leads to legislative supremacy, not to the unitary executive, whose originalism is faux originalism.

Liberals, while suspicious of too much power in the hands of any one institution, nevertheless do believe that government action to solve problems and right wrongs is necessary and at times commendable. Yes, such power is at times abused, yet without it, we would not have made the progress toward civil rights, equality for women, environmental protection, and a host of other issues. Politics can be dangerous, yet we are far worse off when we leave the future to the hands of an unregulated market than when the people empower our government to act on our behalf.

Liberal presidentialism is therefore and necessarily indispensable to modern American governance, but it is bearable for democratic sensibilities only when bounded by constitutionalism. The vagueness of Article II did and does open the door to presidential activism, but "ambition must be made to counteract ambition"[71] in the 21st century no less than in the 18th, and the weak participant in the modern interbranch dynamic, Congress, can best fulfill its role when the president is kept broadly within the constitutional box. No presidential power paradigm that views executive power as "limitless" and that contemplates the ability of presidents to "bypass laws at his discretion"[72] can be acceptably subsumed as within any justifiable notion of presidential activism as long as our political system makes any claim to democratic values and Republican governance.

Notes

1. Terence Ball and Richard Dagger, *Political Ideologies and the Democratic Ideal* (New York: Pearson Longman, 2009), chapter 3.
2. Gordon S. Wood, *Empire of Liberty: A History of the Early Republic, 1789–1815* (New York: Oxford University Press, 2009), 10.
3. Wood, *Empire of Liberty,* 8.
4. Arthur Schlesinger Jr., *The Age of Jackson* (Boston: Little, Brown, 1945), 517. Schlesinger's book won the Pulitzer Prize.

5. James MacGregor Burns, *Presidential Government* (Boston: Houghton Mifflin, 1973), chapter 1.

6. Harold J. Laski, *The American Presidency* (New York: Grosset & Dunlap, 1940), 19–20.

7. Laski, *The American Presidency*, 21.

8. Laski, *The American Presidency*, 278.

9. The intellectual tradition of presidential hero worship and strong presidency advocacy among political scientists and historians is carefully chronicled, and dissected, in Raymond Tatalovich and Thomas S. Engeman, *The Presidency and Political Science* (Baltimore: Johns Hopkins University Press, 2003); Louis Fisher, "The Law: Scholarly Support for Presidential Wars," *Presidential Studies Quarterly* 35(September 2005): 590–607; and Fisher, "Political Scientists and the Public Law Tradition," in *The Oxford Handbook of the American Presidency*, George C. Edwards III and William G. Howell, eds. (New York: Oxford University Press, 2009), 797–815. Despite party-based differences, the public continues to reflect support for strong executives. See Joel D. Aberbach, Mark A. Peterson, and Paul J. Quirk, "The Contemporary Presidency: Who Wants Presidential Supremacy?" *Presidential Studies Quarterly* 37(September 2007): 515–530.

10. Clinton Rossiter, *The American Presidency* (New York: New American Library, 1960), 14.

11. Rossiter, *The American Presidency*, 228.

12. Clinton Rossiter, *Constitutional Dictatorship: Crisis Government in the Modern Democracies* (New York: Harcourt, Brace & World, 1948).

13. Quoted in Stanley I. Kutler, *The Wars of Watergate* (New York: Knopf, 1990), 614. The comment was from Nixon's interview by David Frost in 1977. Nixon later disavowed the comment.

14. Arthur Schlesinger Jr., *The Imperial Presidency* (Boston: Houghton Mifflin, 1973), ix.

15. See Fisher's thorough and revealing analysis of the about-face of Schlesinger, historian Henry Steele Commager, and others in "Political Scientists and the Public Law Tradition."

16. Alexander Hamilton, James Madison, and John Jay, *The Federalist Papers* (New York: New American Library, 1961), 322.

17. Thomas A. Bailey, *Presidential Greatness* (New York: Appleton-Century-Crofts, 1966); Robert J. Spitzer, *The Presidency and Public Policy* (Tuscaloosa: University of Alabama Press, 1983), 10–15; Spitzer, *President and Congress* (New York: McGraw-Hill, 1993), 88–104; Marc Landy and Sidney M. Milkis, *Presidential Greatness* (Lawrence: University Press of Kansas, 2000).

18. An exemplar of this new analysis was Fred I. Greenstein's *The Hidden-Hand Presidency: Eisenhower as Leader* (Baltimore: Johns Hopkins University Press, 1994; first pub. 1984).

19. James David Barber, *The Presidential Character* (Englewood Cliffs, NJ: Prentice Hall, 2008; first pub. 1972); Stephen Skowronek, *The Politics Presidents Make* (Cambridge, MA: Harvard University Press, 1993).

20. William Howard Taft, *The President and His Powers* (New York: Columbia University Press, 1916), 139–140.

21. James Burnham, *Congress and the American Tradition* (Chicago: Regnery, 1959); Herman Finer, *The Presidency* (Chicago: University of Chicago Press, 1960); Willmoore Kendall, *The Conservative Affirmation* (New York: Harcourt Brace, 1963); Alfred

DeGrazia, *Republic in Crisis* (New York: Federal Legal Publications, 1965). An important, contemporary statement of the traditional conservative view of the presidency is Gene Healy, *The Cult of the Presidency: America's Dangerous Devotion to Executive Power* (Washington, DC: Cato Institute, 2008).

22. Robert J. Spitzer, *Saving the Constitution From Lawyers* (New York: Cambridge University Press, 2008), 92–95; Steven M. Teles, *The Rise of the Conservative Legal Movement* (Princeton, NJ: Princeton University Press, 2008).

23. An early statement of this general philosophy is Terry Eastland, *Energy in the Executive* (New York: Free Press, 1992). See also Steven G. Calabresi and Christopher S. Yoo, *The Unitary Executive* (New Haven, CT: Yale University Press, 2008); John Yoo, *Crisis and Command* (New York: Kaplan Publishing, 2009).

24. Garry Wills, *A Necessary Evil* (New York: Simon & Schuster, 1999), chapter 5.

25. Spitzer, *President and Congress,* chapter 2.

26. Spitzer, *Saving the Constitution From Lawyers,* 92–98; Spitzer, "The Post-Bush Presidency and the Constitutional Order." Paper presented at the annual meeting of the American Political Science Association, Toronto, Canada, September 3–6, 2009.

27. Robert J. Spitzer, "Saving the Presidency From Lawyers," *Presidential Studies Quarterly* 38 (June 2008): 329–346; Louis Fisher, "The Unitary Executive and Inherent Executive Power," *Journal of Constitutional Law* 12 (February 2010): 569–591; Ryan J. Barilleaux and Christopher S. Kelley, eds., *The Unitary Executive and the Modern Presidency* (College Station: Texas A&M University Press, 2010).

28. For example, see Louis Fisher, "Lost Constitutional Moorings: Recovering the War Power," *Indiana Law Journal* 81 (Fall 2006): 1199–1254; Spitzer, *Saving the Constitution From Lawyers,* chapter 4.

29. Theodore J. Lowi argues persuasively that America has indeed undergone de facto regime change, whereby the constitutional system has changed so fundamentally that we are, in effect, in a different Republic than that in which we began. See *The Personal President* (Ithaca, NY: Cornell University Press, 1985).

30. Louis Fisher, *Congressional Abdication on War and Spending* (College Station: Texas A&M University Press, 2000).

31. Michael A. Genovese and Robert J. Spitzer, *The Presidency and the Constitution* (New York: Palgrave Macmillan, 2005).

32. Spitzer, *President and Congress,* chapters 5 and 6; Harold Hongju Koh, *The National Security Constitution* (New Haven, CT: Yale University Press, 1990), chapters 5 and 6.

33. http://www.hpol.org/fdr/chat/, accessed April 24, 2010.

34. Jeff Shesol, *Supreme Power: Franklin Roosevelt vs. the Supreme Court* (New York: W.W. Norton, 2009).

35. Quoted in James MacGregor Burns, *Roosevelt: The Lion and the Fox* (New York: Harcourt Brace Jovanovich, 1956), 421.

36. Peter Irons, *War Powers* (New York: Henry Holt, 2005), 129–30; Francis D. Wormuth and Edwin B. Firmage, *To Chain the Dog of War* (Urbana: University of Illinois Press, 1989), 64.

37. Robert J. Spitzer, *The Presidential Veto* (Albany, NY: SUNY Press, 1988), chapter 2.

38. American Bar Association, "Task Force on Presidential Signing Statements and the Separation of Powers Doctrine," July 23, 2006, 7; Christopher N. May, "Presidential Defiance of 'Unconstitutional' Laws: Reviving the Royal Prerogative," *Hastings*

Constitutional Law Quarterly 21(Summer 1994): 929. According to May, Monroe apparently abided by the terms of the law. Monroe actually issued a second such statement in 1822.

39. May, "Presidential Defiance," 932.
40. Ryan J. Barilleaux and David Zellers, "Executive Unilateralism in the Ford and Carter Presidencies," in *The Unitary Executive and the Modern Presidency*, Ryan J. Barilleaux and Christopher S. Kelley, eds. (College Station: Texas A&M University Press, 2010), 41–76.
41. Early questions about the constitutionality and propriety of some of these signing statements were raised in Marc N. Garber and Kurt A. Wimmer, "Presidential Signing statements as Interpretations of Legislative Intent: An Executive Aggrandizement of Power," *Harvard Journal on Legislation* 24 (Summer 1987): 363–395; Spitzer, *The Presidential Veto*, 138–139.
42. Christopher S. Kelley, "The Law: Contextualizing the Signing Statement," *Presidential Studies Quarterly* 37 (December 2007): 739.
43. Steven G. Calabresi and Daniel Lev, "The Legal Significance of Presidential Signing Statements," *The Forum* 4, no. 2 (2006): 1.
44. Christopher S. Kelley, "A Matter of Direction: The Reagan Administration, the Signing Statement, and the 1986 Westlaw Decision," *William and Mary Bill of Rights Journal* 16 (October 2007): 283–306.
45. Shirley Anne Warshaw, *The Co-Presidency of Bush and Cheney* (Stanford, CA: Stanford University Press, 2009), chapter 9.
46. Spitzer, *Saving the Constitution From Lawyers*, 96; http://www.users.muohio.edu/kelleycs/ accessed May 1, 2010.
47. Phillip J. Cooper, "George W. Bush, Edgar Allen Poe, and the Use and Abuse of Presidential Signing Statements," *Presidential Studies Quarterly* 35 (September 2005): 518, 531.
48. T. J. Halstead, "Presidential Signing Statements: Constitutional and Institutional Implications," CRS Report for Congress, September 17, 2007, 2.
49. Steven G. Calabresi and Daniel Lev, "The Legal Significance of Presidential Signing Statements," *The Forum* 4 (2006): Article 8, 1–9.
50. George W. Bush, "Statement on Signing the Intelligence Authorization Act for Fiscal Year 2005," December 23, 2004, *Weekly Compilation of Presidential Documents*, December 21, 2004, 3012. This brief, five paragraph signing statement actually includes five separate signing statement provisions that assert alterations of language in the bill Bush signed into law.
51. "Senate Resolution 22—Reaffirming the Constitutional and Statutory Protections Accorded Sealed Domestic Mail, and for Other Purposes," *Congressional Record— Senate*, January 10, 2007, S394.
52. Quoted in "Senate Resolution 22."
53. Taft, *The President*, 78.
54. May, "Presidential Defiance," 979; Louis Fisher, "Signing Statements: What to Do?" *The Forum* 4 (2006): Article 7, 1.
55. For the case of Bush's signing statement challenge to a 2005 law barring the use of torture, see Spitzer, *Saving the Constitution From Lawyers*, 94–95.

56. James P. Pfiffner, *Power Play: The Bush Presidency and the Constitution* (Washington, DC: Brookings Institution Press, 2008), 196.

57. Pfiffner, *Power Play,* 2.

58. George Will, "The 'Unitary Executive,'" *The Washington Post,* May 4, 2008, B7.

59. Bruce Fein, "Executive Nonsense," *Slate Magazine,* July 11, 2007, accessed October 14, 2008, http://www.slate.com/id/2170247/; Fein, "Carts Before Horses," *Slate Magazine,* accessed August 31, 2007, http://www.slate.com/id/2173106/. See also Fein, *Constitutional Peril: The Life and Death Struggle of Our Constitution and Democracy* (New York: Palgrave/Macmillan, 2008).

60. David Iglesias, "Out of Bounds," *Slate Magazine,* June 13, 2008, accessed June 14, 2008, http://www.slate.com/id/2193365/.

61. Joseph Baldacchino, "Conservatism Can Be Revived: Unmasking Neocons Just a Beginning," *Epistulae* No. 3, September 25, 2008.

62. Claes G. Ryn, "Power Play," *The American Conservative,* October 6, 2008, accessed October 15, 2008, http://www.amconmag.com/article/2008/oct/06/00025/.

63. Gene Healy, *The Cult of the Presidency* (Washington, DC: Cato Institute, 2008), 19–33. For more on the problems with Yoo's view of the power of the commander in chief, see Spitzer, *Saving the Constitution From Lawyers,* 103–114.

64. Spitzer, *Saving the Constitution From Lawyers,* 92–98. See in particular John C. Yoo's article, a kind of talisman for the second Bush presidency's claim to vast executive powers in foreign affairs: "The Continuation of Politics by Other Means: The Original Understanding of War Powers," *California Law Review* 84 (March 1996): 170–305.

65. Robert J. Spitzer, "Is the Separation of Powers Obsolete?" *Understanding the Presidency,* James P. Pfiffner and Roger H. Davidson, eds. (New York: Pearson Longman, 2007), 313-27.

66. Lowi, *The Personal President,* xi. Lowi dubs the modern era the American "Second Republic." See also Theodore J. Lowi, *The End of Liberalism: The Second Republic of the United States* (New York: W.W. Norton, 1979).

67. Gordon Silverstein makes a similar argument in *Imbalance of Powers* (New York: Oxford University Press, 1997), chapter 9.

68. *Jefferson's Letters,* arranged by Willson Whitman (Eau Claire, WI: E. M. Hale & Co., 1950), 108.

69. Wills, *A Necessary Evil.* Will concludes his book by saying that, in fact, government is "a necessary good" (297).

70. Quoted in Michael A. Genovese, *The Power of the American Presidency,* 1789–2000 (New York: Oxford University Press, 2001), 48.

71. Hamilton, Madison, and Jay, *The Federalist Papers,* No. 51, 322.

72. Charlie Savage, "New Justice To Confront Evolution In Powers," The *New York Times,* May 8, 2010, A10.

CHAPTER 4

Toward a Constitutional Presidency

David Gray Adler

What a Constitutionalist Believes

The term "constitutionalist" may mean different things to different people. In the context of my thinking and writing, it means that all governmental actions—if they aspire to be legal—must be grounded in constitutional norms. In his opinion for the Supreme Court in *Reid v. Covert,* Justice Hugo Black gave voice to what I've characterized as the first principle of American Constitutionalism: "The United States is entirely a creature of the Constitution. Its powers and authority have no other source. It can act only in accordance with all the limitations imposed by the Constitution."[1] The principle that the government has only those powers—express or implied—granted to it by the Constitution was an article of faith for the founders, and should be, I submit, a constant for every generation of American citizens.[2] Governmental subordination to the Constitution, what the framers of the Constitution regarded as the essence of the rule of law, is all the more important to a political system committed to government based on the "consent of the governed."[3] That doctrine, indispensable to republicanism, declares, in the words of John Adams, principal author of the world's oldest written Constitution—the Massachusetts Constitution of 1780—and four other state constitutions drafted at the founding, "The people have a right to require of their . . . magistrates an exact and constant observance" of the "fundamental principles of the Constitution."[4] The passage of time has disturbed neither the force nor the vitality of that requirement. If it were otherwise, it would be necessary to acknowledge that we have abandoned governance based on preestablished rules and embraced governance grounded on the whims of those who wield power. "That might result in a benevolent despotism," Justice Benjamin Cardozo rightly observed, "if the judges," or presidents, for that matter, "were benevolent men." In any case, he added, it "would put an end to the reign of law."[5] And not merely an end to the rule of law, it must be added, but to republican principles as well. "In a government of laws," Justice Louis Brandeis justly cautioned, "existence of the government will be imperiled if it fails to observe the law scrupulously."[6] It is for this reason, as Madison pointed out, that "it is our duty . . . to take care that the powers of the Constitution be preserved entire to every department of Government; the breach of the Constitution in one point, will facilitate the breach in another."[7]

While effectuation of the rule of law may more than occasionally escape our grasp, owing largely to the interests of those who exercise power, it is worthy of our effort and admiration, as victims of Auschwitz and Buchenwald would attest.[8] The rule of law maintains the principle of limited government, promises to thwart arbitrariness, pledges government conduct in accord with known laws and procedures, applies brakes to unlimited discretion and power, provides a sense of certainty and predictability, and fulfills the will of the people, as manifested in their ratification of the Constitution. In practice, the rule of law means that governmental officials may not undertake acts that are prohibited by the Constitution. It means, as well, that what John Hart Ely said of the Supreme Court applies equally to Congress and the president. The Court, he wrote, "is under obligation to trace its premises to the charter from which it derives its authority."[9]

The concept of governmental power exercised in accord with constitutional principles captured the framers' understanding of the rule of law. As a result, governmental actors have no authority to displace the choices made by the people. In the Constitutional Convention, Madison declared that "it would be a novel and dangerous doctrine that a legislature could change the Constitution under which it held its existence."[10] Hamilton agreed: "[A] delegated authority cannot alter the constituting act, unless so expressly authorized by the constituting power. An agent cannot new model his commission."[11] Manifestly, the people are the "constituting power" and the Constitution the "constituting act." No governmental actor— president, legislator, or judge—has been granted an exemption or dispensation from adherence to the Constitution, to which he has sworn an oath to defend. Governmental violation of the Constitution mocks the fundamental principles of constitutional government and the concept of popular sovereignty. [12]

The Constitution reflects the fundamental choices made by the American people; the government has the solemn duty to enforce them, to effectuate the "consent of the governed." "The people," explained James Iredell, one of the most acute constitutional theorists of the founding period, "have chosen to be governed under such and such principles. They have not chosen to be governed or promised to submit upon any other."[13] Accordingly, as Chief Justice John Marshall stated in *Marbury v. Madison,* once limits are established, they may not "be passed at pleasure." It was owing to the perception of constitutions as bulwarks against oppression, he explained, that "written constitutions have been regarded with so much reverence."[14]

It is only fair that I briefly explain the constitutional scaffolding on which my interpretive platform rests. Because I embrace the doctrine of popular consent, take the Constitution seriously, and believe that governmental officials have a solemn duty to obey the Constitution, I feel obliged, regardless of party affiliation or partisan concerns, I feel obliged to criticize those actors who violate constitutional norms. Thus, Republicans and Democrats, conservatives and liberals alike, have been within my sights at one time or another. I heartily endorse, moreover, Chief Justice Marshall's observation that "the peculiar circumstances of the moment may render a measure more or less wise, but cannot render it more or less constitutional."[15] James Wilson had given voice to the same principle in the Convention, when he noted that laws "may be unjust" and yet "constitutional."[16] The constitutionality and the desirability of policies belong, in my view, to separate realms. As a constitutional scholar, my allegiance is to the Constitution. I might embrace a policy as wise or necessary, but if it conflicts with constitutional principles then I am left to seek either statutory revisions or a constitutional amendment. At all events, I try to avoid converting the Constitution into what Jefferson called a "thing of wax." As a consequence of my endorsement of the Wilson–Marshall principle, I have criticized, for example, President Jimmy Carter's termination of the 1954 Mutual Defense Treaty with Taiwan as a violation of the Constitution which, I believe, does not confer on the president a unilateral authority to terminate treaties, even though I supported the wisdom of the measure as a means of normalizing relations with China. In my view, the termination of a treaty requires joint action by the president and Senate, which reflects the symmetry that characterizes the creation of a treaty. Similarly, while I supported as a policy measure President Bill Clinton's decision to order air strikes against Serb President Slobodan Milosevic to halt ethnic cleansing of Albanians, I nevertheless criticized the act as an exercise in presidential usurpation of the war power. The Constitution, I believe, requires congressional authorization of hostilities.[17] My criticisms of presidents who have usurped the war power run the range from Harry Truman, Richard Nixon, and Lyndon Johnson, to Jimmy Carter, Gerald Ford, and Ronald Reagan, to George H. W. Bush, Bill Clinton, and George W. Bush. As the reader can see, partisan interests and ideological values have not been a consideration in my analyses of executive aggrandizement over the past 60 years. The substitution of a judge's personal or ideological values for clearly established constitutional rules would, as Justice Cardozo stated, "put an end to the rule of law." Scholars, I believe, receive no dispensation from that judicial standard. Impartiality is not easily achievable, and one's best efforts may fall short, of course, but there remains the duty to strive for such detachment.

My emphasis on governmental adherence to the Constitution, moreover, does not place the government in a straitjacket any more than it reduces the Constitution to a suicide pact, two metaphors advanced by those who would free the president of constitutional restraints. In truth, the derisive and misleading terms—straitjacket and suicide pact—are, in the hands of some, a euphemism for a presidential revisory power or justification for resort to the doctrine of necessity. The use of the metaphor of a straitjacket to portray a government rendered impotent in the face of foreign affairs and national security challenges is ill-suited to America, which boasts a Constitution, as Hamilton explained in *Federalist* No. 23 and Madison in *Federalist No.* 41, that provides all powers necessary to conduct foreign relations and to provide for the common defense. All of the requisite foreign relations powers that the nation—any nation—might require have been vested in the federal government, from the authority to initiate war to the authority to repel invasions to the authority to make security and economic agreements with other countries; these have been duly conferred upon the government of the United States. Hamilton pointed out in *Federalist* No. 23 that "no constitutional shackles can wisely be imposed" on those powers necessary to the nation's defense. Madison famously declared in *Federalist* No. 41 that it would be "in vain to oppose constitutional barriers to the impulse of self-preservation."[18] Nobody has contended that the American government lacks the powers necessary to its preservation. Similarly, Hamilton and Madison attested to the fact that the means necessary to the efficient use of national security powers must be conferred, as indeed, they have been, for without sufficient means, the grant of a power would be self-defeating. This, of course, was the point of *McCulloch v. Maryland* (1819), in which Chief Justice Marshall stated, "The power being given, it is the interest of the nation to facilitate its execution. It can never be their interest, and cannot be presumed to have been their intention, to clog and embarrass its execution, by withholding the most appropriate means."[19] The *means,* Marshall explained, follow the allocation of *powers.*

In all likelihood, those who are eager to cast the term "straitjacket" into discussion are critical of the constitutional allocation of powers. In that case, their fight is with the framers of the Constitution—those who drafted the document—and the American people who ratified it. If we were to start anew from a blank sheet and proceed to write a Constitution that reflects our views and values on the question of assigning governmental powers, perhaps we would produce a document that differs from that produced in Philadelphia. But absent a fresh start, or even invocation of the Amendatory Clause to alter constitutional provisions, an approach to separation of powers revisions that receives no serious discussion, the fact remains that the president has no authority to slip the chains of the Constitution, which is to say that there is no repository of authority for the president to revise the meaning of the Constitution. We shall consider the problem of emergency, within the context of the Constitution as a suicide pact, for it is within that frame that the issue is apt to arise. Nevertheless, the assertion that the government should follow the Constitution, except when the president determines that it need not do so, as when adherence to the law would reduce the Constitution to the status of a suicide pact, is a plea for a presidential power to act above the law. As we have seen, however, neither the text of the Constitution nor the debates in Philadelphia offer even a hint of executive power to defy the Constitution.

The requirement of governmental adherence to the Constitution was, for the founders, the linchpin of American Constitutionalism. In 1785, Madison had declared that rulers "who overleap the great barrier which defends the rights of the people . . . are tyrants."[20] The denial to government of authority to replace the choices of the people with their own values, to ignore the norms and principles enshrined in the Constitution, constituted subversion of the Constitution through rank usurpation of power—one of the most serious of impeachable offenses. Thus Justice Joseph Story, the most scholarly of Justices, wrote, "We are not at liberty to add one jot of power to the national government beyond what the people have granted by the constitution."[21] Usurpation was no idle word for a generation that imposed on its agents the duty to swear an oath to uphold the Constitution, violation of which was impeachable.[22] In his Farewell Address, George Washington acknowledged the seductive nature of occasional acts of usurpation, but he reminded the American citizenry of its destructive consequences for the rule of law and republican values:

> If in the opinion of the People, the distribution or modification of the Constitutional powers be in any particular wrong, let it be corrected by an amendment in the way in which the Constitution designates. But let there be no change by usurpation; for though this, in one instance, may be the instrument of good, it is the customary weapon by which free governments are destroyed. The precedent must always greatly overbalance in permanent evil any partial or transient benefit which the use can at any time yield.[23]

Washington's declaration that usurpation represents a "permanent evil" is comprehensible within the ideological context of the framers' fundamental commitment to the rule of law and government grounded in consent of the people, the *sine qua non* of a generation that wrote the Declaration of Independence, waged war against an empire which it perceived as repressive, and ushered into world history a radical conception of the right of the people to create a government of their choosing. For the framers, the rule of law was hardly unattainable, for if it were, the cardinal principle of a government founded on the consent of the people would be but a chimera. It was, after all, through the creation and, subsequently, the ratification of the Constitution that the people gave their assent to be governed by a particular Constitution with a particular allocation of power and no other. The implementation of the Constitution—and governmental adherence to it—breathes life into the rule of law and makes possible, as Abraham Lincoln famously put it, a "government of the people, by the people and for the people."

Above all, the framers feared the exercise of power which, at least since the revolutionary period, was viewed in America as a threat to liberty.[24] The menace of arbitrary power—aggrandizement of power, abuse of power, usurpation of power, and violation of the Constitution—represented to their generation the mortal enemy of the rule of law, limited government and civil liberties, for it awakened in their memories a pattern of tyranny and repression. They well knew, as Madison observed in *Federalist* No. 48, that all "power is of an encroaching nature, and that it ought to be effectually restrained from passing the limits assigned to it."[25] Lord Radcliffe described the framers' studied response to the problem: "One attitude is to be afraid of power. That is not a poor or cowardly attitude in face of the reckless use that men have made of their authority over other men. But if mistrust is the dominant note, then it may be best expressed by such constitutional devices as those of the American Constitution. Power is placed under restraint; it is deliberately shared out so that it cannot all be grasped in the same hand."[26]

The mistrust of power, particularly the concentration of power, represented the dominant theme of the Constitutional Convention. It was the framers' fear of power, bulked by a keen sense of history and mankind's struggle for freedom and liberty across the centuries, that propelled them down the path toward a written Constitution. Justice Hugo Black justly observed that the historical struggle to establish a *written* Constitution was "to make certain that men in power would be governed by *law*, not the arbitrary fiat of the man or men in power."[27] As Thomas Jefferson stated, "It is jealousy and not confidence which prescribes limited constitutions to bind down those whom we are obliged to trust with power. . . . In questions of power, then, let no more be heard of confidence in man, but bind down from mischief by the chains of the Constitution."[28] The founders' finely tuned antennae, their ability to sniff out and anticipate the abuse of power, indeed, their "distrust of official power," as Willard Hurst, the eminent legal historian, described it, constituted "a very basic principle of our constitutionalism" and inspired their commitment to written limits on governmental power.[29]

The fears and "distrust" of official power that permeated the Constitutional Convention were spiked when delegates turned their attention to the creation of the presidency. The framers' deep-seated aversion to unrestrained executive power colored their discussions and debates on the allocation of power to the president. At all events, they aimed to confine presidential power within the four corners of Article II. There was, within the Convention, no expressed interest in what has been variously termed executive "prerogative," "emergency," or "inherent" powers. Rather, the drafters aimed, in Madison's explanation, to "confine and define" presidential power. Indeed, the framers rejected the concept of inherent executive power, despite contemporary assertions from scholarly corners and the offices of White House lawyers and supporters that fill the pages of law review articles and books.

The Constitution, Prerogative, and Emergency Powers

The issue of whether the president possesses an inherent or emergency power has long absorbed the wit and energies of American academics, politicians, and lawyers. The assertion that the framers of the Constitution endowed the president with the Lockean Prerogative, which exalts powers independent of those enumerated in Article II, including, in the face of an emergency, the authority to act either in the absence of legislation or in violation of it, raises questions of great moment and plumbs the depths of the controversies about the relationship between the executive and the law that have raged in the Anglo-American world since the early years of 17th-century England.[30] Does the Constitution confer upon the president authority to violate the law? Is there, indeed, room in the Constitution for governmental actors to defy the instrument from which they derive their authority? Assertions of an executive authority to trample constitutional restraints invites Chief Justice Marshall's rejoinder in Marbury: "To what purpose are powers limited, and to what purpose is that limitation committed to writing, if these limits may, at any time, be passed by those intended to be restrained?"[31] The Bush Administration's assertion that the president's inherent executive power encompasses a "commander in chief override," if necessary to meet the nation's security needs, is an assertion drawn straight out of the pages of the Stuart King's doctrine of the Royal Prerogative. Is it possible for governmental officials to swear an oath to uphold the Constitution and at the same time to ignore its provisions or assert the authority to violate the Constitution and the laws of the land? May a president who perceives a grave emergency invoke inherent authority to stay in office for six years rather than four? Does the president possess a revisory power? The answer to each of these questions, emphatically, is "no."

Advocates of inherent presidential power have sought, primarily, to ground presidential prerogative in the Vesting Clause. Their assertions, however, find no support in the text of the Constitution, the debates in Philadelphia, the discussions in the various state ratifying conventions, or in contemporaneous writings. According to the Vesting Clause, "The executive Power shall be vested in a President of the United States of America." The question of whether this provision will bear the weight assigned it may be illuminated by what delegates to the Convention actually said. It is instructive as well to recall the understanding of the term "executive power" on the eve of the Convention. The renowned legal historian Julius Goebel observed that "executive"

> [a]s a noun . . . was not then a word of art in English law—above all it was not so in reference to the crown. It had become a word of art in American law through its employment in various state constitutions adopted from 1776 onward. . . . It reflected . . . the revolutionary response to the situation precipitated by the repudiation of the royal prerogative.[32]

The use of the word "prerogative," as Robert Scigliano has demonstrated, was, among the founders, a term of derision, a political shaft intended to taint an opponent with the stench of monarchism.[33] The rejection of the use of the word "prerogative" in favor of the new and more republic-friendly noun "executive" necessitated discussion and explanation of its scope and content. The provisions of the state constitutions, moreover, conveniently frame and illustrate the meager scope of authority granted to state executives. In his 1783 work, "Draft of a Fundamental Constitution for Virginia," Thomas Jefferson stated, "By executive powers, we mean no reference to those powers exercised under our former government by the Crown as of its prerogative. . . . We give them these powers only, which are necessary to execute the laws (and administer the government)."[34]

This understanding of "executive power" and its implementation was reflected in the Virginia Plan, which Edmund Randolph introduced to the Constitutional Convention and which provided for "a national executive . . . 'with power to carry into execution the national laws' . . . [and] to appoint to offices in cases not otherwise provided for." For the framers, the phrase "executive power" was limited, as James Wilson observed, "to executing the laws, and appointing officers." Roger Sherman "considered the Executive magistracy as nothing more than an institution for carrying the will of the Legislature into effect. . . ." Madison agreed with Wilson's definition of executive power. He thought it necessary "to fix the extent of the Executive authority . . . as certain powers were in their nature Executive, and must be given to that departmt. [sic]," and he added that "a definition of their extent would assist the judgment in determining how far they might be safely entrusted to a single officer." The definition of the executive's authority should be precise, thought Madison; the executive power "shd. [sic] be confined and defined. . . ."[35]

And so it was. In a draft reported by Wilson, the phrase "The Executive Power of the United States shall be vested in a single Person" first appeared. His draft included an enumeration of the president's power to grant reprieves and pardons and to serve as commander in chief; it included as well the charge that [If] it shall be his duty to provide for the due & faithful exec—of the Laws." The report of the Committee of Detail altered the "faithful execution" phrase to "he shall take care that the laws of the United States be duly and faithfully executed. . ." This version was referred to the Committee on Style, which drafted the form that appears in the Constitution: "The executive power shall be vested in a president of the United States of America. . . . [H]e shall take care that the laws be faithfully executed. . . ."[36]

To the extent that there was a debate on "executive power," it centered almost entirely on the question of whether there should be a single or a plural presidency. There was no challenge to the definition of executive power held by Wilson, Sherman, and Madison, nor was an alternative understanding advanced. Moreover, there was no argument about the scope of executive power; indeed, any latent fears were quickly allayed by Wilson, who assured his colleagues that "the Prerogatives" of the Crown were not "a proper guide in defining Executive powers."[37]

Edward Corwin's observation that Wilson was the leader of the "strong executive" wing of the Convention may be affirmed by noting that no member of those proceedings promoted a conception of executive power that exceeded his stated parameters—to execute the laws and make appointments to office.[38] That view, which echoed Jefferson's and was shared as well by delegates to the various state ratifying conventions, provides the historical context within which to view the founders' conception of executive power. The framers severed all roots to the royal prerogative. The framers' rejection of the British Model, grounded in their fear of executive power and reflected in their derision of monarchical claims and prerogatives, was repeatedly stressed by defenders of the Constitution. William Davie, a delegate in Philadelphia, explained to the North Carolina Convention "that jealousy of executive power which has shown itself so strongly in all the American governments, would not admit" of vesting the treaty powers in the president alone, a principle reaffirmed by Hamilton in *Federalist* No. 75: "The history of human conduct does not warrant that exalted opinion of human virtue which would make it wise in a nation to commit . . . its intercourse with the rest of the world to the sole disposal" of the Senate.[39] Hamilton, in fact, was at the center of Federalist writings that attempted to allay concerns about the creation of an embryonic monarch. In *Federalist* No. 69, he conducted a detailed analysis of the enumerated powers granted to the president as commander in chief, a narrative that laid bare the framers' refusal to vest in the president unilateral authority over matters of war and peace.

Hamilton's Federalist essays fairly reflect the constitutional "sketch" that he laid before the Convention. His ruminations in Philadelphia, aired in a lengthy speech on June 18, 1787, have inspired in the scholarly fraternity some misconceptions that require attention at this juncture. On the floor of the Convention, Hamilton noted his admiration for the British system. He admitted that in his "private opinion he had no scruple in declaring . . . that the British Gov't. was the best in the world."[40] The "Hereditary interest of the King was so interwoven with that of the Nation," Hamilton stated, that he was beyond "the danger of being corrupted from abroad."[41] Accordingly, as it has often been observed, he preferred an "Executive . . . for life." But it is often overlooked that he also preferred that "one branch of the Legislature hold their places for life or at least during good behavior."[42]

After giving flight to his personal preferences, entirely hypothetical given the context of his speech, Hamilton acknowledged that they had no application to America and the republican enterprise in which he and his fellow delegates were engaged. In his own "plan" for a Constitution, which amounted to ideas that he would contribute to Edmund Randolph's proposals, which were submitted as the Virginia Plan, Hamilton proposed an executive that reflected Wilson's views. The executive, he stated, would have responsibility for "the execution of all laws passed." The president, moreover, would be required to obtain the Senate's approval for making treaties and appointing ambassadors. Hamilton preferred a presidential pardon power weaker than the design that ultimately prevailed, for he would prohibit the president from issuing pardons in cases of treason without the approbation of the Senate. In another rebuke to the monarchical model, Hamilton would vest in the Senate "the sole power of declaring war."[43] In the end, Hamilton's conception of executive power mirrored the views of presidential power advanced by Wilson, Madison, and Sherman.

The confined nature of the presidency, a conception rooted, for example, in Wilson's observation that the president is expected to execute the laws and make appointments to office, or in Sherman's remark that "he considered the Executive magistracy as nothing more than an institution for carrying the will of the Legislature into effect," represented a characterization that was *never* challenged throughout the Convention.[44] No delegate to the Convention, it is to be emphasized, advanced a theory of inherent power. Madison justly remarked: "The natural province of the executive magistrate is to execute laws, as that of the legislature is to make laws. All his acts, therefore, properly executive, must presuppose the existence of the laws to be executed."[45] Manifestly, the concept of an inherent executive power, a Lockean Prerogative to "improvise" law to act in the absence of legislation or in violation of it, does not "presuppose the existence of the laws to be executed."

At the time of the American Revolution, it was widely understood that the principle of the rule of law implied executive subordination to the law. In fact, it was clear that republican government differed from the monarchies of Europe in precisely this respect. The framers, it may be said, did not even squint in the direction of presidential prerogative. Certainly there is nothing in Philadelphia that would provide footing for such a claim, nothing at all in the arguments, discussion, or train of thought of the Convention. There is, finally, no evidence to suggest that the founders, who in 1776 had introduced the term "executive power" to avoid the stench of prerogative, had by 1787 found the odor any less repugnant. Proponents of inherent power will need to look beyond the framers' conceptions of executive power to justify presidential prerogative powers.

If the framers rejected the concept of a presidential emergency power, as I believe they did, then what was their solution to the problem of emergency? After all, it was understood that the law could not provide an immediate remedy for every conceivable situation that the nation might encounter. And, if the existence of an emergency did not serve to redistribute the powers of the government allocated by the Constitution, what mechanism lay within the grasp of government to meet the emergency?

In brief, the solution to the problem of emergency was found in the doctrine of retroactive ratification, a practice rooted in England and one with which the founders were familiar. Lord Dicey explained the method that emerged in English law: "There are times of tumult and invasion when for the sake of legality itself the rules must be broken. The course which the government must then take is clear. The ministry must break the law and trust for protection to an act of immunity."[46] This doctrine was adopted and followed in America. In its application, if the president perceived an emergency, he could act illegally and turn to Congress for ratification of his actions. Congressional ratification would hinge on the question of whether Congress shared the president's perception of an emergency. The chief virtue of this practice was that it left to Congress, as the nation's lawmaking authority, the ultimate determination of the existence of an emergency, and it prevented the president from sitting in judgment of his own cause, a principle of overarching importance in Anglo-American legal history.[47] Only an exceedingly bold and arrogant declaration of High Prerogative could justify the view that a president might judge his own act of usurpation, for such a doctrine would place the laws of the nation at his mercy. Further virtue in the practice of legislative immunity or indemnification may be drawn from the fact that it is likely to temper presidential claims of emergency. Since resort to Congress for vindication and exoneration represents an admission of executive usurpation, a president is unlikely to respond to an emergency with extralegal measures, and as a consequence, he risks his own fate and fortune, unless he is confident that the legislature would likewise view his acts as an indispensable necessity. In any event, it is apparent that the doctrine of retroactive ratification, which incorporates elements of both the doctrine of separation of powers and checks and balances, maintains a semblance of constitutional government. At all events, the framers, as Justice Robert Jackson wryly observed, were familiar with emergencies: "They knew what emergencies were, knew the pressures they engender for authoritative action, knew, too, how they afford a ready pretext for usurpation. We may also suspect that they suspected that emergency powers would tend to kindle emergencies."[48]

American history reflects the founders' commitment to the doctrine of retroactive ratification. It was utilized, for example, during the American Revolution, invoked during the congressional investigation into the allegation that Secretary of the Treasury, Alexander Hamilton, had violated appropriations laws, and invoked by President Thomas Jefferson in 1807, in the aftermath of his decision to spend unappropriated funds during the Chesapeake Crisis.[49] Perhaps the most famous exercise of retroactive ratification, however, occurred during the presidency of Abraham Lincoln. It is testimony to Lincoln's commitment to constitutional government that while caught in the clutches of America's gravest crisis, he nevertheless refrained from laying claim to a theory of High Prerogative but, in fact, adhered to the practice of legislative ratification. In the context of defending the Union after the Confederacy attacked Fort Sumter on April 12, 1861, and initiated the Civil War, President Lincoln, it is familiar, assumed powers not granted to him by the Constitution. While Congress was in recess, Lincoln issued proclamations calling forth state militias, suspending the writ of habeas corpus, and instituting a blockade on rebellious states. He also spent public funds without congressional authorization.[50] When Congress convened, Lincoln explained that his actions, "whether strictly legal or not, were ventured upon under what appeared to be a popular demand and a public necessity, trusting then, as now, that Congress would readily ratify them." After Congress reviewed the circumstances and concluded that Lincoln had acted out of necessity, it passed an act approving, legalizing, and making valid all "the acts, proclamations, and orders of the President . . . as if they had been issued and done under the previous express authority and direction of the Congress of the United States."[51]

Since the attack on the United States on September 11, 2001, and President Bush's declaration of the "war on terror," the scope of presidential power in the realm of foreign affairs has become the issue of the season. President Bush never sought retroactive authorization from Congress, but that is readily explicable: His administration held such a sweeping view of presidential power that it believed the president had not exceeded the scope of his authority. The outpouring of books, articles, essays, and pamphlets examining the Bush Administration's claims of executive power has been rivaled in recent American history by only the extensive commentary that surrounded the Vietnam War and Watergate. The fresh assessment of presidential power represents a welcome awakening from scholarly slumber and indifference that largely ignored the flight of the imperial presidency for the past half-century. And rightly so, for few issues in the life of a nation rival in importance the maintenance of national security, the conduct of foreign policy, and decisions on matters of war and peace. The premise is as true today as it was for the framers of the Constitution, for whom the search for an efficient foreign policy design was a primary and animating purpose of the Constitutional Convention. The framers' blueprint for the conduct of foreign affairs, as we shall see, reflected a commitment to the virtues and values of collective decision making and a thorough repudiation of the ideology of executive unilateralism. Chief among the framers' purposes was to assign to Congress the sole and exclusive constitutional authority to determine matters of war and peace. Indeed, the bulk of the nation's foreign relations powers has been conferred upon Congress. Yet, this constitutional design has been overwhelmed by the accumulation of power in the executive. The repeated violations of the constitutional blueprint for the formulation, management, and conduct of American foreign policy constitutes the greatest constitutional crisis that our nation faces. This crisis is directly attributable to the concentration of power in the executive and the consequent diminution in the separation of powers, checks and balances, and limitations on power. In sum, the flow of power to the president has been at flood tide for decades, and there is no sign that the flow will be halted.

The framers, it is familiar, rejected the English Model—the monarchical model, a design that emphasized executive unilateralism—for the conduct of foreign affairs. The concept of unilateral executive control of foreign policy was, for the founders, intolerable and never within their sights. In their view, the executive model was obsolete; it belonged to an earlier age, the world of monarchy, one ill-suited to the new age of republicanism. As a consequence, their constitutional design for foreign affairs embodied the principle of collective decision making—shared powers, discussion, debate, and checks and balances—in the formulation, management, and oversight of American foreign policy.[52] Yet, no feature of recent government practice has more vexed, betrayed, and disfigured the Constitution than executive aggrandizement of war and foreign affairs. For a nation committed to the rule of law, an understanding of the constitutional design in foreign affairs, so critical in matters of security and survival, is of paramount importance. As Arthur Schlesinger Jr. justly wrote, "If citizens are unwilling to study the processes by which foreign policy is made, they have only themselves to blame when they go marching off to war."[53]

The Constitutional Convention was called for the purpose of correcting the deficiencies of the Articles of Confederation. Chief among the deficiencies were those that weakened the international position of the United States. Under the Articles, for example, Congress lacked effective authority to generate revenues, enforce treaties, raise armies, or wage war. In *Federalist* No. 15, Alexander Hamilton lamented: "We have neither troops nor treasury, nor government."[54] There was broad agreement among American leaders that the foreign affairs flaws of the Articles of Confederation stemmed *not from an absence of an independent executive but from the lack of authority granted to Congress.* Fundamentally, Congress lacked coercive power over the states. The inadequacies of the Articles on this score—mainly the debilitating weakness of the national government—supplied a critical focal point for the framers' deliberations. The Convention's decision to create the Supremacy Clause was a pivotal move; indeed, the declaration in Article VI that "[t]his Constitution, and the laws of the United States and all Treaties, . . . anything in the Constitution or the laws of any states to the contrary notwithstanding," signified the end of state sovereignty and enabled the federal government to wrest control of foreign policy from recalcitrant states. While the Supremacy Clause certainly had profound implications for areas other than diplomacy, there is no exaggeration in the observation that it provided the *sine qua non* of a vital and vibrant national foreign policy. It is to be borne in mind then, despite occasional assertions to the contrary, that the foreign affairs flaws in the Articles did not generate calls in the Constitutional Convention for unilateral executive power over matters of war and peace and national security. The delegates in Philadelphia had no more interest in a president who would act as the sole organ of American foreign policy than they had in state domination of the nation's international relations.

The framers' rejection of the English Model for foreign affairs resulted in an arrangement that vested the lion's share of foreign affairs powers, including the exclusive power over matters of war and peace, in the hands of Congress. A textual review of the Constitution is dispositive, of course, but the argument for presidential unilateralism is bereft of evidence as gleaned from the debates in Philadelphia. By the end of the proceedings, it should be recalled, no delegate left the Convention with an understanding that the president would enjoy unilateral power over America's foreign relations. The preference for collective, rather than unilateral, decision making runs throughout the constitutional provisions that govern the conduct of American foreign policy. Article I vests in Congress broad, explicit, and exclusive powers to regulate foreign commerce, raise and maintain military forces, grant letters of marquee and reprisal, provide for the common defense, and initiate hostilities on behalf of the United States, including full-blown war. As Article II indicates, the president shares with the Senate the power to make treaties and appoint ambassadors. The Constitution assigns to the president only two exclusive powers. He is designated commander in chief of the armed forces although, as we shall see, he acts in this capacity by and under the authority of Congress. The president also has the power to receive ambassadors, but the framers viewed this as a routine, administrative function, devoid of discretionary authority.[55] This list exhausts the textual allocation of foreign affairs powers to Congress and the president. The president's constitutional powers are few and modest, and they pale in comparison to those vested in Congress. The American arrangement for the conduct of the nation's foreign affairs bears no resemblance to the English model.

The Problem

Executive assertions of authority have launched the presidency on a trajectory toward the realm of unfettered power, the netherworld of American Constitutionalism. This is the condition—and the crisis—of the presidency: an overgrown office swollen with powers subject to few limitations. This is not a problem of recent vintage, but rather one that has evolved over the past half-century as constitutional limitations on executive power have been corroded by executive branch missives that have stoked the fires of presidential aggrandizement and encouraged legislative abdication and judicial acquiescence. Fueled initially by Cold War fears and rekindled by the "war on terror," the rise and exaltation of presidential power reflects a consistent historical trend. Justice Felix Frankfurter justly observed, "The accretion of dangerous power does not come in a day. It does come, however slowly, from the generative force of unchecked disregard of the restrictions that fence in even the most disinterested assertion of authority."[56] While widespread concerns about the scope of presidential power have intensified, in reaction to some of President George W. Bush's unprecedented claims of authority, they reflect a long period of unease, anxiety, and fear of executive power, which harken to the dawn of the republic. Forty years ago, no less a personage than the late Senator Sam Ervin questioned, in the course of hearings on the unchecked practice of impoundment, "whether the Congress of the United States will remain a viable institution or whether the current trend toward the executive use of legislative power is to continue unabated until we have arrived at a presidential form of government." Senator Ervin justly criticized executive aggrandizement of legislative authority, but he also found Congress culpable for the rise of presidential dominance: "The executive branch has been able to seize power so brazenly only because the Congress has lacked the courage and foresight to maintain its constitutional position."[57]

It makes little difference whether we refer to this condition as the personal presidency, as Theodore Lowi has described it, or the imperial presidency, as Arthur Schlesinger Jr. has characterized it, or whether we consider it in light of the popular exaltation of the president as Superman, as Thomas E. Cronin has explained it, for the innovation of "Presidential Government" is triumphant in America.[58] The model for executive dominance found clear expression in the presidency of Richard Nixon, as manifested in the usurpation of war-making authority and the aggrandizement of foreign affairs powers and in the extended claims of impoundment authority, executive privilege, and secrecy. Professor Schlesinger ably explained the problem: "The imperial presidency, born in the 1940s and 1950s to save the outer world from perdition, thus began in the 1960s and 1970s to find nurture at home. Foreign policy had given the president command of peace and war. Now the decay of the parties left him in command of the political scene, and the Keynesian revolution placed him in command of the economy. At this extraordinary historical moment, when foreign and domestic lines of force converged, much depended on whether the occupant of the White House was moved to ride the new tendencies of power or to resist them."[59]

In his expansion of executive claims and powers, President Nixon had models. Harry Truman, for example, usurped the war power when he unilaterally plunged the nation into the Korean War and legislative authority when he invoked an "inherent" executive power to seize the steel mills. Truman, it is familiar, was the first president to assert unilateral executive authority to initiate war on behalf of the American people. Previous presidents had understood that the Constitution vests in Congress the sole and exclusive authority over matters of war and peace. In this assertion of power, he ignored the Constitution and embraced theories of executive power urged by Stuart Kings. To a man, delegates to the Constitutional Convention had rejected the executive model for foreign affairs and national security, which rested on the concept of unilateral executive power, in favor of the principle of collective decision making. The constitutional design, however, was of little consequence for Truman. And Nixon has had imitators. Each of his successors—Gerald Ford, Jimmy Carter, Ronald Reagan, Bill Clinton, and George H. W. Bush—has asserted untrammeled executive authority to initiate war. Like Nixon, they have aggrandized foreign affairs powers, including the authority to reinterpret and terminate treaties, negotiate executive agreements at the expense of congressional participation, and to order covert actions, military and otherwise. Presidents since Nixon, including Barack Obama, have asserted broad claims of executive privilege and secrecy.[60]

In his capacity as a wartime president who advocated the theory of a "unitary presidency," President George W. Bush advanced, in the name of national security, broad authority under the banner of inherent presidential power and the Commander in Chief Clause in terms that traduce the doctrines of separation of power and checks and balances. In several key areas, President Bush's assertions of authority soared beyond the claims of his predecessors. The president, according to the Bush Administration, may initiate preventive war without authorization from Congress. As commander in chief, he has the sole and exclusive authority to conduct war. Congressional directions and instructions are invidious, constitute micromanagement, and represent an encroachment on presidential power. The president may institute domestic surveillance of Americans' telephone calls and e-mails as part and parcel of his authority to wage war on terrorism. Statutes in conflict with the president's policies represent a violation of executive authority. It was contended, moreover, that the president may designate, seize, and detain any American citizen as an "enemy combatant" and imprison him in solitary confinement, indefinitely, without access to legal counsel and a judicial hearing. The Constitution, it was asserted, provides to American citizens no right of habeas corpus. In addition, it was claimed that President Bush possessed the authority to suspend the Geneva Convention and the federal laws that prohibit torture. Among other powers asserted, the president, as commander in chief, may establish military tribunals, terminate treaties, order acts of extraordinary rendition, and take actions that he perceives necessary to the maintenance of national security and the common defense. Under this theory, any law that restricts the commander in chief's authority is presumptively unconstitutional. At all events, the president might exercise an "override" authority in the unlikely event that Congress would by statute seek to restrain the president. Courts, it was maintained, have no role to play in matters of war and peace, but if they do entertain lawsuits, they should defer to the president and refrain from second-guessing his foreign policy.[61]

With the possible exception of Richard Nixon, no American president has asserted such a thoroughly Cromwellian view of executive power.[62] And that may be unfair to Nixon. Former Nixon White House Counsel, John Dean, an outspoken critic of the Bush Administration, has aptly characterized the Bush White House as "worse than Watergate."[63] Bruce Fein, a former Reagan Justice Department attorney and another ardent critic of the Bush Administration, has perceived in the Bush theory of presidential power a distressing agenda: "It's part of an attempt to create the idea that during conflicts, the three branches of government collapse into one, and it is the president."[64] The sheer breadth of the aggregate powers asserted, and the Machiavellian tendencies of the Bush Administration, with its apparent though unarticulated embrace of the philosophy that the "ends justify the means," threaten to render the Constitution superfluous, an obstructive and cursed scrap of paper. The administration's disdain for constitutional government may be glimpsed in the remarks of then White House Counsel and U.S. Attorney General Alberto Gonzales, who declared in the "Torture Memos" that concerns about constitutional principles in the context of the "war on terrorism" are "quaint."

The mushrooming growth in executive power also finds its roots in congressional abdication of its constitutional powers, which might strike a novitiate as counterintuitive, but an understanding of Congress yields the conclusion that most members are more concerned with "themselves and their reelection chances" than with the preservation of institutional authority. Unmindful of the prohibitions imposed by the delegation doctrine, Congress has granted sweeping powers to the president. Unmoved by concerns to protect and preserve its exclusive authority over appropriations, Congress has facilitated executive control of the budgetary process and spending determinations. Unconcerned about the maintenance of its lawmaking function, Congress has urged upon willing executives the concept of a line-item veto and, incredibly, the bizarre notion of an "inherent" line-item veto. It hardly seems necessary to mention, moreover, that Congress has been unwilling to defend its broad powers over matters of war and foreign affairs; on the contrary, members seemed relieved to unburden themselves of constitutional duties, responsibilities, and powers that they swore an oath to defend.

Presidential government, built atop aggrandizement, usurpation, and abdication, has become firmly entrenched in the United States. This was the condition of the presidency that George W. Bush inherited when he assumed office. It was imperial when he came to it and imperial when he left it. From a constitutional perspective, President Bush made no effort to curtail executive aggrandizement of power or to stem the tide of legislative abdication, nor did he seek to restore congressional authority. Like his predecessors, Bush chose to ride the "tendencies of power" rather than "resist them." It is too early in the Obama presidency to assay its view of executive power, but there is nothing in the recent historical record to suggest that President Obama will resist the direction that the institution of the presidency has been traveling.

At a minimum, the imperial, or what we might call a plebiscitary presidency, is suffused with swollen conceptions of executive power. It assumes that democracy is enhanced "if the capacity to govern is lodged in the White House," and it exhibits general indifference toward constitutional restraints so critical to the preservation of the enumeration of powers.[65] In its glory, it speaks of the investment of the sovereignty of the nation in the chief executive, and it exhibits contempt for the rule of law. Before Attorney General Gonzales dismissed the Constitution as "quaint," we are loathe to remember, there was the specter on May 19, 1977, of former President Nixon, in the context of his third television interview with the

British broadcaster David Frost, declaring that, like the Stuart Kings, the president could do no wrong. Not only was the president above the law, Nixon explained, but he could "authorize" staff members to violate the law as well.[66]

The assertion of the doctrine of necessity, whether boldly stated or masked by euphemisms of emergency, crisis, national security, or reason of state, as a justification for executive unilateralism in the field of foreign relations, is intended to silence debate and win acquiescence and abdication. Advocacy of executive emergency powers, rightly perceived by the framers as a threat to constitutional government and the rule of law, emerged after World War II in full sprint, undeterred by constitutional limitations. Scholarly promotions lent encouragement, despite the devastation wreaked upon the world by executive absolutism. Clinton Rossiter, for example, published in 1948 a widely read book, *Constitutional Dictatorship,* in which he asserted the necessity of institutionalizing the position of an executive dictator in times of grave crisis to preserve the constitutional order. Rossiter wrote, "A great emergency in the life of a constitutional democracy will be more easily mastered by the government if dictatorial forms are to some degree substituted for democratic, and if the executive branch is empowered to take strong action without an excess of deliberation and compromise."[67] Rossiter's book, it may be said, found a home in the administration of George W. Bush, which asserted unbridled executive powers that defied the metes and bounds of the Constitution. Professor Sanford Levinson has justly declared, "An executive branch that believes itself 'empowered to take strong action without an excess of deliberation and compromise' is, I believe, an almost perfect description of the Bush Administration."[68] A president who describes the "war on terror" as indeterminate, with no forseeable end in sight, and asserts in the same breath unilateral executive powers that are coterminous with the scope of the emergency, even though they violate the strictures of the Constitution has, I think, answered Rossiter's prescriptions.

It is true, of course, in matters of national security and survival, that the question of emergency power is bound to arise. The problem is as old as antiquity, one characterized as "reason of state," which counsels survival no matter how repugnant or noxious the means to the ends may be. In his masterful *History of the Peloponnesian War,* Thucydides grappled with the problem. In the justly celebrated discussion between the Athenians and the Melians, the Athenians embraced reason of state. Might makes right, and "by a necessity of their nature wherever [men] have the power they always rule."[69] Justice exists only among equals, and "the powerful exact what they can, while the weak yield what they must."[70] In this view, the allure of a strong man who would meet and resolve emergencies has long possessed the minds of philosophers and decision makers. Equally appealing is the notion of a benign dictator who would exercise emergency powers until the crisis had passed and return power to the people with liberty intact. Is such a proposal, shared by

Professor Rossiter, realistic or mere fancy? Is it indeed possible to preserve liberty and democracy while assailing their precepts and principles?

The celebrated Montesquieu, who was focused on the fall of the Roman Republic, wondered at the question in a little known work described by Carl J. Friedrich, in which there occurs a discussion between Sylla, the Roman dictator, and his friend, Eukrates.[71] In the conversation, Sylla justifies his actions as part of a design to restore liberty. He explains that he has relinquished his authority and submitted his actions to the judgment of fellow Romans, with the explanation that his emergency actions were necessary. Eukrates, however, is unwilling to accept Sylla's claims: "In taking over the dictatorship, you have given an example of the crime which you have punished. Here is an example that will be followed, and not that of a moderation which one can only admire. When the Gods suffered Sylla to make himself dictator in Rome, they banished liberty forever."[72] In sum, Montesquieu sought to emphasize that Sylla's aggrandizement of power had so warped Roman virtue that his act of returning power to the people was ultimately an act in futility. The life, ways, and practices of the republic, it seemed, had been eclipsed. Once conscripted, liberty could not be recovered.

The framers of the Constitution, as we have seen, rejected the concept of an emergency, or inherent, presidential power, and with it, Rossiter's advocacy of a "constitutional dictator." In his concurring opinion in the *Steel Seizure Case,* Justice Robert H. Jackson rebuked the "plea for a resulting power to deal with a crisis or an emergency according to the necessities of the case, the unarticulated assumption being that necessity knows no law."[73] The framers, as Justice Jackson pointed out, wisely perceived that executive possession of emergency power "would tend to kindle emergencies" and confront the republic with the menace, he said, of an illimitable power, which "either has no beginning . . . or no end."[74] A presidential emergency power, Jackson wrote, "need submit to no legal restraints," an observation that lays bare the oxymoronic quality of Rossiter's "constitutional dictator." If, in fact, necessity is the measure of power, why should any consideration be given to legal constraints or constitutional limitations? And, by what measuring stick may the legality of an extralegal act be evaluated? The ancient conception of reason of state, like its modern kin, national security, often invoked as justification for foreign affairs actions, including interrogation methods, surveillance, imprisonment by executive decree, as well as other tactics and strategies necessary to the conduct of war, can be fatal to the enterprise of constitutional law and government, as Montesquieu observed. The problem is hardly new. In anticipation of claims advanced by the Bush Administration, reason of state was adduced in Parliament in the 17th century to justify the authority of the king, as Francis D. Wormuth observed, "to imprison by special warrant without naming a cause and to hold the prisoner without bail."[75] Thus, Sir Edward Coke perceived reason of state as a "trick to put a man out of the right way; for when a man can give no reason for a thing, then he flieth to a higher Strain, and saith it is a Reason of State."[76]

Given the framers' rejection of an executive emergency power, how did they handle the issues of security and survival? That is no mean question for a generation which, more than once, had faced devastation on the battlefield at the hands of an invading empire. Manifestly, they rejected the doctrine of necessity and executive prerogative, as well as an institutionalization of a constitutional dictatorship. Indeed, they never entertained those widely maligned concepts which were at war with the values and principles of republicanism. The framers, moreover, went beyond Montesquieu's innovative prescription of an amending process to overcome static laws that would deny to government the flexibility it required to confront emergencies, since this tool, critical to the success of the constitutional enterprise, nonetheless lacked the crucial element of immediate response.[77] The prospect of an emergency greatly concerned the framers, for they well knew that law could not provide a remedy for every conceivable situation or crisis that the nation might encounter. The founders' response to emergency, as we shall see, lay in the doctrine of retroactive ratification.

But let us first consider the other "fountainhead" of sweeping executive authority, the attribution to the president of vast authority to identify, promote, and implement "democratic" values. This broad presidential role is manifested in various ways, both foreign and domestic, but it is conspicuous in the articulation of justifications for use of military power, deployment of troops, and invasions of foreign countries. President Bush's invasion of Iraq in March of 2003 was advanced, in part, as a means of bringing democracy to a people who had suffered under the brutal regime of Saddam Hussein. President Bush's assumption of the opportunity to invoke democracy as justification for military action was but the most recent use of a hallowed ideology which finds, perhaps, its most prominent justification in President Woodrow Wilson's declaration that World War I was waged to make the "world safe for democracy." Whether sincere or not, the conscription by executives of the foundation stone of democracy—government by consent of the people—has been recognized as a clever means for winning popular support for a variety of policies and causes, irrespective of constitutional allocation of powers, duties, and responsibilities.

At a minimum, the imperial, or what we might call a plebiscitary, presidency is suffused with swollen conceptions of executive power. It assumes that democracy is enhanced "if the capacity to govern is lodged in the White House," and it exhibits general indifference toward constitutional constraints so critical to the preservation of the enumeration of powers.[78] In its glory, it speaks of the investment of the sovereignty of the nation in the chief executive, and it exhibits contempt for the rule of law. There is no intrinsic harm in presidential efforts to promote their agendas, as Theodore Roosevelt explained, by "appealing over the heads of the Senate and House leaders directly to the people, who were masters of both of us," an Aristotelian approach firmly rooted in politics and aptly described by Sam Kernell and others as "going public."[79] The harm that occurs is a direct attribute of a president-centered government. Whatever the public will support, or even at a minimum, condone, becomes acceptable fare for a presidential agenda. The full measure of this harm may be grasped when it is recalled that White house efforts to build consent for its policies and actions may be rooted in its release of selective information, including reports and announcements tipped with deception.

Arthur Schlesinger Jr. has captured the theory of the plebiscitary presidency in a passage worth quoting at length:

> What Nixon was moving toward was something different: it was not a parliamentary regime but a plebiscitary Presidency. His model lay not in Britain but in France—in the frame of Louis Napoleon and Charles de Gaulle. A plebiscitary presidency, unlike a parliamentary regime, would not require a new constitution; presidential acts, confirmed by a supreme court of his own appointment, could put a gloss on the old one. And a plebiscitary presidency could be seen as the fulfillment of constitutional democracy. Michels explained in *Political Parties* the rationale of the "personal dictatorship conferred by the people in accordance with constitutional rules." By the plebiscitary logic, "once elected, the chosen of the people can no longer be opposed in any way. He personifies the majority and all resistance to his will is anti-democratic. . . . He is, moreover, infallible, for 'he who is elected by six million votes carries out the will of the people; he does not betray them.'" How much more infallible if elected by 46 million votes! If opposition became irksome, it was the voters themselves, "we are assured, who demand from the chosen of the people that he should use repressive measures, should employ force, should concentrate all authority in his own hands." The chief executive would be, as Laboulaye said of Napoleon III, "democracy personified, the nation made man."[80]

Schlesinger's appraisal may be fortified by recalling, among other factors, Nixon's portrayal of the president as above the law, routine acts of executive usurpation and aggrandizement of legislative powers by presidents since Nixon, the largely unstemmed flow of legislative authority from the legislature to the executive, and the Supreme Court's obeisance to the president in foreign affairs cases, including its bizarre dictum in *United States v. Curtiss-Wright Export Corp.* (1936) that the president embodies the "sovereignty" of the nation in its external relations.[81] In truth, in the context of American politics, the term "plebiscitary presidency" is an "exaggeration," as Professor Lowi has pointed out, "but by how much? Already we have a virtual cult of personality revolving around the White House."[82] The term may not be too wide of the mark, for the measure of its utility is to be found, in part, in the acquiescence of the public and Congress in presidential acts of usurpation and aggrandizement of powers assigned by the Constitution to Congress and in both extravagant claims of executive powers and presidential interest in assuming powers not vested in the office. No recent president has even remotely suggested the curtailment of executive power, and neither Congress nor the public has sought it. President Clinton's abuse of the pardon power, perhaps for motive of political gain and fund-raising interests, and his reliance on the doctrines of privilege and immunity in the Jones and Lewinsky matters, are stark reminders that presidents will grasp for power and exercise it unilaterally to satisfy personal as well as political agendas. If Clinton's exercise in the abuse of power is too remote for the citizenry, then it may be helpful to recall the myriad examples of the executive abuse of power in the Bush Administration, some of which, including extraordinary rendition, have been adopted by the Obama Administration. Presidential abuse of power is not the preserve of either party; both Republicans and Democrats have been adept in its ways. The framers regarded such temptations as a natural response to both opportunity and pressure. Madison echoed the sentiments of fellow delegates in Philadelphia when he observed that it is an "axiom that the executive is the department of power most distinguished by its propensity to war; hence it is the practice of all states, in proportion as they are free, to disarm this propensity of its influence."[83] The framers wisely took their own counsel on this score. They created an executive with few and sharply limited powers. But they could not have anticipated that subsequent generations of Americans, principally those whose voices in the latter half of the 20th century wielded power and influence, would embrace monarchical views of executive authority that the founders rejected. The problem of executive power may be stated as simple as that.

The imperial presidency remains in full flight. It never was grounded, even if it did occasionally fly at a somewhat lower altitude. It remained aloft under Gerald Ford and Jimmy Carter, two presidents whose terms often are derided as disappointments or failures and whose actions, even on their best days in office, it seemed, led to their characterization as "caretaker" presidents. Yet both abused the war power—Ford in the Mayaguez incident and Carter in the aborted effort to rescue American hostages in Iran. And Carter, it will be recalled, did not shrink from claiming unilateral authority to terminate treaties, a claim hardly consistent with the constitutional blueprint for foreign affairs. In the hands of more aggressive executives, Reagan, Bush, Clinton, and Bush—the embrace of unilateralism and the cacophony of capacious claims of presidential power were undeterred by constitutional constraints.

There is, moreover, no evidence that this trend will be curtailed. In the aftermath of the impeachment of Bill Clinton, academics, journalists, and public officials, among others, engaged in a national dialogue on the future of the presidency: Had Clinton's contretemps weakened the presidency? In light of the tremendous concentration of power vested in the presidency of George W. Bush as a response to the September 11 outrage, it is hard to believe that there was even a question about it. The fact is, as scholars have observed, the presidency is virtually indestructible. Presidential power was not diminished by Nixon's actions, nor was it sapped of its vitality by Clinton's deeds and misdeeds. On the contrary, presidential government was firmly entrenched when Clinton came to the presidency, and it remained firmly entrenched when he left it. Impeachment, or even the threat of impeachment for executive abuse of power, provides no deterrent. Proof is found in President's Bush's aggrandizement of power.

The framers of the Constitution believed that certain political powers must be exercised only by Congress if republican government were to survive, among them, the lawmaking authority, the war power, and the spending power. For the framers, history suggested that a strong executive might pose a continuous threat to the republic; American history has demonstrated it. Accordingly, they improvised a system that confined the executive. But they could not have imagined a Congress unwilling to assert and defend its constitutional authority, seemingly indifferent to institutional responsibilities, and one apparently uninterested in preserving its status and strength. Power, we are told, cannot resist a vacuum. Perhaps the rise of presidential government was irresistible, after all. Given the failings of Congress, a substantial body of literature extolling the alleged virtues of a strong executive and the emergence of a virtual cult of the presidency in America, perhaps the more interesting question to be addressed is, why did it take so long for the United States to succumb to presidential government?

It is not necessary to explore every angle of an answer to that question, for it is clear that the plebiscitary or imperial presidency represents an assault on the rule of law which, as Lord Dicey explained, requires at a minimum that "absolute supremacy or predominance of regular law as opposed to the influence of arbitrary power, and excludes the existence of arbitrariness, or prerogative, or even of wide discretionary authority on the part of the government."[84] It is not possible, as Alexander Bickel observed, for governmental officials to swear an oath to uphold the Constitution and at the same time to ignore its provisions or assert the authority to violate the Constitution and the laws of the land:

> There is a moral duty, and there ought to be, for those to whom it is applicable—most often officers of government—to obey the manifest Constitution, unless and until it is altered by the amendment process it itself provides for, a duty analogous to the duty to obey final judicial decrees. No president may decide to stay in office for a term of six years rather than four, or, since the Twenty-Second Amendment, to run for a third term. There is an absolute duty to obey; to disobey is to deny the idea of constitutionalism, that special kind of law which establishes a set of pre-existing rules within which society works out all its other rules from time to time. To deny this idea is in the most fundamental sense to deny the idea of law itself.[85]

Presidential disregard of what Professor Bickel describes as the "manifest Constitution" haunts American Constitutionalism. Executive usurpation and aggrandizement of power have become a commonplace in a nation which, ostensibly, is committed to the rule of law. If, as we assume, the denial of arbitrary power—to Congress, the president, and the judiciary alike—was a preeminent goal of the Constitutional Convention, we are left to wonder at the means necessary to achieve that worthy goal. Let us turn to the challenge of solutions to the condition of the presidency—an office overgrown with power, indifferent to constitutional limitations.

The framers knew, as Madison noted in *Federalist* No. 48, that all "power is of an encroaching nature, and that it ought to be effectually restrained from passing the limits assigned to it."[86] Is the remedy for unconstitutional executive unilateralism—the restoration of a constitutional presidency—to be found in the Constitution itself? There seems little wrong with the constitutional blueprint; the principal problem lies, rather, in the unwillingness of the men and women in positions of power, those at the helm, duly to perform their duties and responsibilities. And, it should be emphasized, if the constitutional arrangement were deficient, its violation by the president could hardly be justified in a nation which exalts the rule of law, a principle that requires executive subordination to the Constitution and the laws of the land. If the constitutional design is perceived to be outdated or unworthy of fealty, then the Amendatory Clause supplies a remedy: Change the fundamental law and render it appropriate to the needs of the nation. Yet, there has been no sustained dialogue or even a hint of national debate on the need for revisions in the allocation of constitutional powers to the president. Where, indeed, are the voices calling for amendments to Article II that might reconfigure those provisions that shape executive power?

Presidential disregard of the Constitution, as we have seen, cannot be justified—without a subsequent appeal to Congress for passage of retroactive ratification. Executive violation of the Constitution, absent such a plea to Congress, is the path traveled by a Machiavellian leader, indifferent to the first principles of American Constitutionalism. For all of the shopworn rhetoric that the Constitution is not a straitjacket, a tactic in some quarters that resembles little more than an invitation to the executive to slip the chains of the Constitution when ideology, policy concerns, inconvenience, or "need" suggest it, few are willing to forthrightly and publicly urge the president to ignore constitutional principles and restraints. The explanation for the absence of such public candor on the part of advocates of executive violation of the law, it seems apparent, is to be found in the nation's pervasive commitment to the rule of law and limited government, fenced by constitutional restraints. Thus presidential assertions of power that, manifestly, violate those restraints and limits are cast in terms that sedulously deny constitutional violations. The problem persists, however, for whether executive actions that violate the Constitution are flatly denied or rationalized by legal fictions they remain, nonetheless, constitutional violations.

The Solution

How, then, can the American people obtain presidential adherence to the Constitution? The question of how to persuade the government to obey the Constitution represented, as Madison eloquently declared in *Federalist* No. 51, the great challenge confronting the nation in 1787: "In framing a government which is to be administered by men over men, the great difficulty lies in this: you must first enable the government to control the governed; and in the next place oblige it to control itself."[87] This, I submit, remains the great challenge confronting America today. We might seek remedies in the resuscitation of constitutional mechanisms, an approach that would impose responsibilities on each of the three branches of government. Let us consider available remedies.

For starters, presidents might actually adhere to constitutional limits. It's possible, if not probable, that a future president might forswear the extravagant claims to power and genuinely seek to navigate the presidency back to its constitutional moorings. Manifestly, this would be the most direct—and ideal—solution to the problem of executive violations of the Constitution. As difficult as it is to imagine this as a remedy, in light of the rise of the imperial presidency and rampant executive abuse of power over the past half-century, there is an older American history to which we might appeal. The practice of war making is instructive. After all, until 1950, no president had ever claimed the constitutional authority to take the nation to war. Prior to that juncture, for more than 150 years, presidents adhered to the understanding that the Constitution vests in Congress the sole and exclusive authority to take the nation to war. Could we turn the clock back and invoke older, well-heeled constitutional understandings and moments? What, we might ask, worked a dramatic transformation in the way presidents viewed the Constitution and the war power? The explanation probably lies in the emergence of the Cold War and the increased expectations and duties that fell upon the president in a world swollen with fear. Americans expected the president to protect the nation and to provide for the "common defense," despite the fact that that constitutional duty is assigned to Congress. In a nation governed by the plebiscitary presidency, constitutional arrangements and allocations of power were of little importance. At the time of the invasion of South Korea, Secretary of State Dean Acheson gave short shrift to the Constitution when he remarked, "The argument as to who has the power to do this, that, or the other thing, is not exactly what is called for from America at this very critical hour."[88] Acheson's dismissal of the constitutional design for matters of war and peace became commonplace over the next 50 years and foreshadowed the arrogance of the White House, which believed that it possessed superior qualifications for the exercise of power. With the fall of the Berlin Wall, one might have reasonably expected that the fears that fueled executive excesses might have subsided, but when presidential power continued on an arc toward unfettered power, armed with the declaration of a "war on terror," it became clear that the founders' fear of the "endlessly propulsive tendency [of power] to expand itself beyond legitimate boundaries" was well-grounded.[89]

A reemergence of executive humility and self-abnegation would constitute the ideal antidote to the arrogance of power that has come to characterize the office of the presidency, but additional assistance from the doctrine of checks and balances may be required, particularly in the form of vigorous oversight and scrutiny from the judiciary and Congress. Judicial checks on the expansion of presidential power can be effective—if they are invoked. There was a time in American history when the courts were assertive in checking executive power, but in truth, the expansion of executive power in modern times has been accompanied by judicial deference to the president. Let us consider judicial power as a solution to the problem of sweeping executive powers.

As we have seen, the courts rendered several rulings in the early hours of the 19th century—little more than a decade after the ink on the Constitution had dried—that restrained presidential power in the crucial areas of foreign affairs and national security. The Quasi-War with France, which ran from 1798 to 1800, gave rise to several important cases that resulted in precedent-setting judicial decisions on the scope of congressional authority over war and the use of military force. In 1800 and 1801, the Supreme Court held that Congress could authorize military hostilities in two ways: by a formal declaration of war or by the passage of statutes that authorized an undeclared war, as it had done in the Quasi-War. In 1800, in *Bas v. Tingy,* the Court held that military conflicts could be "limited," "partial," and "imperfect," without requiring a congressional declaration of war. Justice Samuel Chase stated as follows: "Congress is empowered to declare a general war, or Congress may wage a limited war; limited in place, in objects, and in time. . . . Congress has authorized hostilities on the high seas by certain provisions in certain cases. There is no authority given to commit hostilities on land." Crucial to the Court's reasoning was that Congress possessed the authority to determine whether hostilities ought to be launched and where they might be waged. Justice William Paterson, who had been a leading delegate to the Constitutional Convention, observed that on matters of war and peace, Congress is the "constitutional organ of our country."[90] Justice Bushrod Washington referred to Congress as the "legitimate authority" in the determination of the initiation and location of hostilities. In 1801, in *Talbot v. Seeman,* Chief Justice John Marshall, who was a member of the Virginia Ratifying Convention, delivered the Court's opinion: "The whole powers of war being, by the Constitution of the United States, vested in Congress, *the acts of that body can alone be resorted to as our guides in this* inquiry."[91]

Congressional power to authorize war entails the power to place limits on what the president may and may not do. During the Quasi-War, Congress enacted legislation that authorized the president to seize ships sailing *to* French ports. President John Adams exceeded his statutory authority when he issued an order instructing American ships to capture vessels sailing *to or from* French ports. In execution of President Adams' order, Captain John Little seized a Danish ship that was sailing from a French port. He was sued for damages and the case came before the Supreme Court. In his opinion for the Court, Chief Justice Marshall acknowledged the difficult nature of the case. He confessed that his first impression of the case, the "first bias" of his mind, strongly favored the conclusion that while President Adams "could not give a right, they might yet excuse [a military officer] from damages." At the outset, Marshall assumed an "implicit obedience, which military men usually pay to their superiors, which indeed is indispensably necessary to every military system." From Marshall's perspective, the nature of the military hierarchy seemed to justify the acts of Captain Little, "who is placed by the laws of his country in a situation which in general requires that he should obey them." Upon further reflection, Marshall changed his mind and decided that Little could be sued for damages: "I have been convinced that I was mistaken, and I have receded from this first opinion. I acquiesce in that of my brethren, which is, that the instructions [by Adams] cannot change the nature of the transaction, or legalize an act which, without those instructions, would have been a plain trespass."[92] In sum, the president is bound to obey statutory directions and instructions, even if they conflict with presidential policies and programs. Presidential orders, even when issued by the commander in chief, are subordinate to the law. The president has no authority to ignore, change or override statutory commands, what Marshall termed the "nature of the transaction."

The moral of the Court's ruling was not lost on anyone, but what about Captain Little, who had duly executed the orders of President Adams? Little was subsequently "exonerated" by Congress, which, in 1807, after determining that he should not have been liable for obeying the president's instructions, passed a private bill to reimburse him for the damages that he had been ordered to pay. The legislative discussions yield no explanation for the action, but it is likely, as Louis Fisher has observed, that "Congress may have concluded that federal law failed to adequately distinguish between lawful orders and unlawful orders."[93] In addition, Congress likely recognized the dilemma that confronted Captain Little when he received President Adams' orders. In 1789, Congress had enacted a statute that reflected the history of military hierarchy: Officers were directed "to observe and obey the orders of the President of the United States."[94] In 1799, in the midst of the Quasi-War and the ideological storm of emotions and loyalties that it inspired, Congress sought in stark terms to reinforce the duty of military officers to obey orders: "[W]ho shall disobey the orders of his superior . . . on any pretense whatsoever" shall be subject to death or other forms of punishment.[95] Captain Little's case probably contributed to further legislation intended to clarify the duty of officers to obey orders issued by their superiors. In 1800, Congress provided that military officers were not required to execute all commands. Rather, they were specifically prohibited from performing the "unlawful orders" of superior officers.[96]

In 1806, a Federal Circuit Court reaffirmed the reasoning of *Little v. Barreme* and the prohibition on presidential war making in a case that brought a bipartisan tone to the issue, since it involved President Thomas Jefferson, Adams' rival in the election of 1800. In *United States v. Smith,* the court reviewed the indictment of Colonel William S. Smith for engaging in actions against Spain. Smith claimed that his military expedition "was begun, prepared, and set on foot with the knowledge and approbation of the executive department of our government."[97] Justice Paterson, riding circuit, rejected Smith's claim that the president might authorize a military enterprise that violated the Neutrality Act of 1794, which, among other actions, forbade persons within the jurisdiction of the United States from aiding or assisting any "military expedition or enterprise" against the "territory of dominions of any foreign prince or state with whom the United States are at peace." Justice Paterson observed that the Neutrality Act is "declaratory of the law of nations; and besides, every species of private and unauthorized hostilities is inconsistent with the principles of the social compact, and the very nature, scope and end of civil government." The president, moreover, had no authority to waive statutory provisions: "If a private individual, even with the knowledge and approbation of this high and preeminent officer of our government [the president], should set on foot a military expedition, how can he expect to be exonerated from the obligation of the law?" Justice Paterson added:

> Supposing then that every syllable of the affidavit is true, of what avail can it be on the present occasion? Of what use or benefit can it be to the defendant in a court of law? Does it speak by way of justification? The President of the United States cannot control the statute, nor dispense with its execution, and still less can he authorize a person to do what the law forbids. If he could, it would render the execution of the laws dependant on his will and pleasure; which is a doctrine that has not been set up, and will not meet with any supporters in our government. In this particular, the law is paramount. Who has dominion over it? None but the legislature; and even they are not without their limitation in our republic. Will it be pretended that the President could rightfully grant a dispensation and license to any of our citizens to carry on a war against a nation with whom the United States are at peace?[98]

Paterson, who had, in *Bas v. Tingy,* referred to Congress as the "constitutional organ" of the nation on matters of war and peace, reiterated in *Smith* his understanding of the War Clause, when he addressed a crucial constitutional question: "Does [the President] possess the power of making war? That power is vested exclusively in congress." If a nation invaded the United States, the president would have an obligation to repel the invasion. But, Paterson declared, there is a "manifest distinction" between going to war with a nation at peace and responding to an actual invasion." "In the former case, it is the exclusive province of congress to change a state of peace into a state of war."[99]

The significance of these early cases cannot be overstated. They represent a period in American history when the judiciary exhibited a strong commitment to constitutional government, separation of powers, and checks and balances. Above all, they represent an admirable model for judicial restraint of executive power. These decisions remain good law, despite the fact that presidents have routinely ignored them for the past half-century in their exercise in unilateral executive war making. Presidential indifference to the Constitution represents a remarkable commentary on the decline of American Constitutionalism.

It may be that the hopes of restoring a constitutional presidency hinge on a genuine resurgence of Congressional power, which requires recovery from its own lethargy, passivity, and impotence and a renewal of its institutional integrity and pride. What cannot be ignored, of course, is that the rise of presidential government has been aided by congressional retreat. There would be no imperial presidency were it not for an impotent Congress, unwilling to assert its powers and defend its turf. What is sorely missing in contemporary America is a Congress that takes the Constitution seriously. Who will sound the trumpet call for a revival of the spirit, fortitude, and integrity of congressional bodies that sought to check executive power, as seen in the assertiveness of the Senate Select Committee that investigated the Watergate scandal or the Church Committee that endeavored to curb the abuses of the CIA?

Is it reasonable to believe that Congress will recover its institutional pride and prevent the further deterioration of the American Republic? In addition to legislative acquiescence in executive usurpation of war and foreign affairs powers, the congressional record since the September 11, 2001, terrorist attacks has been desultory. It has unconstitutionally delegated the war power to President Bush through the passage of the Authorization to Use Military force (AUMF) in the fall of 2001, and again in the fall of 2002 in the Iraqi Resolution; ceded control over the appropriations power in the form of a $10 billion blank check to the president in the days following the 9–11 outrage and stood idly in the fog created by the event while the president usurped the congressional legislative power to create offices as well as the Senate's share of power in cabinet-level appointments when President Bush created the Department of Homeland Security and named Pennsylvania governor Tom

Ridge to the post. When President Bush unilaterally terminated the Anti-Ballistic Missile Treaty with Russia in December 2002, few members of the Republican-controlled Congress seemed to notice, and fewer still raised any constitutional objections, as leading conservative Senator Barry Goldwater had a generation earlier when he rightly brought suit against President Jimmy Carter for unilaterally terminating the 1954 Mutual Defense Treaty with Taiwan. In the reign of George W. Bush, Congress had been quiescent and it granted the president's wishes: AUMF, the USA Patriot Act, legislation stripping federal courts of habeas corpus jurisdiction, and revisions in the foreign Intelligence Surveillance Act (FISA), among others.

As a body, Congress has been gripped by both partisanship and a paucity of institutional pride. Of course, this is by no means a new story. But if America hopes to find its legislative branch asserting its oversight function, for example, with the admirable vigor of the Church Committee and its vast foreign affairs powers in a robust manner befitting its central role in the constitutional system for the purpose of renewing a moribund doctrine of checks and balances, Congress must regain its institutional character and curb its partisan loyalties to the occupant of the White House. It may be difficult, of course, but it can be done, as seen in the work of the Church Committee.

This congressional reversal will require leadership, certainly, and quite possibly the leadership that arises from an aroused citizenry triggered by a renewed appreciation for virtues and values of constitutionalism. In what was one of his greatest and most impassioned speeches, a speech that lasted two days in the Virginia Ratifying Convention and one that shook the earth when he reached his peroration— "Must I give my soul, my lungs to Congress?"—Patrick Henry brought a razor's edge to our problem: "If you depend on your President's and your Senator's patriotism, you are gone. . . ." In a republic, there is no substitute for a vigilant citizenry. "The only real security for liberty," James Iredell declared, "is the jealousy and circumspection of the people themselves. Let them be watchful over their rulers." In his state's ratifying convention, Edmund Randolph told his fellow Virginians, "I hope that my countrymen will keep guard against every arrogation of power."[100] Heightened public awareness about presidential usurpation of power and the subversion of the Constitution, as seen in the public repudiation of Richard Nixon's "Saturday Night Massacre," can trigger profound political change, as it played a key role in driving Nixon from the White House. It may well be that the acid test of a republic is whether a president could survive in the face of a resolute public repudiation of his illegitimacy.

Critical to a resurgent citizenry is a better understanding, indeed, a greater knowledge of the Constitution, particularly as it pertains to the separation of powers. The public revolt against the Nixon White House reflected an informed citizenry that appreciated the constitutional and historical dimensions of Nixon's actions. It is in this area that the academic world can provide important assistance. One of the primary functions of scholarship, of course, is to heighten public awareness about presidential abuse of power. Scholarly exposure of executive acts of usurpation is critical to any reform movement, and that includes a recitation of fundamental principles that fence and hedge presidential power. Facts, information, and truths are especially important in a government grounded on the consent of the people and governmental accountability. No president can last very long if a credibility gap is exposed and publicized, as Richard Nixon learned. Knowledge of the Constitution, particularly as it pertains to the creation of the presidency, can be advanced to measure and evaluate executive behavior.

An accurate recovery and rendition of the work of the Constitutional Convention, moreover, assumes vital importance when judges, presidents, and commentators draw upon the debates in Philadelphia to adduce constitutional meaning. "[L]egal history," Justice Frankfurter wrote, "still has its claims."[101] "[A]ll questions of constitutional construction," Justice Horace Gray observed, "[are] largely . . . historical question[s]," a view embodied in the works of Coke, Blackstone, Holdsworth, and a host of distinguished legal historians, who ventilated thorny issues with insights from the past.[102] But the use of history by lawyers and judges, occasionally pockmarked by assertions of evidence wrenched from its context, other distortions, and blatant manipulation—a practice colorfully characterized a half-century ago by eminent historian Alfred H. Kelly as "law-office" history and deliciously captured by Robert Spitzer in a hard-hitting work, aptly characterized by its title, *Saving the Constitution From Lawyers*—invites scorn and skepticism.[103] Historical pitfalls and miscues aside, the Court's regard "for the original intent of the framers of the Constitution remains high. . . ."[104] Alexander Bickel rejected "the proposition that the original understanding is simply not relevant. For arguments based on that understanding . . . have been relied on by judges well aware that it is *a constitution* they were expounding."[105] Invocations of the original understanding of the Constitution were renewed by the Bush Administration in an effort to expound a theory of expansive presidential power. But these efforts, which purported to rely on the words of Alexander Hamilton, represented, I have attempted to show, a disservice not only to the American people but to the reputation of Hamilton.[106] The arguments advanced by White House lawyers, which sought foundation and credibility in the magic of Hamilton's name, further confused Americans' thinking about presidential power and undercut their ability to challenge assertions of expansive executive powers.

That problem—lack of knowledge about the constitutional dimensions of presidential power—has been pervasive, and it requires correction. In many ways, Americans' lack of understanding of executive authority is attributable to White House missives that assert virtually unlimited powers, but also to representatives of the media, who exaggerate the scope of presidential power. Then, too, considerable blame should be placed at the porch of the academy, which, for many years, as we have seen, extolled the virtues of broad executive authority and paid scant attention to the constitutional allocation of powers. Academics, as Tom Cronin pointed out nearly 40 years ago, heralded the president as "Superman." A few years ago, in a study in which I stood on the shoulders of Professor Cronin, I brought attention to the wayward manner in which American government textbooks either ignore those constitutional provisions that govern the presidency or, regrettably, exalt presidential power above and beyond constitutional norms.[107] The consequences for our nation of misleading depictions of presidential power are enormous. For the more than one million college and university students who annually enroll in *Introduction to American Government 101,* that course may represent their only classroom exposure to a subject of critical importance to the maintenance of constitutional principles and republican values. When those students leave their academic environs, they will be ill-equipped to challenge presidential claims to power. Without the knowledge necessary to undergird a stout challenge to presidential usurpation of power, as well as an understanding of the failure of Congress to assert and defend its constitutional powers, we may well harbor doubts about the capacity of the American citizenry to demand governmental adherence to the Constitution.

Impact of My Solutions

In the presidency of George W. Bush, the trumpet sound of the rule of law was reduced to tinkling crystal. Monarchical prerogatives and pretensions, the framers recognized, were irreconcilable with republican values. As a consequence, the president's powers were constitutionally "confined and defined," as Madison observed, by a design that the framers believed would protect the nation from an overweening executive and maintain the rule of law. The framers were entitled to believe that they had succeeded in their quest. However, they could not have anticipated the breakdown, indeed, the utter collapse of the doctrine of checks and balances and the acquiescence of Congress in the face of presidential usurpation of power, particularly in the areas of war making and foreign affairs. The abdication by Congress of its foreign affairs powers and responsibilities has shredded the constitutional design for the conduct of American foreign policy. As a result, the presidency has grown autocratic. Its penchant for unilateralism at the expense of the framers' preference for collective decision making represents a permanent threat to the republic.

The implementation of my proposals would renew governmental adherence, particularly presidential adherence, to the Constitution and the rule of law. This is no mean achievement. It spells the difference between a legitimate and an illegitimate government, between one that respects the concept of popular consent and one that mocks it. In the realm of foreign affairs and war making, the principle of collective decision making, not executive unilateralism, would guide and control our policies. A likely impact would be fewer foreign wars and "police actions." As a body, Congress would be less willing to authorize invasions than a president acting alone. Confronted by the harsh realities of facing constituents whose children have been sent to war, members of Congress would recoil from wars of choice. Of course, war is necessary, on occasion, and the understanding of members of Congress, that they would be held accountable for their decisions to initiate war, would force them to demand clear and compelling intelligence before they put the United States on a war footing. In addition to these manifestations of my prescriptions, there would be, as well, less emphasis on the personality of the president, which might help to diminish a "cult of the executive" that has been so injurious to other nations. There is, for the nation, moreover, a great psychological benefit to be derived from knowledge that the government is actually following the law, rather than violating it. Adherence to the rule of law, as Justice Brandeis pointed out, breeds loyalty and commitment among the citizenry, rather than scorn, skepticism, and doubt.

My solutions to the crisis of presidential power—presidential humility, a resurgence of checks and balances in the form of congressional vitality and judicial oversight, and a concerned citizenry aroused to action—represent, fundamentally, *constitutional* solutions. Each of these mechanisms is embedded in the Constitution and reflects age-old hopes and aspirations. If they fail to correct the problems that have arisen with the emergence of the imperial or plebiscitary presidency, then it appears that the problem would elide constitutional mechanisms. But if that is true, then the premise and promise of republicanism and constitutional government exceed our grasp. Ultimately, there is a measure of truth in the explanation of our problem: We need better people occupying the presidency, men and women who would embrace constitutional limitations. The same might well be said of those who hold seats in Congress and on the courts. But, as we have learned from Aristotle and Churchill, and countless others who have weighed in on the perennial debate about the interrelationship and relative influence of individuals on institutions and institutions on individuals, individuals do affect institutions, and institutions affect individuals. There is little point in a narrative that explains the fact of presidential government as a personal tragedy, for there is no denying that it is an institutional tragedy as well.

A revitalized system of checks and balances, spurred by the citizenry, is capable of redressing the problems that our nation faces. For inspiration, we may, again, turn to our own history. America was born as a result of a constitutional crisis, much of it stemming from executive claims to power. The founding generation rejected the English Constitution and created its own constitutional brand. The Civil War resulted in the gravest constitutional crisis that our nation has witnessed, but America persevered and, when it sorted out the most fundamental constitutional sorts of quarrels, it forged ahead into a period of prosperity and growth. The current problem of seemingly boundless presidential power can be fixed as well. As they say, we've done it before and we can fix it again.

Conclusion

Scholars and concerned citizens alike have proffered remedies: presidential humility, congressional resurgence, and judicial responsibility, in one form or another, have been recommended as antidotes. Yet, the institutional prescriptions are yet unavailing. Is it too late to recover republican principles? There is little doubt that the challenge becomes more daunting by the day, particularly in the "age of terrorism," in which governmental officials are tempted to exploit the public's fears to facilitate their circumvention of constitutional provisions. Yet, there remains hope. For those of us who would embrace a renewal of the doctrine of checks and balances, driven by renewed interest in republican governance among the citizenry as a means of recovering a constitutional presidency, there is a need to brace ourselves for comparisons to Don Quixote. Are we tilting at windmills? For those who have little confidence in the citizenry, it may help if Americans summon the ghosts of 1776, those harpies of power that compelled a generation to answer the trumpet call: an imperious executive, oppression, assaults on liberties, absolutist pretensions, disregard for constitutional principles and limitations, and the assertion of arbitrary power. The rule of law is fleeting. It remains within our grasp, however tenuous, but we must seize it. As the historian Charles McIlwain wrote, in the context of a postwar world in which the future of constitutionalism was in doubt, "The two fundamental correlative elements of constitutionalism for which all lovers of liberty must yet fight are the legal limits to arbitrary power and a complete responsibility of government to the governed."[108]

Notes

1. *Reid v. Covert,* 354 U.S. 1, 16–17 (1957). In 1819, in his landmark opinion in *McCulloch v. Maryland,* Chief Justice John Marshall stated: "We admit, as all must admit, that the powers of government are limited and that its limits are not to be transcended." 17 U.S. 316, 421 (1819).
2. For the founders, Julius Goebel observed, "The principle that government must be conducted in conformity with the terms of the constitution became a fundamental political conception." Goebel, *Antecedents and Beginnings to 1801, Vol.* 1 *of The History of the Supreme Court of the United States* (New York: MacMillan, 1971).
3. Alexander Hamilton, writing in *Federalist* No. 22, ably captured the framers' understanding of the crucial linkage between popular sovereignty and governmental actions: "The fabric of American empire, ought to rest on the solid basis of THE CONSENT OF THE PEOPLE." Hamilton, *Federalist* No. 22, 141 (Mod. Lib. Ed., 1937). James Wilson had earlier expressed the principle when he observed that, "The binding power of the law flowed from the continuous assent of the subjects of law." Quoted in Bernard Bailyn, *The Ideological Origins of the American Revolution* (Cambridge, MA: Harvard University Press, 1967), 174.
4. Article XVIII, Benjamin P. Poore, ed. Federal and State Constitutions, Colonial Charters, 2 vols., 1:959; New Hampshire (1784), Article 38, 2 Poore 1283; North Carolina

(1776), Article XXI, 2 Poore 1410; Pennsylvania (1776), Article XIV, 2 Poore 1542; Vermont (1777), Article XVI, 2 Poore 1860.

5. Benjamin N. Cardozo, *The Nature of the Judicial Process* (New Haven, CT: Yale University Press, 1921), 136.

6. *Olmstead v. United States,* 277 U.S. 438, 485 (1928).

7. 1 Annals of Congress, 500.

8. "The government of the United States," Chief Justice Marshall famously wrote in *Marbury v. Madison,* "has been emphatically termed a government of laws and not men." 5 U.S. (1 Cranch) 137, 163 (1803).

9. John Hart Ely, "The Wages of Crying Wolf: A Comment on Roe v. Wade," *The Yale Law Journal,* 82 (1973): 920, 949.

10. Max Farrand, ed., *Records of the Federal Convention of 1787,* 4 vols. (New Haven, CT: Yale University Press, 1966), 292.

11. Alexander Hamilton, "Letters of Camillus," in *Works of Alexander Hamilton,* 12 vols., ed. H. C. Lodge (New York: Putnam, 1906), 166.

12. Julius Goebel observed that in colonial America: "The principle that the government must be conducted in conformity with the terms of the Constitution became a fundamental political conception." Goebel, *Antecedents and Beginnings,* 89.

13. G. J. McRee, ed., *Life and Correspondence of James Iredell,* 2 vols. (New York: Appleton, 1857–1858),145.

14. 5 U.S. (1 Cranch) 137, 178 (1803).

15. Gerald Gunther, ed., *John Marshall's Defense of McCulloch v. Maryland* (Palo Alto, CA: Stanford University Press, 1969),190–191.

16. Farrand, *Records,* 73.

17. See David Gray Adler, *The Constitution and the Termination of Treaties* (New York: Garland Press, 1986); Adler, "The Constitution and the Termination of Treaties: A Matter of Symmetry," *Arizona State Law Journal* 1981 (1981): 891–923; Adler, "The Clinton Theory of the War Power," *Presidential Studies Quarterly* (2000): 155–168.

18. *Federalist* No. 23, 142; *Federalist* No. 41, 262.

19. 17 U.S. (4 Wheat.) 316, 408 (1819).

20. Gaillard Hunt, ed., *The Writings of James Madison,* 9 vols. (New York: Putnam, 1900–1910), 185. Oliver Ellsworth, speaking in the Connecticut Ratifying Convention, echoed the principle when he stated that Congress may not "overleap their limits." Jonathan Elliot, *Debates in the Several State Conventions on the Adoption of the Federal Constitution,* 2nd ed., 4 vols. (Washington, DC: Government Printing Office, 1836), 196.

21. *Houston v. Moore,* 18 U.S. (5 Wheat.) 1, 48 (1820), dissenting opinion.

22. For discussion of impeachable offenses, see Raoul Berger, *Impeachment: The Constitutional Problems* (Cambridge, MA: Harvard University Press, 1973), 56–108.

23. J. Fitzpatrick, ed., *The Writings of George Washington,* 39 vols. (Washington, DC: Government Printing Office, 1940), 228–229.

24. See, generally, Bernard Bailyn, *The Ideological Origins,* particularly 55–93.

25. *Federalist* No. 48, 321.

26. Lord Radcliffe, *The Problem of Power* (London: Secker and Warburg, 1952), 100.

27. In re Winship, 397 U.S. 358, 384 (1970), dissenting opinion.

28. Elliot, *Debates*, 543. Such was the founders' commitment to a written Constitution that Jefferson's fellow Virginian, Francis Corbin, told his colleagues in his state ratifying convention, "Liberty is secured, sir, by the limitation of its [the government's] powers, which are clearly and unequivocally defined." Elliott, *Debates*, 543.

29. Discussion in Edmond Cahn, ed., *Supreme Court and Supreme Law* (Bloomington: Indiana University Press, 1954), 75.

30. See, generally, Francis D. Wormuth, *The Royal Prerogative* (Ithaca, NY: Cornell University Press, 1939); William D. Holdsworth, *History of English Law*, 12 vols. (London: Metheun, 1903–1938), 428–431; Margaret A. Judson, *The Crisis of the Constitution* (New Brunswick, NJ: Rutgers University Press, 1949); Donald W. Hanson, *From Kingdom to Commonwealth* (Cambridge, MA: Harvard University Press, 1970). See also the fine essay by Robert Scigliano, in which he explains that the so-called Lockean Prerogative does not imply authority to violate the law with impunity. Rather, the executive, acting in defiance of the law, without authority to do so, would be required to seek retroactive authorization from the legislature. Scigliano, "The President's Prerogative Power," in *Inventing the American Presidency,* Thomas Cronin, ed., (Lawrence: University Press of Kansas, 1989), 236–259.

31. *Marbury v. Madison*, 5. U.S. (1 Cranch), 137, 176, (1803).

32. Goebel, "Ex Parte Clio," Columbia Law Review 54 (1954):450, 474.

33. Scigliano, "The President's Prerogative," 248.

34. Quoted in Charles Warren, *The Making of the Constitution* (Cambridge, MA: Harvard University Press, 1947), 177.

35. Farrand, *Records,* 62–70.

36. Farrand, *Records,* 171,185, 597, 600.

37. Farrand, *Records,* 65.

38. Edward Corwin, "Conceptions of the Office," in *The President: Office and Powers,* 1787–1984, 5th ed., ed. Randall Bland (New York: New York University, 1984), 11.

39. Elliot, *Debates,* 120. Hamilton, *Federalist* No. 75, 487.

40. Farrand, *Records,* 288.

41. Farrand, *Records,* 289.

42. Farrand, *Records,* 289.

43. Farrand, *Records,* 292. For discussion of the abuse of Hamilton's writings, see David Gray Adler, "Presidential Power and Foreign Affairs in the Bush Administration: The Use and Abuse of Alexander Hamilton," 40 *Presidential Studies Quarterly* 40 (Sept. 2010): 531–544; Louis Fisher, "John Yoo and the Republic," Presidential Studies Quarterly 41 (March 2011): 177–192, 184.

44. Farrand, *Records,* 65.

45. Letter from James Madison to Thomas Jefferson, August 11, 1793, in *The Writings of James Madison 1790–1802,* edited by Gaillard Hunt, 145. New York: Putnam, 1900–1910.

46. A.V. Dicey, *Introduction to the Study of the Law of the Constitution* (London: Macmillan, 1889), 339.

47. In Dr. Bonham's Case, Sir Edward Coke observed that for centuries, common law had prohibited a man from judging his own cause. 8 Co. Rep. 113b, 77 Eng. Rep. 646 (1610).

48. *Youngstown Sheet & Tube Co. v. Sawyer,* 343 U.S. 650 (1952).

49. For discussion of the doctrine of retroactive ratification, see Adler, "The Steel Seizure Case and Inherent Presidential Power," *Constitutional Commentary* 19 (2002): 155, 173–179.

50. James D. Richardson, *A Compilation of the Messages and Papers of the Presidents, 1789–1903* (Washington, DC: Government Printing Office, 1903), 3225.

51. 12 Stat. 326 (1861). The Court took judicial notice of the retroactive ratification in the Prize Cases, 67 U.S. (2 Black) 635 (1863).

52. In the first Congress, Roger Sherman, who had been a delegate to the Constitutional Convention, argued in defense of the shared-power arrangement in foreign affairs: "The more wisdom there is employed, the greater security there is that the public business will be done." 1 Annals of Congress, 1123. The framers' attachment to collective decision making reflected, in part, their distrust of executive unilateralism. Hamilton had explained in *Federalist* No. 75 that the treaty power—the essential vehicle for formulating foreign policy, in the minds of the framers—was withheld from the president since it was not "wise" to commit such awesome authority to a single person. Similarly, James Wilson explained to his colleagues at the Pennsylvania Ratifying Convention that the War Clause was designed to prevent a "single man" from rushing the nation into war. Elliot, *Debates,* 528.

53. Schlesinger, "Foreword," in *The Constitution and the Conduct of American Foreign Policy,* eds. David Gray Adler and Larry N. George (Lawrence: University Press of Kansas, 1996), ix.

54. *Federalist* No. 15, 87.

55. See Adler, "The President's Recognition Power," in *American Foreign Policy,* eds. Adler and George, (College Station: Texas A&M University Press, 2000), 133–157.

56. *Youngstown Sheet & Tube Co. v. Sawyer,* 343 U.S. 579, 594.

57. Quoted in Louis Fisher, *Congressional Abdication on War and Spending* (College Station: Texas A&M University, 2000), 119.

58. See Lowi, *The Personal President: Power Invested, Promise Unfulfilled* (Ithaca, NY: Cornell University Press, 1985); *Schlesinger, The Imperial Presidency* (Boston, MA: Houghton Mifflin, 1966); Cronin, *The State of the Presidency* (Boston, MA: Little, Brown, 1980); Burns, *Presidential Government* (Boston, MA: Houghton Mifflin, 1966).

59. Schlesinger, *Imperial Presidency,* 212.

60. For discussions of unilateral presidential war making, see, for example, Adler, "The Constitution and Presidential War Making: The Enduring Debate," *Political Science Quarterly* 103 (Spring 1988):1–36; Louis Fisher, *Presidential War Power,* 2nd ed. (Lawrence: University Press of Kansas, 2004).

61. For discussion, see Adler, "George Bush and the Abuse of History: The Constitution and Presidential Power in Foreign Affairs," *UCLA Journal of International Law and Foreign Affairs* 12 (Spring 2007): 75–144.

62. While it is true in important respects that some of Bush's predecessors laid claim to similar powers, for example, the assertion of a unilateral executive power to initiate war, it remains the case that, in the aggregate, Bush's aggrandizement of power represents not merely a difference of degree, but a difference in kind.

63. Dean, *Worse Than Watergate: The Secret Presidency of George W. Bush* (New York: Viking, 2004).

64. Bob Egelko, "Gonzales Says the Constitution Doesn't Guarantee Habeas Corpus," *San Francisco Chronicle*, January 24, 2007, A–1.

65. Lowi, *Personal President*, xi.

66. James N. Naughton, "Nixon Says a President Can Order Illegal Actions Against Dissidents," *The New York Times*, May 19, 1977, A–1.

67. Rossiter, *Constitutional Dictatorship* (Princeton, NJ: Princeton University Press, 1948), 288.

68. Levinson, "Constitutional Norms in a Permanent State of Emergency," *Georgia Law Review*, 40 (2006): 699, 739.

69. Thucydides, *History of the Peloponnesian War Books V–VI*, Book V., ch. 105, trans. C. F. Smith (Cambridge, MA: Harvard University Press, 1921), 167.

70. Thucydides, *History*, 159 (Book V, ch. 89).

71. This discussion is indebted to Friedrich's portrayal of the conversation between the two friends. Friedrich, *Constitutional Reason of State* (Providence, RI: Brown University Press, 1957), 50–51.

72. Friedrich, *Constitutional Reason*, 50.

73. 343 U.S. 579, 646.

74. 343 U.S., 650.

75. Wormuth, *Royal Prerogative*, 78.

76. Wormuth, *Royal Prerogative*, 78.

77. Friedrich, *Reason of State*, 51.

78. Lowi, *Personal President*, xi.

79. Kernell, Going Public: New Strategies of Presidential Leadership, 3rd ed. (Washington, DC: Congressional Quarterly, Inc., 1997), 228.

80. Schlesinger, *Imperial Presidency*, 258.

81. 299 U.S. 304 (1936). For a discussion of the Court's reflexive bow to the president in foreign affairs jurisprudence, see Adler, "Court, Constitution and Foreign Affairs," in *The Constitution*, eds. Adler and George (Lawrence: University Press of Kansas, 1996), 19–56.

82. Lowi, *Personal President*, xi.

83. Madison, "Letters of Helvidius," in *Writings*, 138.

84. Dicey, *Lectures Introductory*, 202–203.

85. Alexander Bickel, *The Morality of Consent* (New Haven, CT: Yale University Press, 1975), 75.

86. *Federalist* No. 48, 321.

87. *Federalist* No. 51, 337.

88. Schlesinger, *Imperial Presidency*, 95–96.

89. Bailyn, *Ideological Origins*, 56.

90. *Bas v. Tingy*, 4 Dall. 37 (1800).

91. *Talbot v. Seeman*, 5 U.S. 28 (1801) (emphasis added).

92. *Little v. Barreme*, 6 U.S. (2 Cir.) 169, 179 (1804).

93. Fisher, *Presidential War*, 26.

94. 1 Stat. 96, sec. 3 (1789).

95. 1 Stat. 711, sec. 24 (1799).

96. 2 Stat. 47 (1800) (Art. 14).

97. *United States v. Smith,* 27 Fed. Cas 1192, 1229 (C.C.N.Y. 1806) (No. 16,342).

98. *United States v. Smith,* 27 Fed. Cas 1229, 1230 (C.C.N.Y. 1806) (No. 16,342).

99. *United States v. Smith,* 27 Fed. Cas 1229, 1230 (C.C.N.Y. 1806) (No. 16,342).

100. Elliot, Debates, 3:148–149; 4:130; 3:207.

101. *Fed. Power Comm'n v. Natural Gas Pipeline Co. of Am.,* 315 U.S. 575, 609.

102. *Sparf v. United States,* 156 U.S. 51, 169 (1895).

103. Alfred H. Kelly, "Clio and the Court: An Illicit Love Affair," 1965 Sup. Ct. Rev. 119, 122 (1965); Spitzer, *Saving the Constitution From Lawyers: How Legal Training and Law Reviews Distort Constitutional Meaning* (Cambridge, UK: Cambridge University Press, 2008).

104. Louis Pollak, "The Supreme Court Under Fire," 6 J. Public Law 428, 441 (1957).

105. Bickel, "The Original Understanding and the Segregation Decision," *Harvard Law Review* 69 (1955): 1, 3–4 (emphasis in original).

106. See Adler, "Presidential Power and Foreign Affairs in the Bush Administration: The Use and Abuse of Alexander Hamilton," *Presidential Studies Quarterly* 40 (September 2010):531–544.

107. Adler, "Textbooks and the President's Constitutional Powers," *Presidential Studies Quarterly* 35 (June 2005):376–388.

108. McIlwain, *Constitutionalism: Ancient and Modern* (Ithaca, NY: Cornell University Press, 1947), 146.

CHAPTER 5

The Unitary Executive

Melanie M. Marlowe

THE PRESIDENCY OF GEORGE W. BUSH was a controversial one from the start. He entered the office having lost the popular vote but having won the electoral majority in a messy election that ended in the Supreme Court. At the time he took office, the Senate was evenly divided between Republicans and Democrats, with Vice President Dick Cheney giving the Republicans a one-vote majority in his position as president of the Senate. But on June 6, 2001, Senator Jim Jeffords became an Independent who caucused with Democrats, handing the majority to the Democrats.[1] The terrorist attacks in New York City and Washington, DC, on September 11, 2001, stunned the nation and altered the policy priorities of the new administration.

Although prior to 9/11 President Bush had exercised unilateral authority in such forms as executive orders and signing statements, it was his administration's response to terrorism and use of the phrase "unitary executive" in documents and speeches that brought heightened attention to the theory. Editorials and news stories insisted that the theory was concocted by President Bush and Vice President Cheney to give them the tools they needed to consolidate their power over the government and the American public.[2]

The unitary executive theory is firmly grounded in the Constitution. Proponents of the unitary executive theory assert that the Constitution gives the president all of the executive power and that the constitutional separation of powers demands he be able to effectively exercise and defend his authority. Those who support the proper form of the theory do not contend that the president is unconfined by either the text or structure of the Constitution. They do not believe that the president is above the law and may use whatever means he can muster to serve his political ends. Instead of being a subversion of the rule of law, the unitary executive theory provides the constitutional and political accountability republican government requires.

The Unitary Executive

I am a proponent of the unitary executive theory of the presidency. Supporters of the theory understand that the Constitution provides three main sources of power for the president: the vesting clause, the "take care" clause, and the oath of office. We also find other constitutional clauses, some of which are discussed later, that buttress and further explain these three.

Article II, Section 1, Clause 1 of the Constitution vests "the executive Power" in "a President of the United States." The president alone possesses the executive power, and not simply part of it, and his constitutional authority is only legitimately diminished when qualified by other particular constitutional limitations (such as the Senate's constitutional role in consenting to certain presidential appointments).

The precise wording of this clause is especially significant when compared to the vesting clauses of the other branches. Article I, Section 1, Clause 1 limits Congress to "All legislative Powers herein granted" and does not confer a general legislative power. In Article III, the "judicial Power" is divided between "one supreme Court" and "such inferior Courts as the Congress may from time to time ordain and establish"; there is also an enumeration of what matters the judicial power "shall extend to."

The president's oath of office, the only oath written in the Constitution, requires him to "preserve, protect, and defend the Constitution of the United States."[3] He must be personally bound to the nation's fundamental law. As his oath is not to another institution, this clause indicates that the president must independently assess the constitutionality of actions taken by his own office as well as by the other branches. Madison explains this authority, known as "departmentalism," or "coordinate construction," in *Federalist* No. 49: "The several departments being perfectly coordinate by the terms of their common commission, neither of them, it is evident, can pretend to an exclusive or superior right of settling the boundaries between their respective powers. . . ."[4]

From the president's perspective, this may be most obvious in the legislative context. When both houses of Congress pass a bill and send it to the president for his signature, he must examine the constitutional propriety of the legislation.[5] If he perceives a violation, he may veto the legislation and return it to Congress for revision, sign the bill without comment and enforce it "as is," or sign the bill but decline to defend or enforce the offending provisions. This is often accomplished through a signing statement, which explains to the other branches and the public the president's disagreements with the bill before him.

Article II, Section 3 directs the president to "take Care that the Laws be faithfully executed." Taking care is an affirmative obligation on the president himself, not on the executive branch. To ensure faithful execution of all the laws, the president requires the assistance of others whom he supervises. But this supervision is more than simply judging whether or not a subordinate officer has fulfilled his duties honestly or on time. Most statutes admit of interpretation and some choice in implementation. As the nation's chief law enforcement officer, the president has the constitutional authority to control any discretion that is part of federal law as he executes the federal laws. If, in the president's judgment, the law has not been or will not be faithfully executed, he has a responsibility to supplant a subordinate's discretionary judgment with his own or remove the official who is behaving badly.[6]

Article II, Section 2 authorizes the president to appoint, subject to Senate confirmation, principal officers of the United States. Because they are people of the president's choosing, it is expected that their loyalty to his endeavors will be secure. Congress may vest the appointment of inferior officers in other governmental departments, but because the president may remove them, the principle of accountability is preserved. Congress may not, consistent with the Constitution, commit the execution of federal law to administrative agencies that are free of presidential control. It does not matter where Congress would like "the executive Power" to be; it *is* in the president.

To support the president in his execution of the law, the Constitution provides that he "may require the Opinion in writing, of the principal Officer in each of the executive Departments, upon any subject relating to the Duties of their respective Offices."[7] The president has a constitutional right to the advice of those who assist him. This information helps the president to coordinate activity and manage resources as he either executes the law himself or instructs subordinates as they do so. While there may be disagreement among department heads and even between the president and principal officers, the president is to make the final decision. In order to ensure candid advice from subordinates, the president may attempt to prevent public disclosure of interbranch communications to the other branches and the public.

The Constitutional Convention decided against an executive council that might lessen the responsibility of the president and permit him to ascribe poor administration to others. The clause protects the office of the president as it prevents Congress from creating officers who keep information about law execution from the president. Finally, it confirms the view that the president is himself the chief executor of the law. It would be silly for him to have a constitutional right to opinions on how independent actors would execute the laws. Alexander Hamilton understood that this clause simply confirmed presidential oversight of the executive branch, as we see in *Federalist* No. 74: "This I consider as a mere redundancy in the plan, as the right for which it provides would result of itself from the office."[8]

Finally, the president is the commander in chief.[9] While not always considered to be a particular part of the unitary executive theory itself, in recent years the two have become closely associated. It is a core executive function—perhaps the highest executive responsibility. As noted earlier, President Bush repeatedly invoked the "unitary executive" as he justified his administration's war policies or sought to avoid congressional interference with military operations. As commander in chief, the president has broad discretion over military strategy, personnel placement, and the execution of national security legislation. A single executive who acts with "vigor and expedition" is most important when it comes to the survival of the nation: "In the conduct of war, in which the energy of the executive is the bulwark of the national security, everything would be to be apprehended from its plurality."[10] Congress has clear constitutional authority to restrain the president's war power through refusal to declare war, appropriate funding for military operations, or raise troops. The president, as the head of state, alone may receive ambassadors, recognize foreign governments, and negotiate treaties (subject to a strong senatorial concurrence).

It should be noted that within the unitary executive school, there are stronger and weaker versions of the theory. A "weak" theorist would acknowledge the president has constitutional authority to direct policymaking in the executive branch. This is largely accomplished by appointing principal officers whom he can trust and removing inferior officers who refuse to accept and implement his directives. A "weak" theorist may consider independent agencies and entities to be constitutionally troublesome.

A stronger view, my view, argues that executive branch officials are subject to the direction and possible removal of the president. But because independent agencies exercise executive power, and the executive power—all of it—is given to the president and not to agency heads, independent agencies are unconstitutional. Congress cannot dispense executive power to agency heads or entities who are not under the direct control of the person who has the executive power—the president. The Supreme Court soundly rejected this view in *Morrison v. Olson*,[11] but I might be called a "bitter clinger" on this constitutional principle. Subscribers to the stronger view would likely also agree that the president may invoke executive privilege on behalf of all executive branch officials who exercise discretion and implement law.

Much is owed to Steven Calabresi, Christopher Yoo, and John Yoo for the current debate about the limits of the unitary executive. In *The Unitary Executive*,[12] a compilation of more than a decade of research on the presidency, Calabresi and Christopher Yoo make the case, president-by-president, that every chief executive from George Washington to George W. Bush has understood the Constitution to charge the president with responsibility for the execution of the law.[13] They argue that presidents have consistently (although not in every circumstance) pressed what they viewed as their constitutional authority to remove and direct executive branch subordinates as they fulfill the obligation of the "take care" clause. This includes individuals who sit on independent commissions. The cases in which presidents have acquiesced in congressional intrusion in the executive's authority over the execution of the law are cancelled out many times over by the number and importance of the cases in which they have objected. Because presidents have steadily insisted these Article II powers belong with the executive against the attempts of Congress to restrict them, there is little merit to the claim that over time, Congress established a legitimate authority to limit the powers.[14]

Calabresi and Christopher Yoo differ from another unitary executive theorist, John Yoo, most notably in the area of war policy. John Yoo, who served in the Department of Justice during the early years of the George W. Bush administration, when initial policy regarding the War on Terror was being formulated, relied on a more expansive vision of executive war power than some unitarians could accept. This view relies on a strong emphasis on not simply "unitary" but "executive" as well: the idea that "Article II vests powers of substance that come to the fore during crises."[15]

John Yoo is impressed with the manner in which Washington and Jefferson shaped and responded to events to protect the nation and further its interests even when physical security was not immediately at stake. However, the subject of his greatest admiration is Lincoln[16] (who, it turns out, is the "hero" of the Calabresi and Christopher Yoo volume[17]). Lincoln relied on constitutional grants of power read broadly to fight the Civil War and prepare for postwar freedom. He called up troops and spent money from the treasury without congressional authorization, he implemented a blockade of the Southern ports, he suspended the writ of habeas corpus, and he issued the Emancipation Proclamation. As he later wrote to A. G. Hodges, "I felt that measures, otherwise unconstitutional, might become lawful, by becoming indispensable to the preservation of the constitution, through the preservation of the nation."[18]

While John Yoo defends the aggressive efforts of President Bush (and his subordinates) in the War on Terror as being a legal exercise of commander-in-chief power and necessary (based on information at the time decisions were made) to prepare for the protection of the nation,[19] Calabresi and Christopher Yoo argue against actions such as most use of military commissions in the United States for both citizens and aliens. They also worry that the secrecy with which the Bush administration formulated and carried out interrogations, the wiretapping program, and other national security actions obscured the political accountability that makes the defense of the unitary executive possible, as well as opened the door to judicial decisions that will restrict legitimate executive power.[20]

To be clear, even a strong view does not mean one believes the president is free to do anything he wants, that for him there is no constitutional wrong.[21] In addition, all lawful power must be exercised with care and prudence. Just because one has the authority to do something does not make it prudent under the circumstances to do it or to be seen doing it. Context and actual manner of application matter.[22] And in the end, the president still has to contend with the political and constitutional arguments of the other branches and public opinion.

The Problem With the Presidency Today

As a unitarian, I think the biggest problem with the presidency today is a Congress that is "everywhere extending the sphere of its activity and drawing all power into its impetuous vortex,"[23] even as it refuses to be responsible for its actions. Presidents are unable to act with the energy, decision, and accountability that are essential to the administration of good government.

Congressional encroachments on executive power are supported by a misunderstanding of the constitutional order, in which the legislature is placed in charge of the president, who simply carries out the will of Congress. According to this view, the threat to republican government is executive power, which must be closely monitored and practically restrained.

In the Revolutionary Era, this was the general political sentiment. Having thrown off the chains of English monarchy, Americans were not anxious to shoulder new ones in the form of an elected despot. Most state constitutions, New York being the prominent exception, carefully circumscribed executive power, including subjecting the governor to act to some extent with a council that had involvement in appointments, removals, pardons, and other traditionally executive prerogatives. Legislatures were given general legislative powers, legislators served short terms, and members were subject to being recalled if they did not sufficiently represent the will of their constituents. The Articles of Confederation established a Congress as the national government. Committees took on specific tasks, but they proved to be slow, lazy, and corrupt.

By the time of the Constitutional Convention, it was apparent that legislatures could also behave tyrannically as they translated the will of the majority into law and exercised executive and judicial power in the enforcement of those laws. Madison, in *Federalist* No. 48, noted the opponents of the Constitution "seem never to have recollected the danger from legislative usurpations, which, by assembling all power in the same hands, must lead to the same tyranny as is threatened by executive usurpations." In Philadelphia, delegates recognized that an executive could actually protect liberty by restraining the passions of popular majorities and acting quickly to resolve crises.

As noted in *Federalist* No. 51, the constant threat to the president would be the legislative branch, which, by virtue of its number, association with the people, and control of the purse, would "necessarily predominate." In *Federalist* No. 48, Madison continues, "It is against the enterprising ambition of this department that the people ought to indulge all their jealousy and exhaust all their precautions."

The way to "remedy [the] inconveniency" of an overpowering legislature was to structure the branches so that encroachments may be effectively resisted. Congress was divided into two houses, each with a different mode of election and length of term and different legislative responsibilities. But this would not be sufficient to restrain a body that possesses the advantages of number, popularity, and control of the national purse. To counteract the formidable strength of the legislature, "the weakness of the executive may require . . . that it should be fortified."[24] Executive selection by the legislature would be rejected in order to give him independence. He would need security in office—a term of four years—with the possibility of reelection if he did his job well. He would possess all the executive power, and he would have a role in the legislative process.

The "legislative usurpations" Madison complained of continue today. Congress interferes with the president's appointment power in a number of ways, including by passing statutes that attempt to limit his choices to names on a list or to people based on party affiliation. When Congress includes its own members on commemorative commissions, it violates the Incompatibility Clause of the Constitution, which is clearly intended to keep the branches independent of one another.[25] Congress also burdens the executive branch with advisory boards.

Congress obstructs the president's removal power by setting "good cause" restrictions on that power or placing it in the hands of someone other than the president himself.

Congress demands information from the executive branch that it does not have a right to possess. Through onerous reporting requirements, Congress attempts to manage the advice presidents receive as they formulate and implement policy. As confidentiality is threatened, presidential advisers are unable to offer candid counsel.

Congress also improperly meddles with the president's commander-in-chief power when it attempts to legislatively define that power and when it presumes to force a strategic policy on him.

These congressional actions are efforts to accomplish what was rejected at the Constitutional Convention: the creation of a plural executive that is tied to the will of the legislature. While Congress may sense that there is something unsettling about discretionary executive power and therefore try to limit it, the fact is that executive actions are not always susceptible of exact legal definition. The president must be able to evaluate information, exercise discretion, and suffer the consequences of those decisions. Law and discretion seem to be in tension. But good administration of the law requires effective employment of discretion. The solution for the framers was that the president would be visibly and totally accountable for the executive branch.

Although Congress encroaches on executive power ceaselessly, presidents are not without fault: They often acquiesce to intrusions, perhaps because they believe the immediate political situation calls for it or because they don't know any better. They accept delegations of policymaking authority to individuals over whom they do not exercise substantive control. They sign laws that unconstitutionally usurp their authority. They admit interference in the decision-making process. Presidents who are inconsistently defensive of their own powers when they are attacked, and insufficiently assertive in their responsibilities, reduce the authority of the office and make the exercise of legitimate power more difficult for successors.

The Solution for Reforming the Presidency Today

I would love nothing more than to believe that Congress could be reformed. I would be thrilled to see a Congress that made *laws*—laws that were general, within the proper scope of the objects enumerated in Article I, Section 8 of the Constitution, and clear enough that we could believe the president and his subordinates were only executing the laws, not making them. I would like to say that Congress as an institution could be more responsible, more concerned with how to craft legislation well, instead of simply holding others accountable for the exercise of discretion later. But at this time I confess to being hopeless on these counts.

I contend that reforming the presidency begins with the president. A president who will reexamine his constitutional power and use it to defend his office against the "enterprising ambition" of the legislature will serve his office and the country well. This might mean taking actions that are unpopular but constitutionally or politically warranted. A president with a proper understanding of the separation of powers will recognize that Congress has legitimate claims to power, too, and that clashes between the branches are normal and even good for public debate about competing policy goals.

We look at recent case studies in three areas of constitutional concern to the president, the legislative process, administration of government, briefly, and military operations, to see how a proper use and defense of his constitutional powers will contribute to a recovery of the energetic executive. This is not a glowing report on presidential power. Some of the clearest demonstrations of how a president should act come from seeing how a feeble or unwise employment of power contributes to a decline in the stature of the office.

I conclude with a few words on how Congress and the Supreme Court fit into this solution.

Impact: What This Would (And Would Not) Look Like
The President's Constitutional Power and Responsibility

Legislative Process. The president has a constitutional agenda-setting role in his State of the Union address and obligation that he recommend measures to Congress.[26] At the end of the legislative process, the president may approve of or reject bills that come before him, according to the provisions of Article I, Section 7. If the president vetoes a bill, he is constitutionally required to publicly state his objections to the law the representatives of the people have passed. While he may have recommended a particular policy and signaled his views on it as the legislative process continued, his most important contribution to legislative deliberation may be to say "No."

We do not see the word "veto" in the Constitution. The word itself has monarchical origins, and it would have had a disagreeable connotation in the minds of the people whose support was needed to ratify the Constitution. Instead, we see that the president may either approve a bill or "return" it to Congress. The framers gave the American president a "qualified" veto—one that could be overridden by two-thirds of both Houses of Congress. This was done to make it more tolerable to both the president and Congress; there was concern that an absolute veto (one that could not be overridden) would be an act of such extreme hostility that it would place the institutions in a state of unmitigated confrontation.[27] To avoid this, the president would simply not use an absolute veto. But the veto would be essential to good government, the framers reasoned, so it must be qualified. Besides the requirement to return the bill with a list of his objections, the president has no constitutional restrictions on this power.

In *Federalist* No. 73, Hamilton explains three times that the veto is primarily a self-defense mechanism. For instance, he notes that the "primary inducement to conferring the power in question upon the executive is to enable him to defend himself."[28] An energetic president, one with "tolerable firmness," in the words of Hamilton,[29] will recognize when he is obligated to veto legislation in order to protect his office.

Nixon was right to veto the War Powers Resolution,[30] even though it was clear that his unpopularity due to the Watergate scandal and the political fallout from the Vietnam War ensured Congress would override the veto. The legislative veto and provisions seeking to define the president's commander-in-chief powers are clearly unconstitutional. In 1989, President George H. W. Bush properly vetoed a foreign operations appropriations bill on the grounds that it would interfere with his constitutional authority to conduct foreign relations. He admitted that there was room in the offending section for a constitutional interpretation in his favor, but the ambiguity of the provision and the importance of the constitutional power at stake required him to veto the bill.[31]

These presidents stood firm in their appropriate defense of the executive office from congressional assaults. They risked (and Nixon suffered) defeat in the form of an embarrassing override, but both presidents understood the constitutional issue to be important enough to do so.

President Reagan did not take the political risk. The Independent Counsel Act placed a prosecutor, appointed by a federal court and subject to report to Congress, in the executive branch to investigate and prosecute wrongdoing in that branch.

While designated an inferior officer (so she could be appointed in a manner prescribed by Congress) in the executive branch, the independent counsel had virtually unlimited power to carry out her function and could only be removed by the Attorney General, subject to judicial review. The constitutional violations in the Act led President Reagan to believe it to be unconstitutional, but citing a public need for confidence in government and the fact that a case involving the Act was in federal court, he signed it anyway.[32] President Reagan's failure to abide by his constitutional judgment and veto the bill in either 1983 or its reauthorization in 1987 resulted in a catastrophic defeat for the executive branch, one that plagued succeeding presidents and ultimately resulted in the impeachment of President Clinton.

Constitutional vetoes may be issued when the powers of the president are not directly at stake. When Andrew Jackson vetoed the Second Bank of the United States, he did so even though the bill supporting it had been passed by Congress and the power of Congress to charter a bank had been previously approved by the Supreme Court in the case *McCulloch v. Maryland*.[33] He argued that "each public officer," including the president, must support the Constitution "as he understands it, and not as it is understood by others."[34] Although the president's judgment might lose to another branch's verdict, he properly stated that he could not abandon his oath to "defend the Constitution."

As Hamilton observes, presidents may also veto bills solely on policy grounds: "The secondary [purpose of the veto] is to increase the chances in favor of the community against the passing of bad laws, through haste, inadvertence, or design."[35] While this may be politically difficult—a bill that has made it through the legislature is likely to have a great deal of public support—the president is to take the larger view. He is to be concerned with the nation as a whole and not simply the narrow interests that might attract the attention of legislators. The president is not a rubber stamp. On a more partisan level, vetoes can be instructive in helping us understand the policy differences between the party holding Congress and the one occupying the White House.

Hamilton noted in *Federalist* No. 73 that strategically, the veto is a power whose use, if credibly threatened, would "have a silent and unperceived, though forcible, operation." The legislature would have to more carefully consider bills if an independent president—one "they cannot control"—might impede an imprudent design. But the threat has to be real. A president who claims he simply cannot accept certain provisions, but in the end agrees to them, weakens his office. Under most circumstances, a Congress can live with a harsh signing statement and will figure that is better than an outright veto. It is the president who will have to abide by what *he* could not live with.

The use of the veto by the president is an important tool. Although it may be used to thwart the will of the people, the president is ultimately politically accountable for exercising it. He must explain his reasons and accept the policy consequences. The veto assists the rule of law by adding a layer of assurance that the laws passed are constitutional and wise.

Signing statements are issued at the time a bill is signed and are a way for a president to inform Congress and the public of his understanding of the law. Most law execution requires discretion, and a president's interpretation of the law gives necessary guidance to executive branch officials as to how they must carry out their duties. In his statement, a president might remind Congress of earlier policy recommendations he made or propose further action. He may note that he is signing legislation in spite of personal policy concern or indicate that there are provisions in the bill that fall into a constitutional gray area. The president should not use a signing statement to alter the bill itself by adding provisions; the Constitution does not permit the president to write laws. While he may explain how he will interpret the law, he should not try to establish a construal of the legislation that clearly contradicts what the bill says.

If the president has serious constitutional concerns about the legislation, the most responsible course of action would be to veto the bill and explain the constitutional violations in his return statement. Even if the bill is popular and might have some good policy outcomes, his constitutional concerns cannot be ignored. Simply approving a bill that he believes is constitutionally suspect does not make it constitutionally whole.

A president will, of course, need good judgment as he makes his determinations. If a bill before him is truly immediately necessary for the public good and he is unsure about constitutionality, he may feel he must make a temporary concession and deal with it later. Presidents Ford and Carter issued 17 signing statements that addressed the constitutionality of the legislative veto, which was ultimately held to be unconstitutional by the Supreme Court.[36] President Reagan signed the Gramm-Rudman-Hollings deficit reduction bill in spite of constitutional concerns about an attack on the executive's appointment power and a legislative veto provision, concerns that were noted in a signing statement. He did, however, support the case against those provisions in court, and his signing statement was included in the majority opinion's first footnote.[37] This, however, is an enormous gamble, as we saw with the Independent Counsel Act being upheld by the Supreme Court.

It also proved to be a bad gamble for President George W. Bush when he signed the Bipartisan Campaign Reform Act on March 27, 2002.[38] As one who disagreed with the bill on both constitutional and policy grounds, George W. Bush would have done well to examine President Jackson's reasoning more carefully. This bill restricted the ability of American citizens to independently purchase political advertisements that supported or criticized political candidates by name 60 days before a general election. It also banned "soft money" contributions to political parties, forcing unions, corporations, and other associations to establish political action committees, which can raise and distribute limited amounts of money according to strict guidelines. This law, which clearly and intentionally regulates political speech, is a flagrant violation of the First Amendment's mandate that "Congress shall make no law . . . abridging the freedom of speech." Additionally, the law (passed by incumbent politicians, of course) increases the advantages of incumbents in political contests. Unknown candidates do not have the trappings of office, a record of constituent service, and a solid contributors' list to aid them in a race. The restrictions on contributions to political parties would severely limit the ability of new entrants in the race to make a credible challenge. During the campaign of 2000, when candidate George W. Bush was asked if he would veto the bill, he said, "[Y]es, I would."[39]

In a statement accompanying the bill, President Bush stated his constitutional concerns:

> Certain provisions present serious constitutional concerns. In particular, H.R. 2356 goes farther than I originally proposed by preventing all individuals, not just unions and corporations, from making donations to political parties in connection with Federal elections. I believe individual freedom to participate in elections should be expanded, not diminished; and when individual freedoms are restricted, questions arise under the First Amendment. I also have reservations about the constitutionality of the broad ban on issue advertising, which restrains the speech of a wide variety of groups on issues of public import in the months closest to an election.[40]

But the president could rest well that night, as he had relieved himself of any constitutional responsibility: "I expect that the courts will resolve these legitimate legal questions as appropriate under the law."

In *McConnell v. FEC,* the Supreme Court did resolve the questions, but not in accordance with the president's earlier wishes.[41] The Court upheld the major provisions of the bill, reinforcing the idea that the Justices are the only governmental actors qualified and authorized to make constitutional judgments.

Christopher Kelley estimates that through signing statements, President Bush raised concerns with almost 1,200 legislative provisions; this is more than twice the number of provisions challenged by all previous presidents.[42] In the statement accompanying the Consolidated Appropriations Act of 2005,[43] the president objected to more than 110 provisions. This is not the strategy of an independent executive. Numerous and vague objections, especially in the same bill, look like petty sniping and weaken the authority of the office. If President Bush understood there to be that much constitutional ambiguity or violation in the bill as a whole, he should have exhibited some "tolerable firmness" and vetoed it.[44]

A proper statement provides other institutional actors insight as to how laws will be enforced and gives them an opportunity to respond. While good administration and the oath of office require the president to veto legislation he considers flatly unconstitutional, signing statements aid in the rule of law when they clarify the president's intentions. As for bills where there are policy disagreements with Congress or constitutional ambiguities, a president may still be able to sign the bill in good conscience and enforce it according to the interpretation he sets forth. This is preferable to a president signing a bill and quietly neglecting its implementation.

The passivity with which President Reagan and President Bush neglected their own constitutional judgment is troubling. The president takes an oath to support the Constitution. Passing on this responsibility is not the kind of defense the framers envisioned. Habitual deference to the judiciary encourages courts to reposition themselves as the final say in important constitutional matters. It becomes a shield behind which the president may hide and avoid responsibility. It incentivizes the president and Congress to accept popular but legally questionable measures; if the Supreme Court overturns a publicly supported measure, it can be blamed.

Administration: Oversight, Appointment, and Removal. Execution of the law requires discretion. Congress statutorily commits authority to executive branch actors. But this policymaking responsibility is divided up among agencies and individuals, and the lack of coordination among them and the fact that they are somewhat accountable to both the president and Congress make organized execution of the law exceedingly difficult.

Since the beginning of the Republic, presidents have made control over the executive branch a serious priority. At a time when the national government did very little compared to what it is responsible for today, George Washington personally examined all correspondence of high executive officials in order to "preserve an unity of object and action among them" and to impose on "himself the due responsibility for whatever was done."[45] As government responsibilities moved into policy areas traditionally managed by state government and private individuals, especially during the New Deal period and beyond, Congress found itself unable to deal with all the regulatory activity of the administrative state. It increasingly delegated broad legislative authority to agencies of its creation and directed them to solve particular problems and meet certain goals. To accomplish this, the agencies could develop "rules" with the force of law.

This has proved to be very convenient for Congress. It can pass measures that are popular with or unknown to the public and move the responsibility for actually crafting policy to the executive branch. If the end result is popular with the public, Congress can claim the praise for initially passing the broad authorization. If mistakes are made in the implementation process or if the measure is otherwise unpopular, Congress can shift political blame to the president, hold hearings, demand executive branch information, and if it so chooses, attempt to overrule the executive action with a regular law.

President Obama has demonstrated a willingness to take control of the executive branch in order to accomplish his regulatory goals. In spite of his earlier concerns about the insertion of the president and politics into rulemaking, he is largely relying on the provisions of Executive Order 12,866, issued by President Clinton, which provides for extensive executive oversight of regulatory activity in order to coordinate policymaking across the agencies.[46] Cass Sunstein, one of the most prominent legal scholars in the United States, was appointed by the president to head the Office of Information and Regulatory Affairs, which reviews draft regulations for compliance with policy goals. He acknowledged in his confirmation hearings that "OIRA has a role to play in promoting compliance with the law and with the President's commitments and priorities."[47]

Helping to shape President Obama's policies and priorities is an unknown and fluctuating number of White House "czars" who deal with issues such as faith-based initiatives, AIDS, domestic violence, and science.[48] Few of these czars occupy positions created by Congress, which require confirmation by the Senate. This puts them entirely in the service of the president and outside of the control of Congress.

Senators such as Kay Bailey Hutchison (R-Texas) and the late Robert Byrd (D-West Virginia) publicly contested the right of the president to have such advisers and claimed separation of powers violations, but there is nothing unconstitutional about these positions. They (czars who have not been confirmed by the Senate) are neither principal nor inferior officers under the appointments clause, and they therefore have no legal authority. When the Senate Judiciary Subcommittee on the Constitution held hearings on the constitutionality of czars, the White House refused to send any officials to meet with the Senators. However, Counsel Gregory Craig submitted a letter in which he reassured members that czars do not "raise valid concerns about accountability, transparency, or congressional oversight" and that the president is committed to protecting "the Constitution and its fundamental system of checks and balances."[49]

Appointments. The appointment power of the president is a primary way for the president to ensure the faithful execution of the laws. Because he appoints principal officers, he can select individuals in whom he can place his trust, and the principle of accountability is protected. The Constitution does not limit the president's choice, but it does require that the nominee be approved by the Senate. However, Congress seeks to control the executive branch through limiting the ability of the president to appoint people of his choosing to positions of trust. For example, a provision in the Omnibus Public Lands Management Act of 2009[50] required the Secretary of the Interior to appoint commission members of the Erie Canalway National Heritage Corridor Commission "based on recommendations from each member of the House of Representatives' whose district encompasses the canal corridor."

President Obama responded to this provision in his signing statement: "Because it would be an impermissible restriction on the appointment power to condition the Secretary's appointments on the recommendations of members of the House, I will construe these provisions to require the Secretary to consider such congressional recommendations, but not to be bound by them in making appointments to the Commission."[51] The president properly defended his constitutional authority from an encroachment that, while it appears to be relatively unimportant in the scheme of things, interfered with his responsibility and may have been used by Congress as a foundation for other restrictions.

Removal. In 2002, Congress passed and President Bush signed the Sarbanes-Oxley Act of 2002. This bill provided for a new Public Company Accounting Oversight Board (PCAOB) to enforce securities laws, commission rules, and accounting standards. The Board is composed of five members serving staggered five-year terms, appointed by the Securities and Exchange Commission (SEC) and removable by them only "for good cause shown." Because the SEC is an independent commission, the president has only limited removal power over its members. Therefore, the members of the PCAOB are doubly insulated from removal by the president.

Eight years after the act went into effect, the Supreme Court correctly, but narrowly, held that this restriction on the president's removal power is an unconstitutional infringement on his duty to faithfully execute the laws, as he is unable to meaningfully supervise Board members.[52] Without a clear hierarchy of responsibility in which the president is at the top, the public is unable to determine where to give praise or lay blame. President Bush should not have supported this bill and the Obama administration should not have defended it in the Supreme Court.

Discretion in the execution of the law is necessary and desirable. Constitutional government requires laws, but it also requires men to make judgments about the enforcement of laws in order for the laws to be effective. Presidents must trust their subordinates and therefore must have practical control over them. Congressional interference should come at the time of confirmation or in shaping public opinion when it is clear an executive branch official is not fit for the job.

Military Operations. As mentioned earlier, the president's power as commander in chief is constitutionally protected. Because of the design of the office, the president is uniquely situated to deal with issues of national self-preservation—the office possesses the secrecy and dispatch required for military and intelligence operations.[53]

But we feel a sort of ambivalence here: The same secrecy and dispatch that is to be employed for our security makes us concerned about the discretion the president exercises. This power is not without limits, but the limits, both constitutional and political, are in some cases hard to define.

Congress has a clear constitutional role regarding national security. Congress may declare war (or, today, authorize military force), advise and consent on treaties and appointments, hold investigative hearings, get information briefings, and fund military and intelligence operations. The last authority is key: There is nothing that can be done without Congress appropriating money for it. This was so essential the framers wisely restricted funding for military purposes to periods of no more than two years in advance. No other enumerated legislative object is so confined. While the president may respond to a clear national security imperative on his own, he cannot continue to act without congressional funding, and he would be wise to seek a specific authorization as George W. Bush did after the terrorist attacks of September 11, 2001. That authorization clearly gave the president the authority to determine the scope of and methods to be used in the War on Terror.[54] Abraham Lincoln sought authorization for his actions during the Civil War, although he waited for more than two and a half months to do so—long enough for him to establish his military program.[55]

The greatest check on a president, however, is public opinion. The president has to make a political case for his actions. A president's claim to action will be weighed against the duration of the operation, perceived strength of the enemy, cost in lives and money, and the political force of domestic opposition. In 2006, Republicans lost the midterm elections, in large part due to the status of the military operations in Afghanistan and Iraq and the inability of the administration to explain what was going on. The president himself could not be unelected, but he was held politically accountable and was forced to fire his Secretary of Defense, Donald Rumsfeld.

The Responsibility of Congress

While Congress in some ways benefits politically from having a large membership and possessing the authority to legislate, it does have institutional qualities that put it at a disadvantage with the president. Because of the number of members, it operates slowly and according to fixed rules. It relies on consensus as the basis of action, which should come after a deliberative process where lawmakers can discuss and debate the merits of legislation. The president may act quickly, changing the rules of the game and forcing Congress (and courts) to acquiesce or respond.

But even with these inconveniences, it is difficult to feel sorry for an institution that cares so little about its own constitutional authority and political responsibility. One need look no further than the Patient Protection and Affordable Care Act of 2010 to see a rather egregious example of this. Whatever one thinks about the policy merits of the legislation, it is not a model of legislative care. The bill is 906 pages long and says "The Secretary shall" 1,018 times.[56] The Speaker of the House said in a speech to a convention of county officials that Congress must "pass the bill, so you can see what is in it, away from the fog of controversy."[57] One member acknowledged that constitutional authority for the law wasn't a concern.[58] Another asked, "What good is reading the bill if it's a thousand pages and you don't have two days and two lawyers to find out what it means after you read the bill?"[59]

So here a Congress delegated an incredible amount of authority to the executive branch without important members having read the bill or considering the constitutionality of it. It is not unreasonable to conclude that in the near future, as executive branch officials start filling in the enormous gaps in the legislation, Congress will not be happy with the results. As rulemaking proceeds and consequences become visible, it is certain that Congress will seek to investigate executive branch decision-making processes and hold others responsible for what should have been done when the law was being created.

Congress could assert itself in constitutional ways that would moderate the president and help make accommodations in times of conflict. Most importantly, Congress could legislate. While discretion is necessary to the execution of law, a Congress that took its legislative responsibility seriously and passed laws instead of delegated authority could bind the president more closely to its will. Instead of attempting to unconstitutionally restrict the president's appointment powers, Congress might use its responsibility to "advise and consent" to hold up confirmations until it is satisfied with the nominees. Congress also holds the purse and can refuse to appropriate money as the president wishes if he is behaving in an arbitrary or unwise fashion. Of course, the biggest constitutional weapon that Congress wields over the president (and other officers of the United States) is impeachment and removal from office. While this has only threatened a few presidents, the possibility of its use could serve as a powerful motivator for proper conduct on the part of the president.

The Role of Federal Courts

This chapter has not much discussed the role of the federal courts in separation of powers issues for the simple reason that I have serious reservations about the wisdom of permitting them to be the final say on what I believe are, for the most part, political questions. The federal judiciary has an important constitutional role in protecting the rights and liberties of American citizens, but in my view, its obligation and ability to resolve interbranch conflicts in areas such as war, executive privilege, and administration are unclear. What is clear is that it is often irresponsible and an abdication of constitutional responsibility on the part of presidents to leave constitutional disputes for the federal courts to resolve. This is true for several reasons.

Judges are not the only smart actors in the American political system. Presidents (and Congress) are capable of exercising good judgment on constitutional matters. Both institutions may have valid claims. How will a court determine who will win and who will lose? What kind of balancing test will be used to come to a conclusion? What kind of evidence will the Supreme Court require each branch to divulge? By what standards will it measure the worth of each claim? Will a court's test be any better than one a president or Congress might say is the best one?

Next, the courts must think about their own legitimacy as they resolve disputes. A federal court might consider whether or not the decision will be enforced, the partisan makeup of the political branches, and the will of the public as much as it may consider the merits of the case.

In addition, while we commonly think of Congress and the presidency as the "political" branches, judges are human and have policy and institutional preferences, too, which may be brought to bear in a constitutional opinion. It is naïve to think that members of the federal judiciary are blind to the stake they have in the outcome of separation of powers questions. Exhibit A is Justice Kennedy's statement in *Boumediene v. Bush,* in which he and four other Justices struck down an act passed by Congress and signed by the president: "[T]he exercise of [the president's commander-in-chief] powers is vindicated, not eroded, when confirmed by the Judicial Branch."[60] The Justice sees the Court as owning *the* stamp of constitutional legitimacy and has confirmed for the Court regular oversight of an area constitutionally committed to the "political" branches.[61]

Finally, it circumvents the political process—even if the "process" includes a long stalemate. At some point, one branch will overplay a hand or another will cave to what it views as necessity. The public will view one institution's claims as more legitimate than the other's or competition between the branches will expose a claim as unjustified. The branches may finally agree on some accommodation of interests. Political power comes and goes. Political debate does not necessarily require and may not be capable of a Court-issued constitutional conclusion. It isn't the job of the Supreme Court to supervise and revitalize the presidency.

While the Supreme Court may be the final word on a matter, that doesn't mean it is the correct one. Presidents have a responsibility to stop unconstitutional measures before they get to the Supreme Court, where a loss has consequences for more than just the current occupant of the Oval Office. Of course, a president risks defeat when he vetoes a piece of popular legislation or enforces the law in a way that he understands is consistent with the Constitution. But a temporary political setback is preferable to a "constitutionalized" judicial loss, and here again, the competition between the elected branches can prove to be useful and instructive.

Conclusion

When there is conflict between the branches, Madison's solution here is best: Ambition must be made to counteract ambition. The governed are controlled, and the government has incentives to control itself. Individual actors must be personally interested in defending their offices. Congress should not attempt to dilute the strength of executive ambition at the expense of its own. Congress has a vital role to play, and when it attempts to impersonate the executive through unconstitutional means, it neglects its own role.

Presidents should not be afraid to make the first move in defending their offices. Waiting for the Supreme Court or a public majority may not be timely or sufficient to overcome a constitutional challenge. Had President Reagan vetoed the Independent Counsel Act, it is likely he would have taken a short-term political hit. But he would have saved the office of the presidency a great deal of trouble, and he would have had an opportunity to instruct the public on the merits of his decision. In the same vein, presidents should display energy in making appointments of high quality and character and removing those who do not prove both. Good administration can be quickly stifled by charges of incompetence and wrongdoing, as was seen in the Clinton and George W. Bush administrations.

An energetic president is a discerning president. Just because he is able to do something does not mean it is done. He must resist the temptation to serve only his immediately political interests and instead think about the long-term consequences of his actions for his office. He will reserve his rhetorical authority to support deliberation and education, not to repeatedly call attention to trivial, short-term matters. He will not label all events "crises" and then misplace energy on matters that do not require it.

The unitary executive is the responsible, constitutional executive. It does not allow the president to "conceal faults and destroy responsibility,"[62] yet it permits discretion in administration and national security. A prudent and consistent defense of the constitutional powers of the president ensures they will be properly preserved for succeeding executives.

Notes

1. United States Senate, "Majority and Minority Leaders and Party Whips," accessed July 29, 2010, http://www.senate.gov/artandhistory/history/common/briefing/Majority_Minority_Leaders.htm.
2. Peter Baker, "Congress; When 535 Take on Number 1," *The New York Times,* October 5, 2008, accessed July 15, 2010, http://query.nytimes.com/gst/fullpage.html?res=9901E3DB1339F936A35753C1A96E9C8B63. "The 'unitary executive' theory he embraced held that because the Constitution provides for only one executive branch, Congress cannot intrude upon the president's duties to manage the government. . . . Mr. Bush and Mr. Cheney advanced their cause for years—the secret deliberations of an energy task force; the Patriot Act; 'signing statements' that express reservations about enforcing a bill; warrantless surveillance; unrestricted detention of terrorism suspects; the reinterpretation of the Geneva Conventions."
3. The oath is in quotation marks in Article II, Section 1. In 2009, Chief Justice Roberts misspoke as he gave President-elect Obama the oath of office. Although it was probably unnecessary, President Obama took the oath again the following day.

4. *Federalist* No. 49, 311.
5. Article I, Section 7. The president may also veto a bill on policy grounds. See *Federalist* No. 73, 439–445.
6. "The persons, therefore, to whose immediate management [the matters of government administration] are committed ought to be considered as the assistants or deputies of the Chief Magistrate, and on this account they ought to derive their offices from his appointment, at least from his nomination, and ought to be subject to his superintendence." Hamilton, *Federalist* No. 72, 434.
7. Article II, Section 2, cl. 1.
8. *Federalist* No. 74, 446.
9. Article II, Section 2.
10. *Federalist* No. 70, 425.
11. 487 U.S. 654 (1988).
12. Steven Calabresi and Christopher Yoo, *The Unitary Executive* (New Haven, CT: Yale University Press, 2008).
13. Ibid., 418.
14. Ibid., 431.
15. John Yoo, "Unitary, Executive, or Both?" *University of Chicago Law Review* 76 (2009): 2018.
16. Ibid., 2004–2017.
17. Calabresi and Yoo, 173.
18. Accessed February 29, 2011, http://teachingamericanhistory.org/library/index.asp?document=423.
19. See, for example, John Yoo, "The Terrorist Surveillance Program and the Constitution," *George Mason Law Review* 14 (2007): 565.
20. Calabresi and Yoo, 411.
21. John Yoo notes, "Presidents can also err when they misread conditions or turn their powers to purposes not envisioned by the Constitution." "Unitary, Executive, or Both?" 2018.
22. For example, President George W. Bush had the right to fire U. S. Attorneys. However, the manner in which the firing of several U.S. Attorneys in 2006 was imprudent, as was the way the administration handled the aftermath. As a result, the public view of the presidency was diminished. See Mark Rozell, "Executive Privilege and the U.S. Attorneys Firings," *Presidential Studies Quarterly* 38, no. 2 (June 2008): 315–328.
23. *Federalist* No. 48, 306.
24. *Federalist* No. 51, 320.
25. President Obama restrained such interference in his Statement on the Signing of the Ronald Reagan Centennial Commission Act, accessed August 12, 2010, http://www.presidency.ucsb.edu/ws/index.php?pid=86243.
26. Article II, Section 3.
27. *Federalist* No. 73, 444.
28. Ibid., 442. See also 441, 443.
29. Ibid., 443.
30. 50 USC 1541–1548 (c. 33). 1973. Richard Nixon, "Veto of the War Powers Resolution," October 24, 1973, accessed August 14, 2010, http://www.presidency.ucsb.edu/ws/print.php?pid=4021.

31. President Bush also opposed a provision in the bill that appropriated money for a United Nations fund that he argued supported coercive abortion. George H. W. Bush, "Message to the House of Representatives Returning Without Approval the Foreign Operations, Export Financing, and Related Programs Appropriations Act, 1990," November 19, 1989, accessed July 29, 2010, http://www.presidency.ucsb.edu/ws/index.php?pid=17835&st=veto&st1.

32. Ronald Reagan, "Statement on Signing the Independent Counsel Reauthorization Act of 1987," December 15, 1987, accessed August 14, 2010, http://www.presidency.ucsb.edu/ws/index.php?pid=33827.

33. *McCulloch v. Maryland,* 17 US 316 (1819).

34. Andrew Jackson, "Veto Message of the Bill on the Bank of the United States," July 10, 1832, accessed July 28, 2010, http://teachingamericanhistory.org/library/index.asp?document=64. He also objected to the bank on policy grounds.

35. *Federalist* No. 73, 442.

36. Christopher S. Kelley, "The Presidential Signing Statement," in *Executing the Constitution: Putting the President Back Into the Constitution,"* ed. Christopher S. Kelley (Albany: State University of New York Press, 2006), 77.

37. Ibid., 78. *Bowsher v. Synar,* 478 US 714 (1986).

38. Public Law 107–155, 116 Stat. 81, March 27, 2002.

39. Robert P. Beard, "Whacking the Political Money 'Mole' without Whacking Speech: Accounting for Congressional Self-Dealing in Campaign Finance Reform after Wisconsin Right to Life," *University of Illinois Law Review,* no. 2 (March 2008), 10.

40. George W. Bush, "Statement on Signing the Bipartisan Campaign Reform Act of 2002," March 27, 2002, accessed August 14, 2010, http://www.presidency.ucsb.edu/ws/index.php?pid=64503.

41. *McConnell v. FEC,* 540 U.S. 93 (2003). The Solicitor General of the United States, Ted Olson, argued this case before the Supreme Court.

42. Charlie Savage, "Obama Looks to Limit Impact of Tactic Bush Used to Sidestep New Laws," *The New York Times,* March 9, 2009, accessed July 18, 2010, http://www.nytimes.com/2009/03/10/us/politics/10signing.html.

43. Public Law 108–447, 2004.

44. President Obama issued a similar statement when he signed the Omnibus Appropriations Act of 2009, accessed July 29, 2010, http://www.presidency.ucsb.edu/ws/index.php?pid=85848. Some sympathy may be felt for presidents on appropriations bills, as the bills have become a way for Congress to manipulate the president.

45. Thomas Jefferson, as quoted in Christopher C. DeMuth and Douglas H. Ginsburg, "White House Review of Agency Rulemaking," *Harvard Law Review* 99 (1986), 1079.

46. Executive Order 12,866, "Regulatory Planning and Review," *Code of Federal Regulations,* Title 3, p. 638 (1993).

47. "OIRA Nominee Sunstein Promises Law and Pragmatism Will Guide Decisions," OMBWatch, May 19, 2009, accessed August 12, 2010, http://www.ombwatch.org/node/10010.

48. President Obama's 'Czars,'" *Politico.com,* September 4, 2009, accessed August 12, 2010, http://dyn.politico.com/printstory.cfm?uuid=870D765C-18FE-70B2-A86B-4FAE48EF7FBB . Presidents have been appointing czars to manage policy initiatives for decades.

49. Gregory Craig, Letter to Senator Russell Feingold, October 5, 2009, accessed August 12, 2010, http://theplumline.whorunsgov.com/wp-content/uploads/2009/10/feingold-letter.pdf accessed April 10, 2011.

50. Public Law 111–11.

51. Barack Obama, "Statement on Signing the Omnibus Public Land Management Act of 2009," March 30, 2009, accessed August 12, 2010, http://www.presidency.ucsb.edu/ws/index.php?pid=85926.

52. *Free Enterprise Fund v. Public Company Accounting Oversight Board*, 561 U.S. __ (2010), accessed August 11, 2010, http://www.supremecourt.gov/opinions/09pdf/08-861.pdf.

53. "Of all the cares or concerns of government, the direction of war most peculiarly demands those qualities which distinguish the exercise of power by a single hand." Alexander Hamilton, *Federalist* No. 74, 446.

54. Public Law 107-40 (2001), "Authorization for the Use of Military Force." Accessed May 21, 2011, http://www.gpo.gov/fdsys/pkg/PLAW-107publ40/content-detail.html.

55. Abraham Lincoln, Message to Congress in Special Session, July 4, 1861. Accessed May 19, 2011, http://teachingamericanhistory.org/library/index.asp?document=1063.

56. Public Law 111–148 (2010). Accessed February 22, 2011, http://www.gpo.gov/fdsys/pkg/PLAW-111publ148/pdf/PLAW-111publ148.pdf .

57. Peter Roff, "Pelosi: Pass Health Reform So You Can Find Out What's In It," *US News Politics and Policy*, March 9, 2010, accessed August 12, 2010, http://politics.usnews.com/opinion/blogs/peter-roff/2010/03/09/pelosi-pass-health-reform-so-you-can-find-out-whats-in-it.html.

58. Congressman James Clyburn, in an interview with Judge Andrew Napolitano, accessed August 12, 2010, http://www.youtube.com/watch?v=ooXcqp46A64.

59. Congressman John Conyers, in Victoria McGraine, "Read the Bill? It Might Not Help," *Politico.com*, September 8, 2009, accessed August 14, 2010, http://www.politico.com/news/stories/0909/26846.html.

60. 553 US 723 (2008). Accessed February 19, 2011, http://supreme.justia.com/us/553/06–1195/.

61. This is most distressing in matters of war, which, compared to other issues, are the least susceptible to judicial discovery and resolution and most in need of the "decision, activity, secrecy, and dispatch" of the executive. *Federalist* No. 70. See also Justice Thomas's dissent in *Hamdi v. Rumsfeld*, 542 US 507 (2004). Accessed May 16, 2011, http://www.law.cornell.edu/supct/html/03-6696.ZD1.html.

62. *Federalist* No. 70.

CHAPTER 6

Libertarians and the Presidency

Gene Healy

What a Libertarian Believes

I am a libertarian. As a libertarian, I believe that people own themselves, the fruits of their labor, and whatever property they peacefully acquire—and that they should be free to run their own lives without interference, so long as they respect the equal rights of others to do the same.[1] I believe, with Thomas Paine, that "government in its best state is but a necessary evil"—and that any government that goes much beyond guaranteeing our basic rights is well on its way toward becoming intolerable.[2]

In the Red-Team/Blue-Team fights that dominate contemporary political discourse, progressives and neoconservatives consider themselves bitter enemies. Yet when it comes to their basic philosophies of government, the two camps are as one. Both are dead set against the libertarian view that securing peace and prosperity is a mission that's ambitious enough by far for any government.

"Wishing to be left alone isn't a governing doctrine," neoconservatives William Kristol and David Brooks chide in their brief for "national greatness conservatism."[3] Modern liberals agree that good governance requires far loftier goals than simply securing Americans' rights to live their lives as they choose. Though they're less bellicose than neoconservatives, latter-day progressives tend to romanticize the notion of "the Good War"—and long for war's "moral equivalent"—some transformative cause that might help us realize our national destiny, uniting Americans in the service of a higher calling.[4] From the perspective of modern progressives and "national greatness conservatives," then, libertarians cling to a woefully cramped and ignoble view of the State's proper role.

Guilty as charged: We libertarians believe, with John Locke, that the sole legitimate purpose of government is to protect individuals' rights to life, liberty, and property. And we hold, with Thomas Jefferson, that governments are instituted among men to secure those rights, deriving their just powers from the consent of the governed.

In fact, Jefferson's first inaugural address neatly sums up what libertarians advocate in domestic and foreign policy. At home, we favor "a wise and frugal Government, which shall restrain men from injuring one another [and] shall leave them otherwise free to regulate their own pursuits of industry and improvement," without taking "from the mouth of labor the bread it has earned." Abroad, we support "peace, commerce, and honest friendship with all nations, entangling alliances with none."[5]

It's more complicated than that, of course. Libertarians are a fractious bunch, given to quarreling over first principles and the policies that flow from them. Wade into the intellectual mosh pit of the libertarian movement, and you'll find yourself slamming up against "libertarian consequentialists" (who favor liberty because it leads to good outcomes) and "libertarian deontologists" (who support strict respect for rights regardless of the consequences). You'll be bounced between "minarchists" (who back a Lockean "nightwatchman state") and "anarcho-capitalists" (who insist that even the minimal state can't possibly be justified).[6]

Skepticism Toward Power

But if there's a common belief unifying the various quarrelsome factions in the political movement I call home—if there's something on which we eccentrics all can agree—it's this: *Human beings are fallible creatures, and they cannot be trusted with unchecked power.*

"The first principle of libertarian social analysis," David Boaz writes in *The Libertarian Reader,* "is a concern about the concentration of power." It's for good reason that Boaz assembled the first set of essays in that tome under the heading "Skepticism Toward Power."[7]

Libertarians' skepticism toward power flows from empirically well-grounded doubts about human nature and man's ability to resist power's temptations.[8] Though as a class, we libertarians contain more than our share of atheists and free-thinkers, most of us would agree with the Catholic intellectual G. K. Chesterton, who wrote that original sin is "the only part of Christian theology which can really be proved."[9]

In this, we libertarians aren't quite as eccentric as we might appear at first. In fact, we're firmly within the American political tradition. As Bernard Bailyn writes in *The Ideological Origins of the American Revolution,* his classic study of founding-era political thought, for the early Americans, "what turned power into a malignant force, was not its own nature so much as the nature of man—his susceptibility to corruption and his lust for self-aggrandizement. On this there was absolute agreement."[10]

The Anti-Federalist opponents of the Constitution are known as "men of little faith."[11] Though the Constitution's partisans favored a more powerful central government, they weren't all that doe-eyed and trusting themselves. As one scholar described the *Federalist Papers,* "A considerable portion of the book might be said to be a development of Lord Acton's aphorism: 'Power corrupts and absolute power corrupts absolutely.'"[12]

By 1789, Bailyn wrote, the Federalists had "scotched the fear of an effective national executive, showed its necessity and benignity in the American situation. But they continued to believe, as deeply as any of the militants of '76, that power corrupts . . . that any release of the constraints on the executive—any executive— was an invitation to disaster."[13]

The Constitutional Presidency

With that in mind, the framers of the Constitution designed a modest presidency with limited powers. At home and abroad, the constitutional president's role was mostly managerial and defensive. On the domestic front, he'd "take care that the laws be faithfully executed," and occasionally check Congress with the veto when it tried to slip its constitutional bonds.[14] In foreign affairs, he'd have the power to "repel sudden attacks" and negotiate treaties for the Senate to ratify if they so chose.[15] But the framers' president had no constitutional power to start wars uni- laterally, much less ignore validly enacted laws when he thought they hampered his pursuit of America's national security interests.

Twenty-first-century Americans, who've grown up with an omnipresent, domineering chief executive, would find it bewildering to hear a president strike the deferential note that President James Monroe did in an 1822 message to Congress:

> Of these [branches] the legislative . . . is by far the most important. The whole system of the National Government may be said to rest essentially on the power granted to this branch. They mark the limit within which, with few exceptions, all the branches must move in the discharge of their respective functions.[16]

And yet, in that address, Monroe accurately described the constitutional struc- ture of the early Republic.

We often hear it said that ours is a government of "co-equal branches," but, as Garry Wills points out, given the relative powers each branch has under the Con- stitution, "co-equal" is a misnomer:

> Congress can remove officers from the other two branches—President, agency heads, judges in district or supreme courts. Neither of the other two branches can touch a member of the Congress. Congress sets the pay for the other two and also for itself. It decides on the structure of the other two departments, creating or abolishing agencies and courts.[17]

Moreover, Article I, Section 8's so-called "Sweeping Clause" gave Congress considerable authority to guard against abuses of executive power by limiting the means by which the president carried out his duties.[18]

The framers didn't conceive of the president as America's "national leader." The very notion raised the disturbing possibility of authoritarian rule by a demagogue, bent on stoking an atmosphere of crisis in order to enhance his power.[19] The legislative branch, not the executive, was to be the prime mover in setting national policy.

That didn't make Congress America's national leader, competent to legislate on every area of human endeavor. The powers of the national government as a whole were "few and defined," and in Congress's case, limited to those enumerated in Article I, Section 8.[20]

As Madison put it in *Federalist* 51, "In a republican government, the legislative authority necessarily predominates." In other systems, that "inconveniency" allowed legislatures to erode checks on their power.[21] In the American system, however, legislative dominance would be tempered by restricting legislative authority, dividing Congress into separate houses, and fortifying the president with the veto power.

By wielding the veto, the president could protect his constitutional prerogatives and interpose himself between Congress and the People whenever Congress acted beyond its authority. Denied the exalted roles of People's Tribune and Chief Legislator, the framers' president got to play a part that was at once humbler and more important: Constitutional Guardian.

Even in foreign affairs, where the chief executive's powers are thought to be broadest, the constitutional president's role was, again, mainly defensive. Just as the president could command the militia to suppress rebellions, should it be "called into the actual Service of the United States," he could lead the Army and the Navy into battle, should Congress choose to declare war.[22]

As " first General" of the United States, in Hamilton's phrase, the president had an important role, but generals do not have the power to decide whether, when, and with whom we go to war.[23] "In no part of the constitution is more wisdom to be found," Madison wrote, "than in the clause which confides the question of war or peace to the legislature, and not to the executive department. . . . The trust and the temptation would be too great for any one man."[24]

The framers knew that mere "parchment barriers against the encroaching spirit of power" wouldn't be enough to keep the federal government limited or to prevent any one branch from securing powers the Constitution denied it.[25] Instead, they thought the constitutional architecture itself would channel man's lust for power in a manner that preserved individual liberty and limited government. The trick, Madison wrote, was "so contriving the interior structure of the government as that its several constituent parts may, by their mutual relations, be the means of keeping each other in their proper places."[26]

The Constitution the framers designed was supported by vertical and horizontal checks on power. And the framers expected government officials at all levels to have the requisite incentive to man the barricades against those who sought to overwhelm those checks.

The states would provide a vertical check against the pressure for centralization, aided in that effort by a Senate appointed by, and dependent on, the state legislatures.[27] In the original design, senators were "ambassadors" from their respective states to the federal Union, and thus could be expected to stand firm against federal encroachments on the states' retained authorities.[28]

Horizontal checks, at the federal level, depended on each branch jealously defending its turf to maintain the separation of powers. "The great security against a gradual concentration of the several powers in the same department," Madison wrote, "consists in giving to those who administer each department the necessary constitutional means and personal motives to resist encroachments of the others. . . . Ambition must be made to counteract ambition."[29]

In the Madisonian vision, then, separation of powers, like federalism, was supposed to be largely self-executing. "The interest of the man"—that is, the ambitions of individual representatives, judges, and presidents—would lead each to defend "the constitutional rights of the place": the authority of the particular branch each occupied.[30] That, not the fond hope that political actors would forever respect the formalities of the national charter, would keep government limited and prevent any one branch from commandeering powers belonging to the others.

And yet, from the long vantage point of 2011, it seems that things haven't quite worked out as planned.

The Problem

From a libertarian perspective, the fundamental problem with the presidency is that the office long ago slipped its constitutional bonds, concentrating enormous, unchecked powers in the hands of one fallible human being. The modern presidency increasingly resembles Madison's nightmare, "the accumulation of all powers, legislative, executive, and judiciary, in the same hands"—a situation he termed "the very definition of tyranny."[31]

As it's become Madison's nightmare, the modern presidency has become a libertarian's nightmare too: an ever-greater threat to individual rights and the rule of law. Those are core libertarian values, but they're core *American* values as well. No American of any political stripe should be entirely comfortable with what the presidency has become: an institution that trusts one man with the power to launch wars at will and reshape vast swathes of American law via executive order.

In fact, many Americans *do* seem distinctly uncomfortable with the powers and privileges the modern "commander in chief" enjoys. All too often, though, that discomfort is clouded by Red-Team/Blue-Team partisanship. Human nature being what it is, people are more inclined to appreciate the virtues of a restrained presidency when "the other team" seizes power. The tendency to support enhanced executive power when one's friends hold the executive branch—aptly dubbed "Situational Constitutionalism"—is a vice to which far too many of us fall prey.[32]

Even so, surely it says something that, for decades now, each new president has faced an increasingly precipitous "decay curve" in his popularity—and that average presidential approval ratings have declined from one president to the next.[33]

Most Americans only see the presidency through a partisan lens, darkly. But more and more are coming to recognize the truth: that the institution has become a constitutional monstrosity—at once menacing and ineffective. It promises everything and guarantees nothing, save public frustration and the steady growth of federal power.

Since diagnosis precedes cure, before we embark on "reforming the presidency," we need to get a clear idea of what's wrong with it—and we need to understand the forces that made the institution the threat to liberty it is today.

Toward that end, in this section, I briefly trace the growth of presidential power abroad and at home. Then, before turning to possible reforms, I examine some of the factors that have transformed the office from a modest "chief magistracy" to an unholy amalgam of national redeemer, all-purpose problem solver, and Supreme Warlord of the Earth.

The Imperial Presidency and the National Security State

Since the middle of the last century, American presidents have effectively enjoyed the power to take the country into war unilaterally—the Constitution's Declare War clause notwithstanding. They can do so either by bypassing Congress entirely—as Harry Truman did in the Korean War—or by intimidating the legislature into punting its power to declare war to the executive branch—as LBJ did with Vietnam.

Korea marked a constitutional Rubicon—the first major conflict in which a U.S. president explicitly asserted that he didn't need legislative authorization to launch a full-scale war. Over 33,000 American soldiers, most of them conscripts, died without the courtesy of an up-or-down vote on the war from their representatives in Congress.

The 58,000 who died in Vietnam got a vote of sorts, but it wasn't worth much. The Gulf of Tonkin resolution, passed on the basis of false testimony from Johnson administration officials, left the final decision about whether to go to war entirely in the hands of the president.[34] LBJ compared the resolution to "Grandma's nightshirt," because it "covered everything."[35] By 1968, according to newly released transcripts from the Senate Foreign Relations Committee's closed-session debates over Vietnam, committee chairman Sen. J. William Fulbright (D-AR) feared that Congress had become "a useless appendix on the governmental structure."[36]

Nothing that's happened since has given us much reason to doubt Fulbright's epitaph for Congress. For the last six decades, the pattern of presidential warmaking has been fairly steady: For small wars like Grenada, Panama, and Kosovo, the Chief won't even bother to seek congressional approval.[37] For larger conflicts, like the last two Iraq Wars, he'll deign to ask for congressional "support," while denying it's in any sense mandatory.[38]

No surprise, then, that the 2002 congressional "debate" over the Iraq War produced the 21st-century equivalent of the Tonkin Gulf resolution: a measure that gave the president all the authority he needed to attack Iraq if and when he decided to and allowed prominent members of Congress to insist (however unconvincingly) that they hadn't really voted to use force.[39]

Today, many conservatives cling to the comforting notion that we can have unbridled presidential discretion abroad and limited government at home.[40] As Madison recognized, though, war is "the true nurse of executive aggrandizement."[41] America's experience in the Cold War and the War on Terror should by now have made that all too clear.

In the mid-1970s, the investigations of a select committee chaired by Senator Frank Church (D-ID) revealed the frightening extent to which the Cold War–era national security state had been turned inward, threatening liberty on the home front. For three decades, the National Security Agency reviewed virtually all telegrams to and from the United States, while Army intelligence operatives maintained a domestic watch list of over 100,000 Americans, including such dangerous security threats as folk singers Arlo Guthrie and Joan Baez.[42] In its concluding report, the Church Committee observed, "Executive power, not founded in law or checked by Congress or the courts, contained the seeds of abuse and its growth was to be expected."[43]

The Church Committee's revelations led to reinvigorated checks on the president's national security powers. But three decades later, in the crisis atmosphere of 9/11, the federal government abandoned most of those checks, as the "War on Terror" blurred whatever line once supposedly insulated the home front from the wartime presidency unbound.[44]

In a "war" that began in lower Manhattan and Northern Virginia, America was a battlefield, President Bush insisted, and on that battlefield, there could be only one commander in chief. Tapping Americans' phones and reading their e-mail became "gathering battlefield intelligence," to be conducted free from judicial oversight.[45] The president could even seize American citizens on American soil and lock them up for the duration of the struggle—that is, perhaps forever—without ever having to answer to a judge.[46]

As the 2008 presidential campaign approached, those who recoiled from Bush's extravagant claims looked to Barack Obama, allegedly America's "first civil libertarian president," to rein in the burgeoning "Terror Presidency."[47]

No such luck: As Jack Goldsmith, former head of Bush's Office of Legal Counsel, put it, despite new "packaging," the Obama administration "has copied most of the Bush program," even "expanded some of it."[48] Nearly three years into the Obama era, it's apparent that what the new president has delivered is the same old imperial presidency—now with new, "hopier" rhetoric.

The Obama team no longer calls terrorist suspects "enemy combatants," perhaps finding the Bush-era term too harsh. But that softer rhetoric obscures a drive for unchecked authority that would do George W. Bush proud. In April 2010, the Obama administration let slip a startling announcement: They'd targeted an American citizen living abroad for summary execution, based solely on the executive branch's determination that he posed a threat to American national security.[49] Just as President Bush once insisted that his Magic Scepter of Inherent Authority allowed him to ignore federal laws against torture, the new administration seems to be arguing "that Obama has the authority as Commander-in-Chief to ignore the foreign-murder statute."[50]

Even before he took office, Barack Obama signaled that, for privacy advocates, his presidency would be heavy on the "Hope," light on the "Change." On the campaign trail, he'd promised to filibuster any legislation granting immunity to FISA-flouting telecom companies. He broke that promise in the summer of 2008, when, as a senator, he voted for the FISA Amendments Act, legalizing large swaths of a dragnet surveillance program he'd long claimed to oppose.[51] Worse still, as president, Obama has embraced the Bush-Cheney position that the State Secrets Privilege bars the courthouse door to litigants who claim they've been harmed by warrantless wiretapping—that, in essence, the government can never be sued for unlawful surveillance.[52]

As the Church Committee hearings documented, during the Cold War, unrestrained surveillance powers allowed the executive branch to shift easily from guarding against foreign threats to spying on peaceful citizens. Even so, the technological limitations of the time provided an upper bound to potential mischief. In the '60s and '70s, keeping tabs on dissenters was a low-tech affair of paper files and index cards, requiring government agents to physically open letters and individually review telegrams.

Our burgeoning 21st-century "National Surveillance State" is a different beast entirely. In July 2010, *The Washington Post* published "Top Secret America," a three-part investigative report on the post-9/11 "Intelligence-Industrial Complex." Over the last decade, the executive branch has erected vast pyramids in the name of homeland security, with some 1,200 agencies filling up nearly three Pentagons of new office space. Now, "every day, collection systems at the National Security

Agency intercept and store 1.7 billion e-mails, phone calls and other types of communications."[53] With modern processing power and data-mining technology, the possibilities for surveillance are staggering. And so is the potential for abuse.[54]

Presidential Imperialism at Home

Surely, though, the modern president's powers are far more limited—and thus less susceptible to abuse—in domestic areas that don't involve national security. After all, as political scientist Aaron Wildavsky posited in an influential 1966 article, we really have "Two Presidencies": one with broad authority over foreign affairs, and another with comparatively limited ability to work its will on the home front.[55]

There's something to the Wildavsky thesis. Though the modern president has a free hand in foreign policy, he can't intone "make it so!" and unilaterally rework our campaign finance system or summarily mandate universal health care coverage.

And yet, in areas far removed from foreign policy, Congress's eagerness to delegate lawmaking authority to the executive has given modern presidents enormous power to reshape the law via executive fiat.

The Constitution vests "All [the] legislative Powers" it grants in Congress and emphasizes that the president is supposed to *execute,* not *make,* the laws.[56] Yet the post–New Deal administrative state leaves most actual lawmaking power in the hands of the executive branch. It happens like this: Congress passes a statute endorsing a high-minded goal—accommodation of the handicapped, reduced air pollution, security against "systemic" financial risk—and leaves it to the relevant executive-branch body to issue and enforce the regulations governing individual behavior.[57] The result is that most of the rules that citizens today have to follow, at pain of fine or imprisonment, are generated by unelected administrative agencies that add over 75,000 new pages to the *Federal Register* each year. That gives the president enormous power to make the laws he's tasked with enforcing, either by exercising his authority over the administrative state, or skipping the middleman, and directly issuing executive orders.

In the first century of the Republic, when Congress still served as the country's principal lawmaker, presidents issued only about 300 executive orders. Yet as his responsibilities expanded, so too did the chief executive's power to govern by decree. From Truman through Nixon, presidents issued over 2,400 executive orders, which became increasingly indistinguishable from legislative acts.[58] "Stroke of the pen. Law of the land. Kinda cool," as President Clinton's adviser Paul Begala once put it.[59]

In the early 1980s, bright young things in the Reagan Justice Department looked at the enormous administrative authority the modern president had accrued and saw a ring of power that could be used for good. The original architects of unitary executive theory in Reagan's Justice Department viewed the presidency as "a friendly institution," and they argued that he should use his constitutional powers to rein in aggressive regulators.[60]

In an era when the GOP held a virtual lock on the electoral college, that idea had great appeal for Republicans. But as former Clinton policy adviser (now Supreme Court Justice) Elena Kagan pointed out in a 2001 *Harvard Law Review* article, after the Democrats lost control of Congress in 1994, President Bill Clinton used his administrative authority to push "a distinctly activist and pro-regulatory agenda." There's little reason, Kagan argued, to think that "presidential supervision of administration inherently cuts in a deregulatory direction."[61]

Thus far, the Obama administration's regulatory policies have more than validated Kagan's observation. *The New York Times* hailed a "new aggressiveness" from Obama's new regulatory "cops on the beat," quoting the president's budget director to the effect that "smart regulation can make people's lives better off."[62] Among the Obama administration's new initiatives is an FDA plan to lower the level of sodium allowed in American food, the better to "adjust the American palate to a less salty diet."[63]

And despite massive resistance to "cap and trade" on the Hill, President Obama believes that he has the authority to implement comprehensive climate change regulation, congressional opposition be damned. Alas, under current constitutional law—which has little to do with the actual Constitution—he's right.[64]

An April 2009 study by the New York University Law School argues—fairly convincingly—that the president has the power to go even further than he's thus far appeared willing to do. "If Congress fails to act on global warming," the authors maintain, "President Obama has the power under the Clean Air Act to adopt a cap-and-trade system."[65] Even staunch supporters of greenhouse gas regulation ought to be a bit unsettled by the notion that, in a democratic country, the president could massively restructure domestic energy use without specific authority from Congress.

In "The Two Presidencies," Professor Wildavsky observed that, on occasion, "great crises" could enhance the president's domestic policy powers, allowing him to shape policy on the home front as thoroughly as he dominates affairs abroad. Rahm Emanuel, President Obama's chief of staff, seemed to understand that intuitively when he declared, "You never want a serious crisis to go to waste. . . . [It] provides the opportunity for us to do things that you could not do before."[66]

Though that statement raised GOP hackles, the financial collapse of 2008 had already driven Congress toward new frontiers in delegation well before Emanuel's boss took office. With the Emergency Economic Stabilization Act of 2008, better known as the "TARP law," Congress handed the power of the purse over to the executive branch, making Treasury Secretary Henry Paulson the modern equivalent of a Roman dictator for economic affairs. During Bush's "last 100 days," Paulson used that near-bottomless font of authority to decide which financial institutions would live and which would die.[67]

In December 2008, after Congress refused to bail out General Motors and Chrysler, Bush announced that he'd decided to use TARP authority to do it anyway.[68] "This is not the way we wanted to deal with this issue," White House spokesman Tony Fratto explained, but what could we do? "Congress lost its opportunity to be a partner because they couldn't get their job done."[69]

Some on Capitol Hill angrily protested, demanding to know how the auto bailout could possibly be authorized by a law allowing the purchase of "troubled assets" from "financial institutions." Yet those terms were so loosely defined in the TARP statute Congress had just passed that Bush and Obama had a colorable argument for reshaping the bailout as they saw fit. Here congressional outrage was more than a day late and $700 billion short.[70]

Thus far, Barack Obama has vigorously exercised the powers George W. Bush left him: doubling the amount of TARP funds available to GM and using the federal government's 60 percent ownership of the automaker's stock to install a Treasury-appointed board of directors that quickly rolled over when the government demanded environmentally friendly cars.[71]

On the campaign trail in 2008, then-presidential candidate Hillary Clinton declared, "We need a president who is ready on *day one* to be *commander in chief of our economy*."[72] That extraconstitutional notion sounded risible at the time.[73] Yet today, we have a president who can appoint a czar to set executive pay at major companies and summarily fire the CEO of GM. "Commander in chief of our economy" isn't far off.

How We Got Here

If the unchecked power the modern president exercises is a problem—and it is—it's worth thinking about how we got the presidency we have. What accounts for the office's transformation from a humble, legally constrained institution, to the awkward, menacing colossus that dominates our politics today? Three factors stand out: our imperial role abroad, flaws in the Madisonian design, and, perhaps most importantly, the American people's apparently insatiable demand for presidential solutions to all manner of national problems.

The modern president's role as the guarantor of international peace greatly increases the odds of war and the centralization of executive power war brings. After all, the *Federalist* reminds us, "It is of the nature of war to increase the executive at the expense of the legislative authority."[74]

Today, the United States spends more on "defense" than the next 18 countries combined and nearly half of what the rest of the world spends put together.[75] By creating a vast empire of 700 military bases in some 144 countries across the globe,

Congress has virtually ensured that the president would have ample opportunity to act first and ask permission later—or, more likely, dare the legislature to cut off funds for the troops he's sent into battle.[76]

Yet our overextension abroad doesn't fully explain how the modern president has come to dominate and overawe Congress. To account for that, we need to consider the flaws in Madison's vision of a constitutionally self-reinforcing separation of powers.

Recall that in the Madisonian theory, the ambition of presidents was to be met and checked by the ambition of legislators. Clearly, when it comes to Congress, that incentive structure has failed. Its failure is, in large part, a result of the divergence between the interests of individual legislators and the interests of Congress as a whole. "Congress" is an abstraction. Congresspeople and senators are not, and their most basic interest is in getting reelected.[77]

For most members, party loyalty appears greatly to outweigh loyalty to the institution, which gives presidents an especially free hand under unified government. When one party holds both branches, presidential vetoes greatly decrease, and delegation of legislative authority skyrockets.[78]

Delegation is a "political shell game," says New York Law School's David Schoenbrod, allowing legislators to "kiss both sides of the apple," taking credit when the executive branch uses its delegated authority wisely and railing against the bureaucracy when it doesn't.[79]

That scam works for Congress in large part because the American public, conditioned by the media's relentless focus on presidential action, views the president as "our perennial main character, occupying center stage during almost all dramas in national political life."[80] The fact that the federal chief executive is front and center on the nightly news whenever there's a significant economic downturn, a hurricane, or a terrorist attack reinforces the view that he alone is responsible for, and capable of, dealing with the emergency of the week, whatever it may be.

Unitary executive theory exploits that atavistic impulse, Cynthia Farina argues: It "tells us a story we want to hear."[81] In the confusing modern world, which seems to present endless complications and threats, we want desperately to believe that someone's "in charge"—to the point of embracing the transparently false notion that a president who sits atop an executive branch of over 2 million employees meaningfully controls what they do and can prevent them from making mistakes. But "president-centered government cannot deliver what it promises," Farina writes—and in the promising, it threatens the careful checks the framers placed on presidential power: "Any power the leader needs to meet the danger becomes his by right, for no ordinary rules can interfere with the duty . . . to preserve the group."[82]

The ordinary voter deserves an enormous amount of blame for the constitutional horror the presidency has become—but so do America's intellectual elites.

The perennial presidential ranking polls—which typically rank the monster Wood-row Wilson in the top 10 and his "normalcy"-protecting successor Warren G. Harding among the worst—have long made clear that most of our scholars and pundits worship the presidents who dream big and dare great things—even if they leave wreckage in their wake.[83]

Indeed, consider the attitude displayed by two regular *New York Times* columnists in May 2010, during the BP oil-spill crisis. It was hard not to conclude that their major complaint with the president was that he'd missed the opportunity to properly exploit the episode to become a more effective demagogue.

Invoking Obama's 11-year-old daughter, who'd asked the president, "Did you plug the hole yet, daddy?" *Times* mainstay Thomas Friedman urged the president to "react to this spill as a child would." "Daddy, why can't you even mention the words 'carbon tax,'" asked Friedman, who, according to his bio, is a grown man of 57.[84]

Maureen Dowd did her part by lambasting Obama for acting like "President Spock," instead of our "Feeler in Chief." How, she demanded, can we possibly survive with a chief executive who "scorns the paternal aspect of the presidency"?[85] I don't know, maybe we could . . . grow up?

Alas, as Theodore Lowi has observed, the "Pogo Principle" is the key factor behind our metastasizing executive branch: "We have met the enemy, and he is us." When we Americans look to the president for salvation from all problems great and small, it's the sheerest hypocrisy for us to complain that the presidency has grown too big, too powerful, and too menacing. And so long as we cling to the anticonstitutional notion of the president as national redeemer, it's hard to imagine that our problems can be solved by clever legislative, or even constitutional, reforms.

The Solution

So what's my solution? Throw up my hands in despair? I kid, sort of. Here's what I *wouldn't* do: perpetuate the comforting—but false—notion that every political problem has a workable solution.

My 2008 book, *The Cult of the Presidency,* spent eight chapters dissecting the pathologies of the modern presidency. When I got to the ninth and final chapter, I (somewhat) cheerfully admitted that I didn't have a good prescription for curing the ills I'd examined at length in the preceding pages:

> After eight chapters spent covering the problems of the presidency, the reader has every right to expect the payoff to come in the last installment, in which the author will provide a series of reforms designed to solve the problems he's outlined. Natural as that expectation is, it's also unrealistic. As Theodore Lowi has put it, "solutions are for puzzles. Big government

is not a puzzle. The plebiscitary presidency is not a puzzle." Instead, over-weening government and the swollen presidency that inevitably accompanies it are the product of incompatible public demands.[86]

So long as Americans cling to the romance of presidential salvation, I argued, so long as we demand what the office can never provide, "even the most well-crafted five-point plan for restoring the constitutional balance of power is likely to fail."[87]

Judging by reader feedback, though, *Cult*'s last chapter was the least popular part of the book. I'll try to do better here, offering a more comprehensive list of reform proposals. But anyone still inclined to shoot the messenger should be forewarned that I haven't abandoned my conviction that there's no simple solution to the problem of presidential power.

I outline my preferred reforms in ascending order of radicalism and descending order of plausibility. That is, the proposals that are most politically feasible come first, followed by more drastic (and less likely) measures—the ones that are so crazy, they just might work.

Presidential "Question Time"

In his underrecognized 1978 book, *The Presidential Experience: What the Office Does to the Man,* political scientist Bruce Buchanan argued that the Oval Office environment itself feeds the arrogance of power and helps make the modern presidency a continuing threat to the rule of law. Per Buchanan, the fact that each new president finds himself ringed by a paramilitary cordon and ensconced in a bubble of sycophants shields the officeholder from necessary feedback and ends up warping his character and ability to make sound decisions.[88]

One way to start puncturing the insular, regal atmosphere of the office, Buchanan argued, was by adopting an American version of a British practice: Prime Minister's Questions, in which the head of government is regularly grilled by his opponents. Buchanan saw "Question Time" as a way to "force the president to expose himself in a setting he did not control."[89]

The "Question Time" idea has gained popularity in recent years. Surprisingly, the prickly Sen. John McCain (R-AZ), who seemed as likely a candidate as any to bristle like Captain Queeg under hostile questioning, proposed it as part of his 2008 presidential campaign.[90]

In 2010, a diverse coalition of political luminaries—including liberals like *Nation* editor Katrina vanden Heuvel and conservatives like Grover Norquist—set up http://demandquestiontime.com, a petition drive aimed at starting "a new American political tradition" of regular, frequent, and public Question Time sessions between the president and the opposition party.[91] Done properly, the signatories believed, those sessions could push presidents off-script, deflate their air of majesty, and force them to listen.

"Internal Separation of Powers"

Disturbed by the Bush-era erosion of external checks on presidential powers, Neal Katyal argues that the solution is to impose internal checks within the executive branch. "A critical mechanism to promote internal separation of powers is bureaucracy," he writes.[92]

By "setting out inter-agency consultation requirements"; enhancing civil-service protections for top executive-branch employees; transferring the Office of Legal Counsel's role as the legal arbiter of executive actions to a "Director of Adjudication," removable only for cause; and other measures—we might be able to replace greatly weakened *external* checks with *internal* ones. "Overlapping jurisdiction, civil-service protections and promotion, and the invigoration of the agency bureaucrat as an elite force will produce modest internal checks," Katyal argues.[93] He doesn't promise that those checks will fully restore the constitutional balance: But, if implemented, some of the movement toward overweening executive power "can be pulled back toward equilibrium."[94]

Statutory Restraints on Executive-Branch Lawmaking and Warmaking

Reformers with loftier ambitions have proposed legislative reforms aimed at narrowing the president's ability to make law at home and war abroad. In 1973, in the midst of the Watergate scandal and public disaffection over the Vietnam War, Congress passed the War Powers Resolution (WPR), an attempt to limit the president's ability to intervene militarily without congressional authorization.[95] In essence, the WPR provides that if the president introduces U.S. armed forces into hostilities or "situations where imminent involvement in hostilities is clearly indicated by the circumstances," he must remove those forces within 60 days (90, if necessary to ensure safe withdrawal), absent congressional authorization or an emergency in which Congress is physically unable to meet because of an armed attack on the United States.[96]

The WPR's time limit is supposed to kick in when the president reports that he has sent American forces into hostilities or situations where hostilities are imminent. However, the statute is ambiguous enough to allow the president to "report" without starting the 60-day clock, and it provides no effective mechanism for reining in unauthorized deployments.[97] As a result, the WPR has been an abject failure: In the 35 years since its passage, presidents have put troops in harm's way over 100 times without letting it cramp their style.[98]

In the Bush years, war powers reform took on new urgency. In 2007, Republican congressman Walter Jones introduced "the Constitutional War Powers Resolution [CWPR]," an attempt to give the WPR "teeth." The CWPR would allow the president to use force unilaterally only in cases involving an attack on the United States or U.S. forces or to protect and evacuate U.S. citizens. Jones's amendments to the WPR would give congressmen standing to trigger the time limit and would cut off funding should Congress refuse to authorize military action.[99]

Foreign-policy luminaries Leslie H. Gelb and Anne-Marie Slaughter proposed an even simpler solution to the problem of presidential warmaking: "a new law that would restore the Framers' intent by requiring a congressional declaration of war in advance of any commitment of troops that promises sustained combat." The Gelb/Slaughter proposal would still allow the president to "repel sudden attacks," but any prolonged military engagement would require a declaration of war, without which "funding for troops in the field would be cut off automatically."[100]

Other reformers have tried to curb presidential unilateralism at home. After the GOP takeover of Congress in 1994, several enterprising Republican freshmen introduced legislation designed to rein in congressional delegation of lawmaking power to the executive branch.

The 1994 "Congressional Responsibility Act" was based on an idea suggested by then-judge, now Justice, Stephen Breyer in 1983. Breyer argued that Congress could constitutionally exercise a "legislative veto" over executive-branch rulemaking with statutory language stating, "The agency's exercise of the authority to which the veto is attached is ineffective unless Congress enacts a confirmatory law within, say, sixty days." Agencies could recommend particular courses of action, but their recommendations would not have the effect of law until they passed through the normal constitutional channels.[101]

The Gingrich-era "Congressional Responsibility Act" went further than Breyer did, applying his confirmatory law requirement to *all* executive-branch regulations. The act's sponsors hoped to ensure "that Federal regulations will not take effect unless passed by a majority of the members of the Senate and House of Representatives."[102] Changes in the House and Senate rules would allow "fast-tracked," up or down votes on proposed rules, requiring the people's representatives to take responsibility for the rules under which we live.

In 1999, Representative Ron Paul (R-TX) proposed another legislative solution to executive overreach at home. Disturbed by President Clinton's late-term flurry of executive orders, Rep. Paul introduced the Separation of Powers Restoration Act, which would have required presidents to identify the specific constitutional or statutory provisions they're relying on to justify any given diktat and allowed congressmen to challenge it in court.[103]

In a way, these measures—the Constitutional War Powers Act, the Gelb/Slaughter proposal, the Separation of Powers Restoration Act, and the 1994 bid to rein in legislative delegation—are *all* "Congressional Responsibility" acts. Each demands that Congress carry the burden the Constitution places upon it: responsibility for national decisions about domestic and foreign policy.

If these measures passed—and *if* they worked—they'd go a long way toward putting the presidency back in its proper constitutional place. But, as we see later, an awful lot hangs on that one unassuming word, "if."

A "No Confidence" Vote

In his provocative 2006 book, *Our Undemocratic Constitution,* Sanford Levinson argues that statutory reforms won't suffice: Stronger measures are necessary. Appalled by President Bush's extravagant claims of uncheckable executive power and his ineptitude at home and abroad, Levinson contends that the Constitution's impeachment provisions have proven far too weak to remove incompetent or abusive presidents.

Like the advocates of presidential "Question Time," Levinson looks to the parliamentary system, which makes replacing the head of government far easier. He points out that in 1990, the British Conservative party "unceremoniously dumped" Margaret Thatcher, then the longest-serving prime minister in history, with a vote of no confidence, moving John Major into Ten Downing Street the next day. In the American system, "the rigidity of the president's term of office" makes that impossible.[104]

Among Levinson's proposals for fixing that problem is a constitutional amendment providing:

> Upon a vote of no confidence by two-thirds of the Congress in joint session, the members of the Congress who are of the same political party as the now-deposed president shall meet and, as soon as is reasonably possible, select someone to serve as president for the remainder of the term of office.

Levinson sees this as one way to right the balance in a system where "the president has taken on the overtones of a monarch." [105]

Carve Up the Executive Branch

The most radical reform proposals look to end the American monarchy by aiming directly at the unitary nature of the American executive. University of Chicago professors Christopher Berry and Jacob Gersen argue that the case for a single officer exercising the whole of "the executive power" has been greatly overstated.[106]

The framers believed that combining all executive powers in one officer's hands would provide "energy in the executive," promote accountability, and maintain the balance of powers among the several branches of government. But those values could be better served, Berry and Gersen contend, by a "partially unbundled executive," in which separately elected officers are given executive power over discrete policy areas. The states provide numerous examples of "special-purpose" executives, including treasurers, comptrollers, utility commissioners, state auditors, and the like. And the state experience provides little reason to fear that partial "executive unbundling" paralyzes government.

One way to break up the executive monolith is to free the attorney general from service at the president's pleasure. Writing in the *Yale Law Journal,* William P. Marshall makes the case for an independent federal attorney general, either elected or appointed, with a fixed term of service, shielded from removal except for cause.

Professor Marshall's proposal addresses a real problem: The Bush years made clear that, "The President's ability to control the Office of the Attorney General makes him effectively the only arbiter of the legality of his actions."[107] As deputy assistant attorney general in the Bush Department of Justice's Office of Legal Counsel, conservative hero John C. Yoo issued a host of legal opinions affirming that no treaty, no statute, and no coordinate branch of government could stand in the president's way when he acts in the name of American national security.[108] Though the president ran into internal resistance when a bedridden attorney general John Ashcroft refused to reauthorize the so-called Terrorist Surveillance Program, Bush was soon able to replace Ashcroft with his personal attorney, Alberto Gonzales, who never met a presidential counterterror initiative he didn't like.[109]

Radical as it might seem, Marshall's brief for an independent attorney general faithfully reflects the American norm virtually everywhere but the federal level. After they threw off British rule in the late 18th century, the states opted for independent attorneys general, and those states that entered the union after the Constitution's ratification "tended to reject the federal model because they were concerned with the concentration of too much power in one executive officer."[110] Today, attorneys general are elected in 43 states. It's only Maine, New Hampshire, and New Jersey that make the governor the sole elected executive officer.[111]

Fears that an independent federal attorney general would lead to a rickety "house divided" within the executive branch are misplaced, Marshall maintains: "History suggests that both governors and attorneys general have generally learned to cooperate effectively within a divided executive framework." That framework would retain the Hamiltonian virtue of "energy in the executive," while preventing the president from arrogating to himself the power to "say what the law is." As Marshall puts it:

> Certainly a President who must work through an independent attorney general . . . to initiate an extensive program of warrantless electronic surveillance or detention of American citizens may be stilled in his efforts.

But having presidents less energetic in testing the boundaries of their powers would also presumably serve the goal of protecting individual liberty.[112]

As for the other proffered virtues of unitariness—accountability and separation of powers—"unbundling" advocates believe they're better served by dividing power within the executive branch.

For the unitary executive, true electoral accountability comes just once every four years, and, as Berry and Gersen note, "a vote for or against a Presidential candidate is remarkably crude," a "weighted average of voter approval of dozens if not hundreds of policy dimensions."[113] Votes for several "special purpose" executives would translate voter preferences less crudely and better promote accountability. Moreover, Marshall argues, "To the extent that requiring the President to consult with an independent officer leads to greater transparency, the interests of accountability are served."[114]

One of the reasons the framers opted for bicameralism was to give a unified executive a fighting chance against a divided legislature. Even so, Madison feared that it "would rarely if ever happen that the Executive constituted as ours is proposed to be would have firmness eno' to resist the legislature."[115]

Today, Madison's fears of legislative dominance seem utterly outdated. Indeed, if, as seems apparent, "the executive, and not the legislature, is now the most dangerous branch, then restructuring the government to reflect the new reality would be consistent with Madison's vision and design."[116]

In a January 2009 *Atlantic Monthly* article, legal scholar Garrett Epps called the presidency "The Founders' Great Mistake." The Bush years, which saw the president "stonewalling congressional oversight; detaining foreigners and U.S. citizens on his 'inherent authority'; using the Justice Department as a political cudgel; [and] ordering officials to ignore statutes and treaties that he found inconvenient" brought home the fact that the framers' creation of the presidency "wasn't their best work."[117]

In a constitutional culture that looks at the Philadelphia convention as, in Jefferson's words, an "assembly of demigods," it's bracing to hear someone argue that that august body got it completely wrong. Bracing—and perhaps necessary—if we want to guard against future abuses of power.

"Some men," Jefferson wrote, "look at constitutions with sanctimonious reverence and deem them like the ark of the covenant, too sacred to be touched. They ascribe to the men of the preceding age a wisdom more than human and suppose what they did to be beyond amendment."[118] But we should be open to the idea that the framers made significant errors when they crafted the Constitution. The *Federalist* itself warns against a "blind veneration for antiquity," and that surely applies to a system whose self-correcting checks and balances have been eroded by congressional abdication in the face of the executive drive for power.[119]

Unfortunately, though, if the presidency was "the Founders' great mistake," it's not one that's likely to be corrected anytime soon.

The Impact

Presidential reformists face daunting odds. Measures that might conceivably pass likely wouldn't work; and those that might work would be nearly impossible to pass.

Thus, arguing for ambitious statutory and constitutional reforms designed to deimperialize the presidency feels a bit like offering the political science version of the old joke about the economist trapped in a pit: "First, we assume a ladder."

Each of the "solutions" I've outlined begs for what we don't yet have: a Congress eager to be held accountable for its decisions, a judiciary with a stomach for interbranch struggles, and, most importantly, a voting public that rewards political actors who fight to put the presidency in its place.

Begin with the narrowest reform explored earlier: Presidential Question Time. It wouldn't take a single power from the president, but it might, so the theory goes, knock him off his pedestal.

Nice work, if we can get it—but presidents can't constitutionally be compelled to appear before members of a coordinate branch and submit to questioning. And, unlike the British, we don't have a long tradition supporting Question Time and shaping its contours. So what incentive do presidents have to adopt the parliamentary practice—or maintain it in a manner that would serve the purposes its advocates intend?

One could imagine a president, like Barack Obama, who's a particularly adept debater, seeing the advantage in regularly confronting Congress. Recall that the event that inspired "Demand Question Time," Obama's January 2010 question-and-answer session before House Republicans in Baltimore, was considered a great victory for the president.[120] And it was structured quite differently than Prime Minister's Questions, with the "Chief" on an elevated stage, symbolically above the assembled congressfolk.

If an American version of Question Time began to undermine presidential dominance, though, what's to stop a president from dropping it altogether or reshaping it according to his purposes, like the other forms of stage-managed "debate" presidents and presidential candidates prefer?

Neal Katyal seeks to impose internal checks on the presidency, undermining its unitary nature with layers of bureaucratic procedures that, in the ordinary course of business, the president couldn't avoid.

But those procedures can only be instituted one of two ways. Either Congress passes "a general framework statute . . . to codify a set of practices,"[121] or a well-meaning president adopts them on his own. The former method is well worth trying, but it faces all the hurdles legislative "fixes" ordinarily confront, including the possibility of a presidential veto. The latter approach demands Cincinnatus-like self-restraint from someone who's struggled mightily—through countless pancake breakfasts in Iowa and New Hampshire—to grasp the ring of power, and who, as president, will be held responsible whenever any of the 2.4 million members of the executive branch make a headline-dominating mistake.

Statutory reforms aimed at reining in delegation and executive warmaking face daunting hurdles as well. They're hard to pass and even harder to enforce.

Rep. Jones's Constitutional War Powers Resolution would require an extraordinary window of political opportunity to make it past a likely presidential veto. Even the deeply flawed WPR we have now only passed in a moment of unusual presidential weakness, in the midst of public revulsion over the "Saturday Night Massacre," when Nixon fired special prosecutor Archibald Cox.

What's more, by seeking to draw the judiciary into the struggle to constrain executive warmaking, Rep. Jones's CWPR ignores the 30-year history of litigation under the WPR, which shows how adept the federal judiciary is at constructing rationales that allow it to avoid picking sides in battles between Congress and the president.[122]

The same goes for the Separation of Powers Restoration Act and the Congressional Responsibility Act. The former purports to force the courts to hear suits by congressmen alleging injuries to Congress's institutional interests, something they've long been reluctant to do.[123] The latter sets out a statutory scheme aimed at precommitting legislators to particular procedures—and those schemes have a terrible track record. No mere statute can truly bind a future Congress. In areas ranging from agricultural policy to balanced budgets, Congress has rarely hesitated to undo past agreements in the pursuit of short-term political advantage.[124]

It's worth thinking about how best to tie Ulysses to the mast. But the problem with legislative schemes designed to force Congress to "do the right thing" is that Congress always has one hand free. Even if any of these measures became law, Congress would remain free to avoid the pinch: ducking responsibility for new regulations and presidential wars.

Moving on to our more radical proposals, we enter a political fantasyland. Professor Levinson's "No Confidence" Vote and Professor Marshall's bid for an independent attorney general require amending the Constitution.[125] Constitutional amendments are notoriously difficult to pass. Even to propose one requires a supermajority of both houses or a convention called by two-thirds of the state legislatures (the latter has never happened), and two-thirds of the states need to ratify it before it becomes law.[126]

It's difficult to imagine a groundswell of popular support for an independent attorney general or a "No Confidence" procedure great enough to leap those hurdles. Indeed, Professors Berry and Gersen admit that their call for an "unbundled executive" has an "air of absurdity" about it: "We estimate the probability of institutional reform in the United States to be approximately zero."[127]

Conclusion: The Audacity of Hope?

More to the point, the reforms I've outlined here aren't just politically difficult—they're superfluous. An America in which they were politically possible would have no need of them. An America that demanded such changes would be a country that had fundamentally changed its orientation toward the presidency—thoroughly rejecting the idea that it's the president's job to deliver us from evil and to invest our lives with meaning. We don't yet live in that country.

Where does that leave us? After our century-long drift away from the framers' vision of a constitutionally constrained chief executive officer, are we doomed to spiral ever downward through successive cycles of crisis and centralization?

Rather than closing on a note of despair, let me suggest that there are at least two long-term trends that could improve our chances of "right-sizing" the presidency.

The first is America's waning dominance abroad. One major factor that led to the growth of the imperial presidency was America's increasing global role in the 20th century and its unrivaled supremacy after the collapse of the USSR. As neoconservative luminary Charles Krauthammer wrote in 1987:

> Superpower responsibilities inevitably encourage the centralization and militarization of authority. . . . And politically, imperial responsibility demands imperial government, which naturally encourages an imperial presidency, the executive being (in principle) a more coherent and decisive instrument than its legislative rival.[128]

As the 21st century progresses, though, the United States is likely to distance itself from those responsibilities—and, perhaps, from the domineering presidency they enabled.

Fareed Zakaria predicts that, in this century, China and India's rise, along with waning U.S. power, will usher in "the Post-American World."[129] A 2008 report from the National Intelligence Council (NIC), the U.S. agency that advises the American intelligence community, bolsters Zakaria's thesis. The NIC report notes, "Shrinking economic and military capabilities may force the US into a difficult set of tradeoffs between domestic versus foreign policy priorities."[130] Fifteen years from now, the United States will retain enormous military power, but economic and technological advances by other nations, coupled with "expanded adoption of irregular warfare tactics by both state and nonstate actors . . . increasingly will constrict US freedom of action."[131]

In the NIC's account, that's a frightening prospect. Yet, properly under-stood, the waning of the American empire is only disturbing if you're the sort of person who overidentifies with U.S. hegemony and can't see the point of being an American unless you can live vicariously through our current ability to bestride the world like a colossus.

But if you're content with an international order that provides ample space for ordinary people to live their lives unthreatened by aggression, then cheer up! In any given year other than 9/11, terrorism kills far fewer Americans than lightning strikes and peanut allergies.[132] Steven Pinker notes that "global violence has fallen steadily since the middle of the twentieth century," with the number of battle deaths in interstate wars declining "from more than 65,000 per year in the 1950s to less than 2,000 per year in this decade."[133] Hard as it is to recognize from our catastrophe-obsessed media, we live in a world that's increasingly secure.

And it's possible that, in the decades to come, shrinking American power and the emergence of new superpowers will encourage the United States to behave more like a normal country in the international sphere. That, in turn, could help enable a shift to a "normalized" presidency.

The second long-term trend that may reduce the presidency's power and importance in American life is growing distrust of government, or what, in keeping with the first section of this chapter, I'd prefer to call "skepticism toward power."

Growing skepticism toward power is one of the most important political developments of the last half-century. In the late 1950s, when pollsters started ask-ing the question, "How often do you trust the government in Washington to do what is right?" nearly three quarters of Americans answered, "Most of the time or just about always"—and most of all they trusted the president. Those numbers collapsed after Vietnam and Watergate.[134]

One of the leading experts on this phenomenon is Vanderbilt political scientist Marc Hetherington.[135] Professor Hetherington leans left, so he takes no joy in reporting what the data have convinced him: that the rise in distrust is going to make it very difficult for any future president to dominate the political landscape with another FDR- or LBJ-style 100 days.[136]

Modern liberals, who generally support an ambitious, redistributive role for the federal government, can't be happy with the fact that distrust's rise has made it difficult to achieve the goals they cherish.[137] But since they also tend to oppose encroachments on civil liberties, liberals should take heart that burgeoning skepticism toward power has also made it more difficult than it was 60 years ago for presidents to permanently evade legal and political checks on their wartime powers.[138]

Hetherington notes that in the four presidential elections following the largest decline in political trust (1968, 1972, 1976, and 1992), the party that held the presi-dency lost it three times.[139] A skeptical public tends to vote for divided government, which in turn leads to greater policing of the executive branch. William G. Howell and Jon C. Pevehouse have found that when the public rewards the opposition party, the result is more vigorous policing of the incumbent administration's conduct, including many more congressional oversight hearings.[140]

Beltway discourse always paints distrust of government as a political pathology, typically equating it with conspiracy theories and reliably invoking Richard Hofstadter's overcited essay, "The Paranoid Style in American Politics."[141] That's a perverse reaction, and it misses the fact that skepticism toward power lies at the heart of our constitutional culture. If resurgent skepticism makes it harder for presidents to do great works, the good news is that it also makes it harder for them to abuse power.

At one point, on the Watergate tapes, Richard Nixon's chief of staff, H. R. Haldeman, made a remarkable statement. Arguing for an aggressive response to the release of the Pentagon Papers, he warned Nixon, "Out of the gobbledygook, comes a very clear thing":

> You can't trust the government; you can't believe what they say; and you can't rely on their judgment; and the—the implicit infallibility of presidents, which has been an accepted thing in America, is badly hurt by this, because it shows that people do things the President wants to do even though it's wrong, and the President can be wrong.[142]

A "very clear thing," indeed. Given what we now know from history, few Americans today could mouth the phrase "the implicit infallibility of presidents" and keep a straight face. Fewer still would be surprised to learn that "the President can be wrong."

In a strange way, that represents progress. Our four-decade journey from the age of the heroic presidency to the modern era of increasing skepticism toward power hasn't quite disabused us of the vain hope that, if we pick the right chief executive, we can heal America and the world. Our current perspective toward the presidency might best be summed in what I'm told was a very popular self-help book: *I Hate You, Don't Leave Me.*[143]

But we're learning, which makes me think it's not too much to hope that the "cult of the presidency" is a *dying* cult.

Notes

1. For general accounts of libertarianism, see David Boaz, *Libertarianism: A Primer* (New York: Free Press, 1997); Murray N. Rothbard, *For a New Liberty*, rev. ed. (San Francisco: Fox & Wilkes, 1973, 1978).
2. Thomas Paine, "Common Sense," (New York: Cosimo Press, 2006), 1.
3. William Kristol and David Brooks, "What Ails the Right," *The Wall Street Journal*, Sept. 15, 1997.

4. See Gene Healy, *The Cult of the Presidency: America's Dangerous Devotion to Executive Power* (Washington, DC: Cato Institute, 2008), 142–145.

5. President Thomas Jefferson, first inaugural address, March 4, 1801.

6. On consequentialist versus rights-based libertarianism, see R. W. Bradford, "The Two Libertarianisms," *Liberty* 22 (March 2008): 37. On anarcho-capitalism, see Rothbard, *For a New Liberty*; David Friedman, *Machinery of Freedom* (La Salle, IL: Open Court, 1973, 1978).

7. David Boaz, ed., *The Libertarian Reader* (New York: Free Press, 1997), 1.

8. See Steven Pinker, *The Blank Slate: The Modern Denial of Human Nature* (New York: Penguin Books, 2002), esp. Chapter 16, "Politics."

9. G. K. Chesterton, *Orthodoxy* (Rockville, MD: Serenity Publishers, 2009), 14.

10. Bernard Bailyn, *The Ideological Origins of the American Revolution* (Cambridge, MA: Belknap Press, 1967, 1992), 59–60.

11. Cecelia M. Kenyon, "Men of Little Faith: The Anti-Federalists on the Nature of Representative Government," *William and Mary Quarterly* 12, no. 1 (3rd Ser. XII, 1955): 3.

12. Benjamin F. Wright, "The Federalist on the Nature of Political Man," *Ethics* 59 (January 1949): 4. n.b.: the precise quote, from a letter written 100 years after the Philadelphia Convention, is "Power tends to corrupt and absolute power corrupts absolutely." *Essays in Religion, Politics, and Morality: Selected Writings of Lord Acton,* J. Rufus Fears, ed., vol. III (Indianapolis, IN: LibertyClassics, 1988), 519. See also James P. Scanlan, "The Federalist and Human Nature," *Review of Politics* 21 (October 1959).

13. Bailyn, 379.

14. U.S. Constitution, Article II, Section 3.

15. James McClellan and M. E. Bradford, eds., *Elliot's Debates, Vol. III: Debates in the Federal Convention of 1787* (Richmond, VA: James River Press, 1989), 451–452.

16. Quoted in James Burnham, *Congress and the American Tradition* (Chicago: Henry Regnery Company, 1959), 92.

17. Garry Wills, *A Necessary Evil: A History of American Distrust of Government* (New York: Simon & Schuster, 2002), 84–85. Indeed, in virtually every important area of federal power, the Constitution gives Congress the last word. Any treaty the president negotiates is invalid without the Senate's ratification. Congress has the power to propose constitutional amendments for the states to ratify, the president has no role in the amendment process, and so forth.

18. That clause empowers Congress to "make all laws which shall be necessary and proper to carry into execution . . . all other Powers vested by this Constitution in the Government of the United States, or in any Department or Officer thereof." It allows Congress to restrict any authority claimed by the executive "beyond that core of powers that are literally indispensable, rather than merely appropriate or helpful, to the performance of [its] express duties" under Article II of the Constitution. William Van Alstyne, "The Role of Congress in Determining Incidental Powers of the President and of the Federal Courts: A Comment on the Horizontal Effect of the 'Sweeping Clause,'" *Ohio Law Journal* 36 (1975): 788, 794.

19. Peter Augustine Lawler, "The Federalist's Hostility to Leadership and the Crisis of the Contemporary Presidency," *Presidential Studies Quarterly* 17 (Fall 1987): 718.

20. *Federalist* No. 45, in George W. Carey and James McClellan, eds., *The Federalist* (Indianapolis, IN: Liberty Fund, 2001), 241.

21. *Federalist* No. 51, 269.

22. U.S. Constitution, Article II, Section 2; Article I, Section 8.

23. *Federalist* No. 69, 357.

24. James Madison, "Helvidius No. IV," in *The Letters of Pacificus and Helvidius (1845) with The Letters of Americanus, A Facsimile Reproduction* (New York: Scholars' Facsimiles and Reprints, 1976), 89–90.

25. *Federalist* No. 48, 256.

26. *Federalist* No. 51, 267.

27. "The Senate of the United States shall be composed of two Senators from each State, chosen by the Legislature thereof," U.S. Constitution, Article I, Section 3.

28. The 17th amendment, which provided for direct election of senators, repealed that important vertical check in 1913. See Todd J. Zywicki, "Beyond the Shell and Husk of History: The History of the Seventeenth Amendment and Its Implications for Current Reform Proposals," *Cleveland State Law Review,* 65 (1997): 176. Zywicki writes, "It is inconceivable that a Senator during the pre-Seventeenth Amendment era would vote for an 'unfunded federal mandate.'"

29. *Federalist* No. 51, 268.

30. *Federalist* No. 51, 268.

31. *Federalist* No. 47, 249.

32. Richard J. Piper, " Situational Constitutionalism and Presidential Power: The Rise and Fall of the Liberal Model of Presidential Government," *Presidential Studies Quarterly* 24, no. 3 (Summer 1994): 577.

33. Tom Jacobs, "Congratulations, Obama. Here's Your Decay Curve," *Miller-McCune: Politics Research in Summary* (January 20, 2009). Accessed April 6, 2011, http://www.miller-mccune.com/politics/congratulations-obama-here-s-your-decay-curve-4002/. "Contemporary presidential approval ratings generally peak 10% to 15% below those achieved at the beginning of the survey era." Marc J. Hetherington, "The Political Relevance of Political Trust," *American Political Science Review*, 92, no. 4 (December 1998): 791. Michael A. Fitts, "The Paradox of Power in the Modern State: Why a Unitary, Centralized Presidency May Not Exhibit Effective or Legitimate Leadership," *University of Pennsylvania Law Review* 144 (January 1996): 836.

34. John Prados, "Essay: 40th Anniversary of the Gulf of Tonkin Incident," George Washington University National Security Archive, August 4, 2004, accessed April 5, 2011, http://www.gwu.edu/~nsarchiv/NSAEBB/NSAEBB132/essay.htm. Asked on the floor of the Senate whether the proposed resolution could be construed to "authorize or recommend or approve the landing of large American armies in Vietnam," then Senate Foreign Relations Committee Chairman J. William Fulbright declared that a full-scale land war in Asia was "the last thing we would want to do. However, the language of the resolution would not prevent it. It would authorize whatever the Commander in Chief feels is necessary." John Hart Ely, "The American War in Indochina, Part I: The (Troubled) Constitutionality of the War They Told Us About," *Stanford Law Review* 42, (April 1990): 886, 888.

35. Jack Beatty, " The One-Term Tradition," *The Atlantic Monthly* 292, no. 2 (September 2003): 1.
36. Elisabeth Bumiller, "Records Show Doubts on '64 Vietnam Crisis," *The New York Times,* July 14, 2010, A8.
37. President Clinton's 78-day air war in 1999 over Kosovo, Operation Allied Force, was the largest commitment of American fighting men and materiel since the Gulf War. To carry it out, Clinton ignored a congressional vote refusing to authorize the war, openly defying the Constitution's Declare War clause and the War Powers Resolution. (The House voted no on declaring war, 427 to 2; no on authorizing the use of ground troops, 249 to 180; and no on authorizing the president to continue airstrikes, 213 to 213.) See Major Geoffrey S. Corn, "Clinton, Kosovo, and the Final Destruction of the War Powers Resolution," *William and Mary Law Review* 42 (April 2001): 1149.
38. In December 1990, Dick Cheney, then George H. W. Bush's Secretary of Defense, told the Senate Armed Services Committee that the president had all the constitutional power he required to expel Iraqi forces from Kuwait. Charlie Savage, *Takeover: The Return of the Imperial Presidency* (New York: Little, Brown, 2007), 61. Years later, at the outset of the Iraq War debate in August 2002, a senior administration official told *The Washington Post,* "We don't want to be in the legal position of asking Congress to authorize the use of force when the President already has that full authority." Mike Allen and Juliet Eilperin, "Bush Aides Say Iraq War Needs No Hill Vote; Some See Such Support as Politically Helpful," *The Washington Post,* August 26, 2002, A01.
39. See Healy, *Cult of the Presidency,* 154–163.
40. That's quite a contrast from the conservative movement of the 1950s, which generally stood athwart the drive for greater presidential power. See Healy, *Cult of the Presidency,* 118–122.
41. James Madison, *Letters and Other Writings,* vol. 4, 491–92.
42. United States Select Committee to Study Governmental Operations with Respect to Intelligence Activities, "Improper Surveillance of Civilians by the Military," in *Book III: Supplementary Detailed Staff Reports on Intelligence Activities and the Rights of Americans* (1976).
43. Church Committee, "Conclusions and Recommendations," in *Book II: Intelligence Activities and the Rights of Americans* (1976).
44. See Andrew Rudalevige, *The New Imperial Presidency: Renewing Presidential Power after Watergate* (Ann Arbor: University of Michigan Press, 2005), see especially Chapters IV and V for a discussion of Watergate reforms and their unraveling.
45. U.S. Department of Justice, "Legal Authorities Supporting the Activities of the National Security Agency Described by the President," January 19, 2006, accessed April 5, 2011, http://www.fas.org/irp/nsa/doj011906.pdf.
46. Jose Padilla v. Commander C. T. Hanft, 389 F. Supp. 2d 678, 690 (D.S.C. 2005).
47. Jeffrey Rosen, "Card-Carrying: The First Civil Libertarian President," *The New Republic,* February 27, 2008, 4.
48. Jack Goldsmith, "The Cheney Fallacy," *The New Republic,* May 18, 2009, A29.
49. Scott Shane, "U.S. Approval of Killing of Cleric Causes Unease," *The New York Times,* May 13, 2010, A1.

50. Kevin John Heller, "Let's Call Killing al-Awlaki What It Is—Murder," *Opiniojuris.org,* April 8, 2010, accessed April 5, 2011, http://opiniojuris.org/2010/04/08/lets-call-killing-al-awlaki-what-it-is-murder/.

51. FISA Amendments Act of 2008, Public Law 110–261, U.S. Statutes at Large 110 (2008). The FISA Amendments Act left very little of the original Foreign Intelligence Surveillance Act standing, removing the requirement for individualized warrants. Instead, FISA Court judges would approve the parameters of executive surveillance programs, without access to information about the targets to be observed or the factual basis for observing them.

52. John Schwartz, "Obama Backs off a Reversal on Secrets," *The New York Times,* February 9, 2009, A12.

53. Dana Priest and William M. Arkin, "A Hidden World, Growing beyond Control," *The Washington Post,* July 19, 2010, accessed April 5, 2011, http://projects.washingtonpost.com/top-secret-america/.

54. See, e.g., Jack Balkin, "The Constitution in the National Surveillance State," *Minnesota Law Review* 93, no.1 (November 2008): 1.

55. Aaron Wildavsky, "The Two Presidencies," *Trans-Action* 4 (December 1966): 7. "Since World War II," Wildavsky observed, "Presidents have had much greater success in controlling the nation's defense and foreign policies than in dominating its domestic policies."

56. U.S. Constitution, Article I, Section 8; Article II; Article II, Section 1.

57. With the new Dodd–Frank financial reform bill, for example, lenders and investors wondering what's legal will have to await some 243 rulemakings from 11 different agencies. "The Uncertainty Principle," *The Wall Street Journal,* July 14, 2010, A18.

58. William J. Olson and Alan Woll, "Executive Orders and National Emergencies: How Presidents Have Come to 'Run the Country' by Usurping Legislative Power," Cato Institute Policy Analysis No. 358 (October 28, 1999), 12–13. Where most of the executive orders issued by Coolidge and Hoover related to administrative matters such as civil service rules, with no more than 10 percent "policy-specific," by the 1960s, executive orders making national policy and affecting private rights "reached 50% and never declined." Lyn Ragsdale and John J. Theis, III, "The Institutionalization of the American Presidency, 1924–92," *American Journal of Political Science* 41 (October 1997): 1288–1290.

59. James Bennet, "True to Form, Clinton Shifts Energies Back To U.S. Focus," *The New York Times,* July 5, 1998, A10.

60. Jeffrey Rosen, "The Power of One," *The New Republic,* July 24, 2006, 8.

61. Elena Kagan, "Presidential Administration," 114 *Harvard Law Review* (June 2001): 2246, 2249.

62. Eric Lipton, "With Obama, Regulations Are Back in Fashion," *The New York Times,* May 12, 2010, A15.

63. Lyndsey Layton, "FDA Plans to Limit Amount of Salt Allowed in Processed Food for Health Reasons," *The Washington Post,* April 20, 2010, A1.

64. Massachusetts v. EPA, 549 U.S. 497 (2007). See Gene Healy, "The Imperial Presidency Comes in Green, Too," *Washington Examiner,* September 29, 2009, 16.

65. Inimai M. Chettiar and Jason A. Schwartz, *The Road Ahead: EPA's Options and Obligations For Regulating Greenhouse Gases* (Report no. 3, New York: Institute for Policy

Integrity, 2009), accessed April 18, 2011, http://policyintegrity.org/publications/detail/the-road-ahead/.

66. Jonathan Rauch, "Is Obama Repeating Bush's Mistakes?" *National Journal,* March 28, 2009.

67. *See* John Samples, "Lawless Policy: TARP as Congressional Failure," Cato Institute Policy Analysis no. 660, February 4, 2010.

68. Brent J. Horton, "The TARP Bailout of GM: A Legal, Historical, and Literary Critique," *Harvard Journal of Law and Public Policy* 14, no. 2 (Spring 2010): 243.

69. David Cho and Zachary A. Goldfarb, "UAW Vows to Fight Salary Concessions," *The Washington Post,* December 24, 2008, D01.

70. Under the law, a "troubled asset" is "any . . . financial instrument" the secretary of the treasury "determines the purchase of which is necessary to promote financial market stability," and "financial institution" is defined as *"any institution,* including, *but not limited to,* any bank, savings association, credit union, security broker or dealer, or insurance company, established and regulated under the laws of the United States or any State, territory, or possession of the United States" (emphasis added). Emergency Economic Stabilization Act of 2008, Public Law 110–343, *U.S. Statutes at Large* 110 (2008).

71. Horton, 249.

72. Patrick Healy, "Clinton Calls for $30 Billion for Home Mortgage Crisis," *The New York Times,* March 25, 2008, A18 (emphasis added).

73. As my colleague Jerry Taylor put it, "We Eagerly Await Your Orders, Ma'am!" accessed April 5, 2011, http://www.cato-at-liberty.org/we-eagerly-await-your-orders-maam/.

74. *Federalist* No. 8, in George W. Carey and James McClellan, eds., *The Federalist,* (Indianapolis, IN: Liberty Fund, 2001), 34.

75. Richard K. Betts, "A Disciplined Defense," *Foreign Affairs* (November/December 2007), 67; Gordon Adams and John Diamond, "Don't Grow the Army," *The Washington Post,* December 29, 2006, B07.

76. Edward F. Bruner, "U.S. Military Dispositions: Fact Sheet," *CRS Report for Congress,* January 30, 2007; Department of Defense, *Base Structure Report (A Summary of DoD's Real Property Inventory),* 2006, 22, accessed April 18, 2011, www.fas.org/sgp/crs/natsec/RS20649.pdf . True, in some ways, the president has always had the power to invade first and ask for permission later. In 1846, James K. Polk showed that the president could usurp Congress's war powers by ordering troops into disputed territory and triggering a war. But the modern president has much more to work with than his 19th-century predecessors.

77. See David R. Mayhew, *Congress: The Electoral Connection* (New Haven, CT: Yale University Press, 1974).

78. Levinson, 953.

79. David Schoenbrod and Jerry Taylor, "The Delegation of Legislative Powers," in *Cato Handbook for the* 108th *Congress* (Washington, DC: Cato Institute, 2002): 157.

80. Bruce Miroff, "Monopolizing the Public Space: The President as a Problem for Democratic Politics," in *Rethinking the Presidency,* ed. Thomas E. Cronin (Boston: Little, Brown, 1982), 220.

81. Cynthia R. Farina, "False Comfort and Impossible Promises: Uncertainty, Information Overload, and the Unitary Executive," *Journal of Constitutional Law* 22, no. 2 (February 2010): 422.

82. Farina, 424.

83. See Healy, 279–281.

84. Thomas Friedman, "Malia for President," *The New York Times,* May 29, 2010, WK8.

85. Maureen Dowd, "Once More, with Feeling," *The New York Times,* May 29, 2010, WK9.

86. Healy, *Cult of the Presidency,* 267.

87. Healy, *Cult of the Presidency,* 268.

88. Bruce Buchanan, *The Presidential Experience: What the Office Does to the Man,* (Englewood Cliffs, NJ: Prentice Hall, 1978); *see also* Healy, *Cult of the Presidency,* chap. 8, "Why the Worst Get on Top . . . and Get Worse."

89. Buchanan, *The Presidential Experience,* 174–175.

90. Christopher Hitchens, "Question Time," *Slate.com,* May 19, 2008, accessed April 5, 2011, http://www.slate.com/id/2191691.

91. http://demandquestiontime.com/.

92. Neal Kumar Katyal, "Internal Separation of Powers: Checking Today's Most Dangerous Branch from Within," *Yale Law Journal* 115, no. 2314 (2006): 2317.

93. Katyal, 2346.

94. Katyal, 2349.

95. Public Law 93–148. In essence, the WPR provides that if the president introduces U.S. armed forces into hostilities or "situations where imminent involvement in hostilities is clearly indicated by the circumstances," he must remove those forces within 60 days absent a congressional declaration of war, specific statutory authorization for the action, or a situation in which Congress is physically unable to meet because of an armed attack on the United States.

96. The president can extend the 60-day deadline by 30 days if he certifies that there is an "unavoidable military necessity respecting the safety of United States Armed Forces," Section 5(b)(3).

97. That occurred in the 1975 Mayaguez affair. See Richard F. Grimmett, "The War Powers Resolution After Thirty Years," *CRS Report for Congress,* RL 32267, March 11, 2004. Of 111 reports submitted from 1975 to 2003, only one president deliberately triggered the time limit, and that was in a case where the fighting had ended before the report was made.

98. The WPR's time limit is supposed to kick in when the president reports that he has sent American forces into hostilities or situations where hostilities are imminent. However, the statute is ambiguous enough to allow the president to "report" without starting the clock, and presidents have exploited that ambiguity. Of 111 reports submitted from 1975 to 2003, only one president deliberately triggered the time limit, and that was in a case where the fighting had ended before the report was made.

99. H.J. Res. 53, introduced September 25, 2007. See also John Hart Ely, "Appendix: Toward a War Powers (Combat Authorization) Act That Works," in *War and Responsibility: Constitutional Lessons of Vietnam and Its Aftermath* (Princeton, NJ: Princeton University Press, 1993).

100. Leslie H. Gelb and Anne Marie Slaughter, "Declare War: It's time to stop slipping into armed conflict," *The Atlantic Monthly* 296, no. 4 (November 2005): 56.

101. Stephen Breyer, "The Thomas F. Ryan Lecture: The Legislative Veto After *Chadha*," *Georgetown Law Journal* 72 (February 1984): 785–799.

102. H.R. 2727, 104th Congress. It's often argued that abandoning delegation would be impossible because Congress simply would not have the time to make the laws we live under. There's some force to that objection, though it ignores the fact that, as David Schoenbrod and Jerry Taylor write, " . . . delegation forces Congress to spend a large chunk of its time constructing the legislative architecture—sometimes over a thousand pages of it—detailing exactly how various agencies are to decide important matters of policy. Once that architecture is in place, members of Congress find that a large part of their job entails navigating through those bureaucratic mazes for special interests jockeying to influence the final nature of the law. Writing such instructions and performing agency oversight to ensure that they are carried out would be unnecessary if Congress made the rules in the first place." David Schoenbrod and Jerry Taylor, "The Delegation of Legislative Powers," in *Cato Handbook for Policy* (Washington, DC: Cato Institute, 2005), 157. But an end to delegation—whether piecemeal (as with the Breyer proposal) or wholesale (as per the Congressional Responsibility Act)—would force Congress to prioritize. That might mean a return to prescriptive laws, a new respect for federalism, and a renewed appreciation of the framers' view that the chief danger to republican government lies in legislative overzealousness, not legislative inaction. A Congress that wanted to reclaim control of the law would have to do less, do it constitutionally, and be held accountable for the results.

103. H.R. 2655, 106th Congress.

104. Sanford Levinson, *Our Undemocratic Constitution: Where the Constitution Goes Wrong (And How We the People Can Correct It)* (New York: Oxford University Press, 2006), 116.

105. Levinson, 120–121.

106. Christopher R. Berry and Jacob E. Gersen, "The Unbundled Executive," Public Law and Legal Theory Working Paper No. 214 (March 2008).

107. William P. Marshall, "Break Up the Presidency? Governors, State Attorneys General, and Lessons from the Divided Executive," *Yale Law Journal* 115 (2006): 2446.

108. See, generally, Charlie Savage, *Takeover: The Return of the Imperial Presidency* (New York: Little, Brown, 2007).

109. Daniel Klaidman, Stuart Taylor Jr., and Evan Thomas, "Palace Revolt," *Newsweek*, February 6, 2006, p. 39.

110. Marshall, 2450–2451.

111. Berry and Gersen, 14.

112. Marshall, 2446.

113. Berry and Gersen, 18.

114. Marshall, 2476.

115. *Debates in the Federal Convention of 1787*, 62.

116. Marshall, 2477.

117. Garrett Epps, "The Founders' Great Mistake," *The Atlantic Monthly* 303, no. 1 (January/February 2009): 68. Among the solutions Epps proposes are these: a shorter interregnum between election and inauguration, revisions to Article II to specify the

president's enumerated powers, a constitutional amendment requiring the appointment of a new cabinet including members of the opposition party when control of Congress switches, and another amendment providing for the separate election of the attorney general.

118. Thomas Jefferson to Samuel Kercheval, 1816 ME 15:40.

119. *Federalist* No. 14, 67.

120. Paul Kane and Perry R. Bacon Jr., "Obama Goes to GOP's House for a Wide-Open Exchange," *The Washington Post,* January 30, 2010, A01.

121. Katyal, 2316.

122. See Richard F. Grimmett, "The War Powers Resolution: After Thirty Years," *CRS Report for Congress,* RL 32267, March 11, 2004.

123. See Raines v. Byrd, 521 U.S. 811 (1997); see also Ryan McManus, "Note: Sitting in Congress and Standing in Court: How Presidential Signing Statements Opened the Door to Legislator Lawsuits," Boston College Law Review 48 (May 2007): 739.

124. David Orden and Robert Paarlberg, "The Withering of Farm Policy Reform," *Cato.org,* April 16, 2002, accessed April 6, 2011, http://www.cato.org/pub_display.php?pub_id=3446; Louis Fisher, *Constitutional Conflicts Between Congress and the President,* 4th ed. (Lawrence: University Press of Kansas, 2007), 207–211.

125. On the latter, see "Proposals Regarding an Independent Attorney General," 1 Op. Off. Legal Counsel 75 (1977).

126. U.S. Constitution, Article 5.

127. Berry and Gersen, 3, 6.

128. Charles Krauthammer, "The Price of Power," *The New Republic,* February 9, 1987, 24.

129. Fareed Zakaria, *The Post-American World* (New York: W.W. Norton, 2008).

130. National Intelligence Council, *Global Trends* 2025: *A Transformed World* (2008), iv.

131. National Intelligence Council, xi

132. John Mueller, *Overblown: How Politicians and the Terrorism Industry Inflate National Security Threats and Why We Believe Them* (New York: Free Press, 2006), 13.

133. Steven Pinker, "A History of Violence," *Edge.org,* accessed April 5, 2011, http://www.edge.org/3rd_culture/pinker07/pinker07_index.html.

134. Table 5A.1, "Trust the Federal Government 1958–2004," *ANES Guide to Public Opinion and Electoral Behavior,* accessed April 6, 2011, http://www.electionstudies.org/nesguide/toptable/tab5a_1.htm

135. See, e.g., Marc J. Hetherington, "The Political Relevance of Political Trust," *The American Political Science Review* 92 (December 1998): 791.

136. See generally, Marc J. Hetherington, *Why Trust Matters: Declining Political Trust and the Decline of Liberalism* (Princeton, NJ: Princeton University Press, 2005).

137. See, e.g., Andrew Kohut, "Would Americans Welcome Medicare If It Were Being Proposed in 2009?" Pew Research Center, August 19, 2009, accessed April 5, 2011, http://pewresearch.org/pubs/1317/would-americans-welcome-medicare-if-proposed-in-2009.

138. Jack Goldsmith and Cass R. Sunstein, "Military Tribunals and Legal Culture: What a Difference Sixty Years Makes," *Constitutional Commentary* 19 (Spring 2002): 282, 289.

139. Marc J. Hetherington, "The Effect of Political Trust on the Presidential Vote, 1968–96," The American Political Science Review 93 (June 1999): 312. Hetherington's article was written before the post-9/11 spike and decline; George W. Bush's reelection would make it three out of five.

140. William G. Howell and Jon C. Pevehouse, "When Congress Stops Wars: Partisan Politics and Presidential Power," *Foreign Affairs* 88 (September/October 2007): 95.

141. Richard Hofstadter, "The Paranoid Style in American Politics," in *The Paranoid Style in American Politics and Other Essays* (New York: Alfred A. Knopf, 1965).

142. "Oval Office Meeting With Bob Haldeman, 3:09 P. M.," Nixon Presidential Materials Project, National Security Archive, George Washington University, June 14, 1971 (emphasis added), accessed April 6, 2011, http://www.gwu.edu/~nsarchiv/NSAEBB/NSAEBB48/oval.pdf .

143. Jerold J. Kreisman and Hal Strauss, *I Hate You, Don't Leave Me* (New York: Harper-Collins, 1989).

Index